PRAISE FOR *EXECUTIVE ENG*

M000103794

'Bev Burgess has the rare talent of being able to unravel complex topics and spell out a practical way forward. This book is about how to build relationships with the most senior prospects. She writes brilliantly and with great clarity, and has filled a major gap in our knowledge.'
Malcolm McDonald, Emeritus Professor, Cranfield School of Management

'Bev Burgess has done it again and produced a comprehensive overview of how to approach a game-changing services marketing activity.'
Ian Hunter, Vice President, North West Europe Marketing, Fujitsu

'Bev Burgess, one of the industry's top thought leaders on marketing and selling complex services and solutions, has written an insightful, pragmatic and consumable playbook on executive engagement that will help anyone looking for new ideas, great examples and a structured process for developing successful business relationships with target executives in today's hypercompetitive market.'
Barbara Robidoux, Senior Vice President, Marketing, Dell Technologies

'Relationships matter. And this book makes an overwhelming case for this, contrary to what many might have you believe, now more than ever. But a successful business relationship demands a strategic, disciplined, structured and intelligent approach. Bev Burgess's latest "how to" is accessible, compulsive and bang on the money. Don't leave home without it.'
Allan Evans, Global Head of Business Development and Marketing, BDO International Limited

'Bev Burgess has a talent for breaking down the complex and sharing pragmatic advice that anyone can follow. This book is no exception, so if you're serious about building great relationships with your customers, this book is a great place to start.'
Stella Low, Chief Communications Officer, Cisco Systems

'In a B2B context, building meaningful relationships with business executives across the organization requires more than just random acts of engagement. You have to consistently learn from the relationship and then apply those lessons to how you execute all touchpoints. Bev Burgess provides a wealth of ideas, practical insight, industry research and real-world examples on the critical aspects of orchestrated executive engagement. Whether you are looking to up your company's game around executive engagement or your own personal success, this book is a must read.'
Keith Pranghofer, Director of Account Based Marketing & Engagement, Microsoft

'In a world where business executives are becoming ever more cynical, time-poor and media-blind, this is a vital and urgently needed book. Given her experience as a marketing practitioner, consultant, author, educator and advocate, there isn't anyone better placed to write this book than Bev Burgess. She writes as she presents at conferences: in a way that is clear, compelling, uncomplicated, unpretentious, engaging and inspiring. She concisely and methodically unpacks and explores the issues relating to this complex challenge. If you only read one book at marketing or business this year, make it this one.'
Joel Harrison, Editor-in-Chief, B2B Marketing

'This is one of those rare business books that's both thoughtful and accessible. It's packed with clear insights into the increasingly complex world of business-to-business marketing, but what really sets it apart is the wealth of practical examples from which organizations of every size and shape can learn valuable lessons.'
Fiona Czerniawska, Joint Managing Director, Source Global Research

'This clear and easy to follow book is essential reading for managers seeking to create and sustain business relationships and successfully engage with key business stakeholders. Bev Burgess distils many years of deep practical experience in complex B2B marketing. An important book for top management, senior marketers and students.'
Adrian Payne, Professor of Marketing, University of New South Wales, Australia and visiting Professor in Marketing, Cranfield School of Management

'Bev Burgess demonstrates that selling successfully to businesses need not be a matter of chance. Rather, by understanding how to engage with senior executives, it can be the result of a carefully considered and controllable

marketing strategy. With plenty of real-world insights and practical examples from someone who's been there and done it themselves, this excellent book shows you how.'
David Sharp, CEO, International Workplace

'As an EMEA CMO in the real estate industry, I can see that this book is going to be on my desk as a core reference to support the practical delivery of our marketing and business development plans. It reinforces the client focus messages for every element of executive engagement, demonstrating that the client journey and experience can be strategically managed to influence success in building relationships and directly supporting the sale.'
Nigel Pyke, Head of EMEA Marketing and Communications, Cushman & Wakefield

'Yes, consumer experiences influence the behaviour of business buyers, but business buyers are truly different. Bev Burgess explains these differences and provides guidance on engaging with executives to create mutual value. Compelling writing, terrific case studies, and action-oriented advice. A great companion piece to her book on account-based marketing!'
Jonathan Copulsky, former CMO, Deloitte Consulting and Lecturer in Marketing, Kellogg School of Management, Northwestern University

Executive Engagement Strategies

*How to have conversations
and develop relationships
that build B2B business*

Bev Burgess

KoganPage

Publisher's note

Every possible effort has been made to ensure that the information contained in this book is accurate at the time of going to press, and the publishers and author cannot accept responsibility for any errors or omissions, however caused. No responsibility for loss or damage occasioned to any person acting, or refraining from action, as a result of the material in this publication can be accepted by the editor, the publisher or the author.

First published in Great Britain and the United States in 2020 by Kogan Page Limited

2nd Floor, 45 Gee Street	122 W 27th St, 10th Floor	4737/23 Ansari Road
London	New York, NY 10001	Daryaganj
EC1V 3RS	USA	New Delhi 110002
United Kingdom		India
www.koganpage.com		

Kogan Page books are printed on paper from sustainable forests.

ISBNs

Hardback	978 1 78966 194 1
Paperback	978 1 78966 192 7
Ebook	978 1 78966 193 4

British Library Cataloguing-in-Publication Data

A CIP record for this book is available from the British Library.

Library of Congress Cataloging-in-Publication Data

LCCN: 2019057812

Typeset by Integra Software Services, Pondicherry
Print production managed by Jellyfish
Printed and bound by CPI Group (UK) Ltd, Croydon, CR0 4YY

For Andy, with love

CONTENTS

ABOUT THE AUTHOR

Bev Burgess is an industry expert in marketing business services, predominantly in the technology sector, and captured that expertise in her book, *Marketing Technology as a Service* (Wiley, 2010). She is best known as an authority on account-based marketing (ABM), which is a strategy to help companies focus on and engage with their most important customers.

In 2017, she published *A Practitioner's Guide to ABM: Accelerating growth in strategic accounts* (Kogan Page).

In addition to running her own strategic marketing consultancy and leading the IT Service Marketing Association's (ITSMA) European operations, Bev has held senior marketing roles at Fujitsu, British Gas and Epson. Today, she leads ITSMA's Global ABM Practice, and delivers consulting and training to companies around the world that are designing, developing and implementing ABM and executive engagement programmes. She is also a principal at strategic brand consultancy Manasian and Co.

Bev is passionate about the role of marketing in business and is a regular contributor through her speaking, training and writing. She holds an MBA in strategic marketing, incorporating an in-depth study of the implications of culture to perceptions of B2B service quality. She also holds a BSc Honours degree in business and ergonomics. Bev is a Chartered Marketer and a Fellow of the Chartered Institute of Marketing, and has served as an international trustee.

LinkedIn: https://in.linkedin.com/in/bevburgess
Twitter: @BurgessBev

ABOUT THIS BOOK

The world is increasingly moving online. As consumers, it's where we look for ideas and inspiration, to explore the brands we aspire and relate to, research purchase decisions and engage with potential suppliers and their content. It's where we buy things, then arrange to have them delivered or to collect them locally.

Some would have us believe that the same is true when we're buying for our businesses. And for small businesses, for low-value, consumable things like office stationery, it probably is, but not for the larger services and solutions that big businesses and public sector organizations rely on. When it comes to the accounting, payroll, banking and insurance services, or the property, facilities, energy, communications and technology they run on day to day, these are high-value, complex solutions. As such, the way they are bought is still mostly offline. People buy from people. Such purchases usually involve a group of buyers and influencers, take weeks or months to complete, feature a range of potential suppliers competing through a structured procurement process, and result in a multi-year, multi-million-pound contract negotiation.

The senior executives making these decisions are incredibly busy. Getting their attention takes more than an e-mail marketing campaign or cold sales call. Sparking and keeping their interest once you've got their attention means knowing what to say, when and how to say it; usually a combination of online and offline engagements leveraging marketing, sales, subject matter experts and your own executives. And building their trust so that they decide to buy from you, and recommend that others do too, requires the kind of customer-centric ongoing engagement that leads to the creation of sustainable, mutual value.

This book explores the conversations and collaborations that build long-term business success. Starting with advice on how to build a solid understanding of senior buyers and the issues they face, it goes on to look at who is best placed to engage with them on their issues and the way to start and maintain conversations around those issues. It provides a step-by-step guide to how buyers want to engage at each step of their B2B buying process, through personalized content and using a combination of online and offline communication channels. Then, it dives into more detail on the best ways to engage, whether with a peer group through large events, online communities and research initiatives, with small groups through seminars, study tours and innovation workshops, or with individuals through briefings and meetings.

The book uses real-life case studies from leading organizations around the world to bring the concepts to life, plus a summary of key takeaways at the end of each chapter. It is a pragmatic, action-oriented tool for anyone marketing or selling complex, high-value business solutions. I hope you find it useful.

FOREWORD

Engaging with executives has always been a critical skill for those working in business-to-business and it is becoming even more important in today's fiercely competitive, fast-paced and ever-changing business environment.

Before I was appointed Director General of the UK's Institute of Directors (IoD) in November 2019, I spent 30 years working in the professional services sector, at both PwC and more recently at Grant Thornton International Ltd. Throughout those 30 years, executive engagement was a core part of my job. It played a role in the way that both firms courted new clients and built long-term value with them all over the world.

At Grant Thornton International, I was responsible for the firm's interest in China, which taught me much about the way cultural differences influence how executives like to engage. Previously, as a global board member responsible for the brand, I was able to take a more holistic view of the way the brand shapes our clients' expectations and helps to bring members of the firm together to deliver great engagement experiences for them.

What's so interesting about this topic we call executive engagement is that it is both tangible and intangible. It is tangible in that, as this book shows, you can develop a framework to give your chances of successful engagement a significant boost. But there are also those intangible elements such as chemistry, relationship management, team working and leadership. Stepping out of your comfort zone can be a good way to hone those sorts of engagement skills even more finely.

For example, in October 2014 I answered an advertisement hidden in the inside pages of a national newspaper. It was a rewrite of Sir Ernest Shackleton's famous but apocryphal 'Men wanted for hazardous journey' appeal for the ill-fated South Pole expedition in 1914–17. After I was selected I endured two years of intensive training, including qualifying as a UK mountain leader, mountain medic and holistic masseur before spending 26 days living in a tent, braving a polar bear attack and temperatures reaching –50 °C to man-haul a 90 kg sledge across the Arctic ice to the North Pole. The lessons I learned about chemistry, relationship building and leadership during this expedition have been invaluable to my business life.

Engagement, in fact, is at the heart of what we are doing at the IoD. We represent the interests of almost 30,000 directors, our members. Founded in

1903 and within three years awarded a Royal Charter to support, represent and set standards for business leaders nationwide, you will find us in all major cities in the UK. Our objective is grounded in the belief that better directors create better business for a better economy and a better world. We also ensure our members' views are taken into account when the government is reviewing policy, legislation or seeking the opinions of the wider business community.

One increasingly common feature I have seen among the directors I represent is how pressured their time is as they strive to adapt to a digital world. They are therefore increasingly selective when being targeted with requests to engage by a myriad of suppliers hoping to start a conversation.

That's why this book is so timely. It is a pragmatic guide to planning and executing a programme for your organization to become experts in engaging with those executives who can determine your organization's success. Beginning with a call to take the time to understand those you want to engage, and then setting out the various techniques you can use to build long-term relationships and value, it is an essential guide to one of the most important growth strategies B2B firms can adopt. It codifies for the first time the random acts of interaction used by most companies today into a well-defined, comprehensive framework we can all use.

Jon Geldart
Director General
The Institute of Directors

ACKNOWLEDGEMENTS

I have so many people to thank for their help in writing this book.

First, thanks to Dave Munn for his support and for allowing me to reproduce so much of the excellent research and case study content that ITSMA has delivered for its members. Our colleagues at ITSMA have contributed through their work on this research, especially Julie Schwartz, our SVP Research and Thought Leadership, who runs all of our studies, including the flagship annual 'How Executives Engage' survey, and who has written many of our resulting publications on executive engagement. SVP Consulting, Rob Leavitt and VP, Vincent Rousselet, have also helped to shape both the thinking and the articles that ITSMA has published on the topic, and on the role that thought leadership plays in engaging executives.

The people whom I work with every day to support clients with their own executive engagement programmes also deserve a mention, since we create ideas as we work, and I have the pleasure of bringing them to life with such a great team. Kate Manasian and the specialists at Manasian and Co deliver programmes that are not only well thought through but are beautifully executed, designed to engage the most senior executives. Gerry Davies has helped me to bring one of these to life for a joint client in the UK, in her interim role there as programme manager. Louise Jefferson is my comrade in arms who makes work a pleasure and keeps me on track to produce our best work for every client, every day. And Victoria Monger keeps us all organized.

I would like to thank the people who have contributed to this book: Jon Geldart who has both written the Foreword and given us an interview on his adventures with executives in China; Jane Hiscock, who was willing to share perspectives and recommendations from her own experience; and Kathy Macchi, the go-to person for advice on how to leverage technology to support your programme. Thanks also to those people who took the time to help create a case study for the book, since these bring the principles behind executive engagement to life and are so valuable to the reader: Andrea Clatworthy, Rudy Dillenseger, Jacqueline Gummer, Mark Larwood, Spencer Lim, Julia Martin, Wim Wensink and Yann Zopf.

There are four people without whom this book simply would not have been published and to whom I am especially grateful: Laura Mazur at Writers 4 Management, whose help with drafting and editing was invaluable as the book took shape, as was her constant encouragement; and Kathy Hunter at ITSMA, who created most of the tables and figures you see in the book. At my publishers, Kogan Page, Anne-Marie Heeney for her editing and kind words and Jenny Volich for commissioning me to write this book on executive engagement and for her ongoing support.

Finally, I would like to thank both Caroline Smith and Alison Baldwin, my friends who kept me sane during the process and understood when I just needed to write. And, of course, my daughters, Katherine and Lauren, who have been there all along and understand that I need to do this as well as be their mother. You rock!

01

Business buyers don't behave like consumers

As the way that we buy for ourselves, our families and our homes continues to change at pace, mostly enabled by advances in technology and moving online in many cases, it would be easy to assume that the way people buy high-consideration, complex solutions for their business is changing in the same way. It isn't.

When there is a lot at stake for a business, people tend to buy from people they know and trust. It's not the same as when they order their groceries, buy a film to watch for the evening or book a holiday.

But the way we behave as consumers is definitely influencing the way we behave as business buyers. We expect to find the information we want quickly, to navigate easily through a supplier's website, to have a seamless experience when we switch channels and speak to a sales person, and, increasingly, to be recognized and have our experiences personalized so that our time is not wasted with irrelevancies.

This chapter explores the way in which people buy at work, how that is influenced by their expectations as a consumer, and what makes it very different indeed.

Changing consumer behaviour

Impact of the information revolution

Anyone with access to the internet has benefited from the ubiquity of information it provides. If we didn't have enough information and choice as consumers before, we certainly do now: we can search for anything, at any time and from any location, with the increasingly powerful mobile networks available.

This has changed both what we buy and how we buy it. We can compare options, see what others who bought the same thing thought and whether they would recommend it. We can buy products and services online and have them delivered to our homes or collect them from a local shop or collection point. Or we can browse online and then go and buy in the store. And it works the other way around: we might see something while we're out and about and then go home and buy it. Even the largest purchases we make – our homes, our cars, our holidays – are increasingly researched, compared, customized and sometimes bought online.

Moreover, the experience of buying is increasingly personalized. If you're a Netflix subscriber, buy from Amazon or listen to music with Spotify, you'll know that machine learning is building up an understanding of you and recommending other products and services you might like. In some cases this works better than others – no one likes to be followed around the internet by ads for the trousers they've only just bought – but it's getting more sophisticated all the time.

All of this is raising our expectations. We expect the same level of service and experience from our utility provider as we get from our favourite store or from our music streaming service. And we expect to be recognized both online and in store, without having to give the same information twice in different channels.

What happens if we don't get it? Well, we're quick to make our feelings known if the service we receive is 'sub-standard'. In fact, we're positively encouraged to rate everything from our satisfaction with the website we used or the server that brought us our meal to how happy we are using our new appliance or with our holiday accommodation. Typically, it's the people who are most or least satisfied that share their thoughts online, as the vast majority of people just move on to whatever's next on their agenda. 'Good enough' doesn't seem to warrant much reflection or promotion.

Other influencing factors

Other factors shape our frame of reference when we buy. Climate change is a major issue that we increasingly take into consideration when we're buying both goods and services. How did the avocados you're buying get to the store? How far have they travelled? Do they need to be individually cushioned in a hard, plastic shell and then wrapped in soft plastic? Is that plastic recyclable? If not, how long will it take to break down?

Corporate social responsibility is another concern. Who made the jacket you're about to buy? Was it a child? If not, was it an adult paid fairly for the work they're doing? Were the raw materials sourced sustainably and at a fair price?

And what if all of the above checks out but no one from the Kardashian family likes what you're buying? How do you feel if there are no bloggers or vloggers recommending your choice? The power of celebrity has always swayed us in our choices, but it has never been as visible and immediate as it is today.

All of these are also at play when people make buying decisions at work, but they have a different impact. There are other, more powerful, forces at work.

What's different at work?

The way we buy at work is different for all but the most 'consumable' of purchases, particularly for the kind of complex, high-value purchases that executives make. These differences include the need to build a business case, the use of buying teams, the professionalization of procurement, risk avoidance, financing, the complexities of the contracting process and forging longer-term relationships.

Making the case

Most organizations require a business case to be created before they will authorize the purchase of anything but the most inexpensive, transactional products and services. At its most basic, the case outlines the problem or opportunity facing the organization, the potential solutions, the likely costs involved, the benefits expected, a break-even or return on investment (ROI) calculation and the preferred solution and/or supplier.

Above all, the business case needs to be quantified. The value the organization will receive from the purchase can be looked at in terms of benefits minus costs. At their most basic, financial benefits could come in terms of increased revenues or decreased costs of doing business. By how much? When will the benefits start to be recognized, how long will they go on and how will they change over that time?

Against this we need to know the total cost of the solution being proposed. How much will it cost in terms of a capital purchase and/or ongoing monthly usage? How much will it cost in terms of the time involved to buy and use the solution given the rates for capital available to the business? How much will any professional services needed to make the purchase, such as lawyers, charge?

In addition, what is the ongoing cost of the solution in terms of maintenance, licences to use it year after year, and supplies to keep it operating, such as new software releases and training on a system, or the energy to run a combined heat and power unit? Many organizations want to calculate the total cost of ownership of whatever it is they are buying, over the lifetime of when they plan to use it.

Organizations also want to know when a planned purchase will 'break even'. How quickly will the costs be recovered? And from that point on, how much more benefit will be received? These calculations help executives to decide between competing possible investments, by comparing the return they will get from each over time and highlighting the most favourable.

After all, as a CEO said to me very early on in my own career, companies outside of the public and third sectors are driven by making money, and they need to make more money from their operations than they would by putting their money in a bank. This might sound obvious, but it always bears repeating.

In public companies, business cases for large purchases will be reviewed by the board of directors, acting on behalf of shareholders to ensure that their investments are protected and the right decisions are being taken for the business in terms of financial, legal, ethical, societal and other considerations. In the public and third sectors, boards of trustees will go through a similar process, to ensure budgets are being spent wisely.

This need for a business case means that business buyers must work through a robust and rational approach to their buying decisions. The most successful suppliers help their clients to do this as part of the sales process and stay involved to help demonstrate that the benefits the organization was expecting have indeed been delivered.

Buying in teams

Business buying is rarely done by a single person. It is both too complicated and too important. Instead, a group of people work together to make the decision, playing different roles in the buying process. This group is commonly referred to as the decision-making unit (see Figure 1.1).

FIGURE 1.1 An illustrative decision-making unit

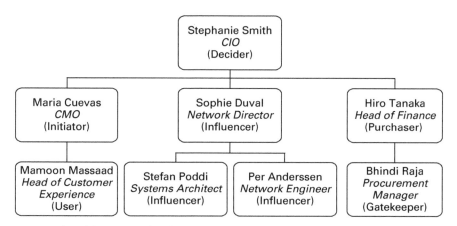

SOURCE Adapted from *A Practitioner's Guide to ABM*, Burgess and Munn, Kogan Page, 2017

In this illustrative example a group of people are buying a new app to give shoppers the chance to find out about stock availability and receive offers as they move around a store. The initiator of the purchase is Maria Cuevas, the chief marketing officer (CMO), who wants to grow customer loyalty and spend in a competitive retail market by improving engagement with millennials in store. The ultimate decider in this instance will be the chief information officer (CIO), Stephanie Smith, whose budget will be used to hire a company to build the new app.

Hiro Tanaka, Head of Finance, will make the purchase, while one of their team members, Bhindi Raja, will manage the purchase process and act as a gatekeeper between potential suppliers and the internal decision makers, controlling the flow of information throughout.

Members of Stephanie's team will have some influence over the purchase, since they will be involved in making sure the new app works in the retailer's technology environment (or in changing the environment to make sure that it does). Finally, the head of customer experience, Mamoon Massaad, will get involved in the decision as a potential user of the app and the information it will provide.

In some cases, there will also be third parties involved in the decision-making process, such as procurement advisors or technical consultants. These external parties can bring a degree of objectivity and experience to the process, either by helping to scope out what the organization is looking for or finding and evaluating potential solutions and suppliers.

Most sales methodologies today take account of the decision-making unit and encourage the mapping out and profiling of those who are a part of it. Engaging with each member – and with external influencers when they're involved – is a key part of the sales and marketing process for complex business solutions.

Procurement as an established profession

Procurement is now a recognized profession and a core function in larger organizations. The UK-headquartered Chartered Institute for Procurement and Supply (CIPS) has offices around the world and is the world's largest purchasing body with a global community of 200,000 professionals in 150 countries. It describes procurement and supply management as 'buying the goods and services that enable an organization to operate in a profitable and ethical manner', with responsibilities ranging from 'sourcing raw materials and services' to 'managing contracts and relationships with suppliers'. The CIPS notes that 'Procurement is often responsible for up to 70 per cent of companies' revenue, so small reductions in costs can have a huge impact on profits'.

And these sums can be substantial. According to figures in one report,[1] 115 major purchasing organizations, such as Barclays, Dell, Kellogg, Microsoft, L'Oréal and Walmart, represent $3.3 trillion in procurement spending.

Malcolm McDonald, Professor Emeritus of Cranfield University School of Management, summarizes the way in which strategic purchasing teams group and deal with suppliers,[2] as shown in Figure 1.2. Suppliers that are doing significant business with the company and are attractive partners are seen as core, receiving a significant degree of support and defended within the organization. Most procurement teams will reduce the number of suppliers in this category to a handful across the company. Potentially attractive partners who aren't yet doing significant business with the company are nurtured, and new opportunities sought to expand the amount of business done together.

Less attractive partners that aren't currently doing much business with the company are seen as a nuisance and are often the ones to have their contracts terminated when organizations go through any kind of supplier rationalization initiative. The less attractive suppliers who are doing significant business with the company find themselves constantly squeezed on price, as procurement teams look for short-term advantage from them in terms of savings while in the long term planning to phase the suppliers out altogether.

FIGURE 1.2 Strategic purchasing

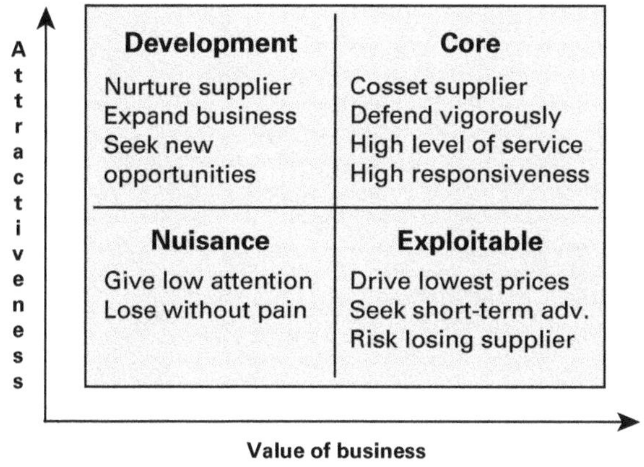

Value of business

SOURCE Professor Malcolm McDonald at ITSMA's European ABM Forum, 2016

The best suppliers recognize that this categorization and management of suppliers is taking place in a professional procurement team, and look to demonstrate their attractiveness to the organization. Ideally, this should go beyond simply demonstrating where a company could save money. McDonald recommends suppliers 'prove that dealing with you will create advantage for your customer, not merely help them to avoid disadvantage'. This is all about co-creating value (more on this in Chapter 5), defined as 'an opportunity-identifying process leading to the creation of new value for all participating parties through the integration and interaction of resources'.

Avoiding risk

Generally speaking, executives are risk averse when buying complex, high-value business solutions, since the stakes are high in terms of the financial and reputational cost to both their organization and their own careers.

This is backed up by research done by the Information Technology Service Marketing Association (ITSMA). Its 2018 'How Executives Engage' study,[3] which looked at the buying process for business solutions worth more than $500,000, found that 71 per cent of the 410 buyers surveyed said that they invited their existing supplier into a shortlist of suppliers bidding for a new opportunity, and 77 per cent of those buyers went on to select the incumbent rather than choosing a new supplier for that project. This means that 55 per cent of the time, incumbent suppliers won those new opportunities (Figure 1.3).

FIGURE 1.3 Selecting existing suppliers for new opportunities

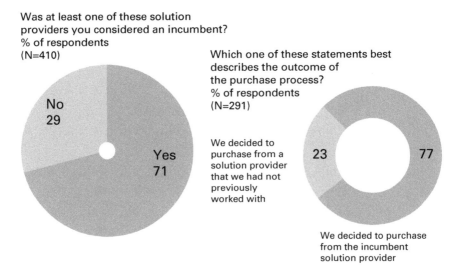

Was at least one of these solution providers you considered an incumbent?
% of respondents
(N=410)

No
29

Yes
71

Which one of these statements best describes the outcome of the purchase process?
% of respondents
(N=291)

We decided to purchase from a solution provider that we had not previously worked with

23   77

We decided to purchase from the incumbent solution provider

SOURCE ITSMA 'How Executives Engage' study, 2018

When making these selection decisions, a number of the most important factors in the decision-making process reflect this risk avoidance. The same ITSMA survey from 2019[4] shows that, of the top five decision criteria, four relate to risk avoidance while the fifth is about pricing (Figure 1.4). After the price, ranked as the most important criterion, the supplier's knowledge and understanding of the buyer's industry comes next, followed by their knowledge of the company's unique issues. Next comes their experience with the technology or solution being bought. In joint fifth place are the quantifiable value of the solution being proposed and the overall trustworthiness of the supplier – something that is much easier for an incumbent to demonstrate than a new supplier.

In fact, more of the other criteria in the list can be seen as helping to reduce the risk of the purchase, whether it be the strength of the supplier's brand (remember the old adage 'you never get fired for buying IBM'?), a proven track record backed by customer references, a recommendation from the board or senior management, an existing relationship, cultural fit or endorsements from third parties.

In addition, the purchases these executives make often have to be signed off at board level, having been scrutinized by a compliance and risk specialist. This gives shareholders the comfort of knowing that everything possible has been done to reduce the risk of the decision taken.

FIGURE 1.4 Minimizing risk when selecting suppliers

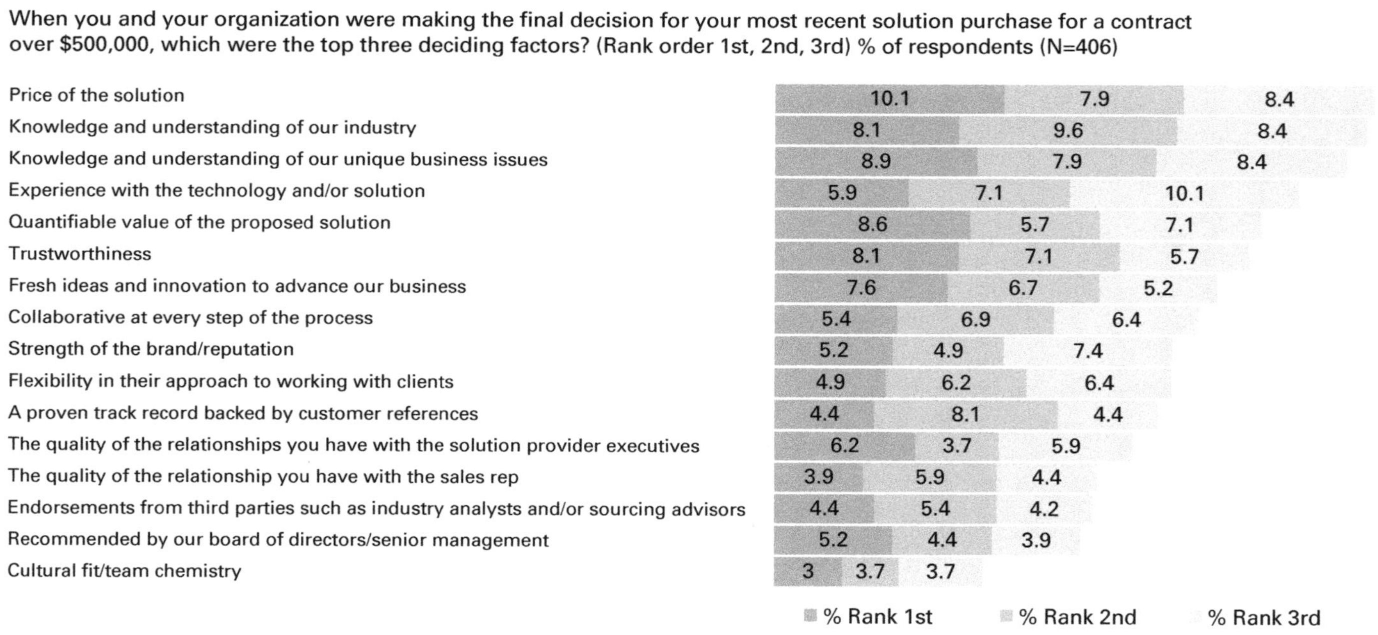

When you and your organization were making the final decision for your most recent solution purchase for a contract over $500,000, which were the top three deciding factors? (Rank order 1st, 2nd, 3rd) % of respondents (N=406)

Factor	% Rank 1st	% Rank 2nd	% Rank 3rd
Price of the solution	10.1	7.9	8.4
Knowledge and understanding of our industry	8.1	9.6	8.4
Knowledge and understanding of our unique business issues	8.9	7.9	8.4
Experience with the technology and/or solution	5.9	7.1	10.1
Quantifiable value of the proposed solution	8.6	5.7	7.1
Trustworthiness	8.1	7.1	5.7
Fresh ideas and innovation to advance our business	7.6	6.7	5.2
Collaborative at every step of the process	5.4	6.9	6.4
Strength of the brand/reputation	5.2	4.9	7.4
Flexibility in their approach to working with clients	4.9	6.2	6.4
A proven track record backed by customer references	4.4	8.1	4.4
The quality of the relationships you have with the solution provider executives	6.2	3.7	5.9
The quality of the relationship you have with the sales rep	3.9	5.9	4.4
Endorsements from third parties such as industry analysts and/or sourcing advisors	4.4	5.4	4.2
Recommended by our board of directors/senior management	5.2	4.4	3.9
Cultural fit/team chemistry	3	3.7	3.7

SOURCE ITSMA 'How Executives Engage' study, 2019

In my experience, even when executives are buying new and innovative solutions, they still need reassurance on these factors. The classic conundrum for suppliers is dealing with buyers who insist their organization is not like any other and the solution they need must be unique, while ironically asking for examples of where you have done this before. The best suppliers manage to achieve this, creating and using advocates from their existing customer base to reassure potential new customers that the risk they are taking is minimal.

Finding financing for big purchases

When an organization buys a high-value, multi-year solution from a supplier, the costs can run into hundreds of millions of pounds. While it may be possible to fund that out of cash reserves, it could also require some form of loan or financing arrangement. This is a key part of the business case analysis and purchasing decision.

Unsurprisingly, some of the biggest and best companies in the world, such as GE, have created financing businesses to help their clients make these large purchases. This then becomes a core part of the value proposition for the buyers.

Typical financing arrangements include leases, sale and leasebacks, and secured debt financing, such as those offered by GE Capital to energy and aerospace clients, or IBM Global Financing for buyers of both IBM and other suppliers' solutions.

Another good example is global infrastructure support services firm Amey. It has been helping to fund vital infrastructure projects such as waste plants and highways developments for nearly 20 years through investment into public–private partnerships (PPPs). It has raised over £4 billion of private finance for clients in the past 10 years, including 'traditional bank debt, bond issues, prudential borrowing and European Investment Bank funding'.[5]

The complexities of the contract process

Once a supplier has been selected to provide a business solution such as a technology system, power plant, infrastructure service or external audit, the contracting process begins. Commercial negotiators and lawyers are often brought in on both sides for this phase, working with the procurement specialists and the decision makers to make sure, once again, that risk is minimized for both parties and that mutual value will be delivered over the life of the contract.

In our 'as a service' world, pricing can be simply agreed on a usage basis, such as per user per month for example. This offers the buyer flexibility to pay only for what is used as the needs of their company vary during the term of the contract. This term is a key point to be agreed, with some contracts running over decades, as are, in parallel, any break clauses in the contract and cancellation notice periods.

Other things to be considered include service level agreements and compensation levels. For instance, what if the service fails for a day? Ownership and protection of intellectual property that is either used or created together is also on the agenda, as are the terms of engagement for the people who will be involved in the delivery of the solution, including non-disclosure agreements and publicity rules.

There are several ways to contract for business-to-business services. The traditional approach is via an input-based service specification, whereby clients pay their suppliers to deliver a specified solution to an agreed level. Input-based contracts are costed in terms of the resources consumed to deliver this solution, usually on a time and materials basis, such as the number of hours an engineer spends mending an air conditioning unit, multiplied by their charge-out rate, added to the cost of the spares and tools needed for the repair.

Output-based contracts are focused on paying for a deliverable, such as a fee for the unit to be working 99 per cent of the time. Outcome-based contracts are for the realization of a business outcome, such as the 99.9 per cent availability of a mobile network for mobile engineers to check their appointment schedules, access and update customer records and take payment after each visit.

Contracting for outcomes comes and goes in terms of its popularity with buyers. Many like the idea of paying suppliers a base-level fee with an upside for shared rewards if the business outcomes anticipated have been achieved, for example. An early instance of this was when an outsourcing supplier (EDS at the time) took over the collection of parking fees in the city of Chicago. It brought in a system that increased parking ticket sales dramatically, and as a consequence saw a significant 'performance bonus' from the contract based on this successful outcome.

However, in more than one case, I've seen contracts renegotiated as the business outcomes achieved have gone beyond anyone's wildest dreams, and the buyer concluded they were ultimately paying over the odds for the solution.

Most contracts are therefore not solely outcome-based. Suppliers also tend to include provisions for service levels in the form of service level agreements monitored by key performance indicators. The benefit of this is that it allows for some compliance to necessary risk management, environmental or quality standards for the operation of the solution. These 'hybrid' contracts usually have contractual rewards tied into the achievement of outcomes, plus regular payments for the delivery of the service to some input or output specification.

The best suppliers ensure that a strong contract is in place but aim to build a relationship way beyond the contract so that any issues arising can be worked on together and settled before either party feels the need to refer to the contract. This is certainly the approach that HCL Technologies prides itself on, with its promise of a 'Relationship Beyond the Contract' publicized widely through its marketing organization.

CASE STUDY
Relationship Beyond the Contract at HCL

HCL Technologies is an India-based multinational IT service and consulting company. Through possibly the worst recession that this generation has witnessed, HCL delivered an extended period of tremendous growth, as measured by business indicators and customer satisfaction, thanks to aggressive sales and effective delivery capabilities.

However, a few years ago their marketing department faced three challenges:

1 Various lines of business within the company were marketing their services independently and with only a suggestive alignment with the core company messaging.

2 There was a need for thought leadership. As HCL took on the role of a more seasoned participant in the IT services market, its customers and prospects wanted to know if it had a vision for IT services that extended past the technology of the season.

3 It is HCL's business strategy to increase its customer base in the top Global 2000 companies. While it had been increasing its customer base overall, the number of Forbes Global 2000 (G2000) customers was still low. Within this elite group of IT service buyers, the company won more than 50 per cent of the deals it participated in, but was only invited to less than 10 per cent of deals to begin with. This was an awareness problem that required immediate intervention.

Programme objective

The objectives of the programme were the following:

- Align all the lines of business under a unified messaging architecture.
- Ensure that messages directly resonated with HCL's core belief.
- Express how the relevance of the brand promise directly translated into the robustness of the business model as the company's vision for the future of IT services.

Programme execution

To crack the integrated communications strategy for an omnichannel customer experience, HCL initiated a global unified messaging campaign called Relationship Beyond the Contract (RBtC).

At the heart of the campaign was a 105-second film that used a father–son relationship over a 20-year period to creatively showcase a simple message: that every relationship has an underlying contract. However, the true joy and memorability of that relationship emerge in moments when the parties go beyond the contract. This was HCL's way of placing its faith and future in the power of its relationships with its customers, and not only on the contract signed with them.

This film received smiles and emotional responses from customers, prospects and employees but, more importantly, became a vehicle to drive multiple communications across various stakeholders leveraging digital, collaterals, website and various other channels.

With its core message of RBtC, the campaign has focused not just on changing but strengthening the brand promise through programmes and artefacts.

Here are some of the sub-initiatives as part of the campaign:

- The Spirit of RBtC Video: 105-second film that used a father–son relationship over a 20-year period, to creatively showcase their simple message.
- The LinkedIn–HCL Collaboration App: HCL collaborated with LinkedIn to create a 'first of its kind in the world' app using LinkedIn's powerful API framework.
- The RBtC Coffee Table Book: showcased 10 iconic relationships from around the world – relationships that the company as a brand could aspire to have with its customers.
- Digital Outreach and Thought Leadership: the CEO's blog on the LinkedIn Influencer platform led to organic media mentions across a variety of top media outlets.

Business results

1 The Integrated Digital Campaign had an exposure of 100 million impressions from G2000 organizations and the online community.

2 G2000 organizations' visits to the HCLTECH website jumped from 300 organizations in June 2014 to 1,300 in June 2015, a 400 per cent jump as a result of the campaign.

3 It was the fastest film in the history of the IT industry to reach 2 million views on YouTube. Fifty per cent of views came from the United States and Europe.

4 A first-in-class digital app was created in collaboration with LinkedIn, with more than 10,000 usages of the app across the G2000 community.

5 From December 2013, 25,000 followers were on HCLTECH social media destinations, an 83 per cent increase in the previous 12 months.

6 RBtC leveraged in 130 large-deal pursuits with a total pipeline value of over $4.5 billion. RBtC-led business campaigns generated a pipeline of $500 million.

7 HCLTECH brand favourability increased by 9 per cent to 29 per cent as measured by a LinkedIn study.

SOURCE ITSMA Marketing Excellence Awards Winner summary booklet, 2015
Reproduced with permission from ITSMA

The purchase is just the start

In order to be a strategic supplier in the eyes of procurement and the wider executive team, suppliers are expected to continue to look for ways to add value to their client. This is what builds a strategic relationship rather than a transactional sale, maximizing the lifetime value of the client.

I once interviewed a number of important clients for a large professional services firm to understand how it could improve its service and differentiate itself from competitors. I was struck by the ability of CEO to put his expectations of his auditor into a succinct phrase. He said: 'I expect my relationship partner at the firm to wake up thinking about my business, like I do.'

Once the buying decision is made, there are a number of areas which executives consider important in the way their supplier continues to work with them, as shown in Figure 1.5.

Buyers want their suppliers to make it easy for them to manage ongoing relationships via tools and processes. This could be through real-time performance dashboards and/or quarterly review meetings, for example. Equally important is the responsiveness of the supplier: executives expect their supplier to do what they ask, even if they disagree with the request.

FIGURE 1.5 Building a relationship post-purchase

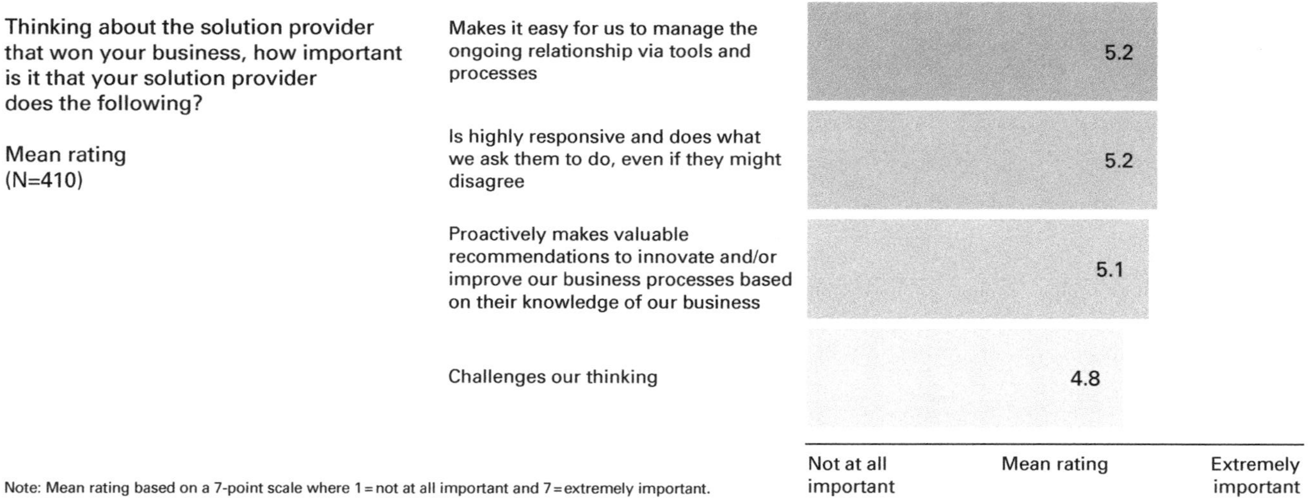

Thinking about the solution provider
that won your business, how important
is it that your solution provider
does the following?

Mean rating
(N=410)

	Mean rating	
Makes it easy for us to manage the ongoing relationship via tools and processes		5.2
Is highly responsive and does what we ask them to do, even if they might disagree		5.2
Proactively makes valuable recommendations to innovate and/or improve our business processes based on their knowledge of our business		5.1
Challenges our thinking	4.8	

Not at all important   Mean rating   Extremely important

Note: Mean rating based on a 7-point scale where 1 = not at all important and 7 = extremely important.

SOURCE ITSMA 'How Executives Engage' study, 2018

Only marginally less important is the supplier's ability to be proactive and bring valuable ideas to the table, based on their knowledge of the client's business. Again, in my experience, this is where many suppliers fall down. They wait until their contract is coming up for renewal before putting in the energy and attention required to suggest improvements and innovations to their client. By then it may be too late, and the client is already researching alternative suppliers to get the innovative ideas they need.

Consider Figure 1.5, based around the following question: Thinking about the solution provider that won your business, how important is it that your solution provider does the following? (Mean rating (N=410), mean rating based on a 7-point scale where 1=not at all important and 7=extremely important.)

Business buyers also look to their suppliers to help them take advantage of the solution they've bought, such as through education or training for the users of the solution so that it can quickly be used effectively across the business. Tools and templates that monitor usage and ROI are valued as well, along with databases of common problems and how to solve them. Best practice examples and case studies on how other companies are using the solution are helpful, as is information on trends affecting their business. Executives are also keen on scorecards, which show how to get better ROI from their purchase, and innovation workshops to explore new technologies and business models that could work for them.

In the world of technology, leading companies such as Microsoft, SAP and Cisco have set up customer success teams to make sure their clients achieve the outcomes they expected and get the best value from both their purchase and their relationship, delivering on many of these client expectations. The case study from NTT DATA shows how the company goes one step further to demonstrate to its existing clients how it is supporting its own teams as they deliver value for their own customers.

CASE STUDY

NTT DATA: Every touch matters

NTT DATA Services partners with clients to navigate and simplify the modern complexities of business and technology, delivering the insights, solutions and outcomes that matter most. As a leading pure-play IT services company, it operates in a highly competitive environment where it constantly identifies ways to provide additional value to clients.

In 2018, the company's challenge was to find ways to better connect with clients and to further differentiate it from competitors to accelerate growth.

Connecting with clients on an emotional level

NTT DATA identified an opportunity to differentiate by better connecting with clients on an emotional level. They mined engagements for compelling stories about its people, who had incredible commitment to their clients' values, training client-facing teams to show and not tell clients why NTT DATA Services is different, appealing to them on both a business *and* emotional level.

'We didn't stop at "show". We wanted to make our clients "feel" our commitment to their values', said Craig Rones, Vice President of Marketing. 'We shifted our communications to focus away from solely traditional business conversation, and instead, we made our clients and their customers the hero. We created deliberate stories with emotional touchpoints that would resonate with our clients' values.'

Telling the client's story

NTT DATA worked to 'cast' brief movies, starring either the client or the client's customer as the hero, and showing how their initiatives were making the world a better place. 'Our delivery people played the role of the supporting team, unravelling IT complexities and giving clients the freedom to focus on their mission. For each story, we used different media – PowerPoint, digital, video, live briefings – to show our employees' strong commitment to our clients' goals and values', added Rones.

'The company provided its sales teams with a new script that stripped away the "us" and focused on how "we" could help our clients and their customers.' The leading role was played by the qualitative emotion, with quantitative data in a supporting role. 'We wanted our clients, after watching our movie and seeing the way our people treated our customers' business as their own, to feel like they had a partner who was part of their business rather than just one who services their business', he pointed out.

Connecting technology and business objectives

To deepen client relationships, NTT DATA needed to first create a winning theme which resonated with its clients' business and IT objectives, and to use tactics which reinforced that theme at every touchpoint. 'We used these win themes as a filter for all client meetings and client-facing content', explained Rones. 'We also created a sub-theme that gave the client three easy-to-remember content "buckets" for deeper context.'

Going through the win-theme exercise and creating a storyboard for client experiences helped ensure the company listened, connected, and ultimately, understood the client's need. It also helped to ensure end-to-end alignment across the extended account team working with that client.

Demonstrating commitment

Beyond showing outstanding technical capability, NTT DATA differentiated itself from its competitors in three ways:

1 personalized hospitality – a consistent, personal experience with each touchpoint and visit;

2 the commitment of its people to their client's values; and

3 client understanding – researching key stakeholders' personal interests and incorporating the learnings into every touchpoint.

Rones concluded: 'By combining all three elements, we demonstrated that we cared not only about our ability to deliver on our contract but also that we had a deep understanding and commitment to our client's values, their objectives, and both their business and personal success'.

Driving growth with customer centricity

NTT DATA changed the way it engaged with clients to focus on both the emotional and business levels. Together, sales and marketing became more customer-centric, allowing the company to showcase its most important differentiating asset: its people and their extraordinary commitment to clients. This change has yielded great results in the first year:

- +1,000 basis-point differential on revenue growth;

- +30 per cent year-on-year (YoY) growth in contractual signings;

- +25 per cent YoY growth in qualified pipeline.

SOURCE ITSMA Marketing Excellence Awards Winner summary booklet, 2017
Reproduced with permission from ITSMA

Summary

1 The way that we buy things for ourselves, our families and our homes is influencing the way we buy for our businesses. There are also other considerations when buying at work.

2 Complex, high-value purchases demand a business case.

3 A group of decision makers and influencers is usually involved.

4 Procurement professionals will support the purchase process, tailoring their approach to reflect how important the supplier is to the business today and their potential for tomorrow.

5 Business buyers are typically risk averse, looking for reassurance from potential suppliers that they are making the right decision for their organization and its stakeholders.

6 Big purchases need financing, and the biggest suppliers have made that part of their offer.

7 Contracting is complicated, and typically done by commercial and legal professionals once the purchase decision has been made.

8 The purchase is just the start. Business buyers look for a range of tools, content and ideas from their suppliers to maximize their ROI and continue to add value to their business.

Notes

1 CDP (2019) 'Cascading Commitments: Driving ambitious action through supply chain engagements', London, (www.cdp.net (archived at https://perma. cc/AML8-AZ5B))

2 Professor Malcolm McDonald's presentation at ITSMA's ABM Forum, June 2016

3 ITSMA (2018) 'How Executives Engage' study

4 ITSMA (2019) 'How Executives Engage' study

5 www.amey.co.uk/our-services/investments/ (archived at https://perma.cc/ 5QD3-3N8B)

02

What is executive engagement?

Executive engagement is about building relationships with senior buyers in the organizations with which you want to do business, and with other senior executives whom those buyers trust. It is a long-term business development strategy aimed at creating mutual value for everyone involved.

For some companies, it encompasses an ad hoc range of disparate activities, such as advisory boards, conferences, innovation events, hospitality and social media outreach, often run by different parts of the organization, and sometimes without any visibility or coordination between them. For others, it is an integrated programme designed and executed with the sponsorship and support of the executive leadership team to achieve agreed business outcomes.

In this chapter, we'll look at how different organizations define and describe executive engagement, and how they select the executives they want to target. We'll explore the goals companies set themselves for their programmes, and how they organize themselves, before reviewing what is typically included in an executive engagement programme.

Defining executive engagement

Executive engagement, at its simplest, is about having conversations and building relationships with your most senior clients and prospects. At its heart lies a belief that sustainable business success comes from really understanding your customers and collaborating with them to deliver value for you both.

It's about cutting through the noise of the market to attract the attention and engage the interest of the executives you want to serve, to secure their permission to meet and talk about their priorities and challenges, and to shape their understanding of your organization and the value it can offer. Ultimately, it's about building your future business with the clients you want to work with.

Executive engagement strategies define the people who will be involved on both sides: first, the external clients, prospects and influencers who will be the focus of the programme, who are typically C-Suite officers or their direct reports; second, the people within your own organization who will communicate and build relationships with these executives, usually your own C-Suite officers, business leaders, subject matter experts (SMEs) and account managers. Occasionally, they will include people from your partner organizations, who also bring value to the programme.

Typically sponsored by business leaders and run by marketing teams, executive engagement programmes cover a whole range of communication and interaction types with the executives in question, from digital marketing and online content exchange through live events and peer sharing down to small group activities or individual meetings. Managing an executive's experience through these many interactions, changing things that don't work, recovering quickly when something goes wrong and making sure that everyone in your team is fully briefed and debriefed for every conversation is no mean feat. It's the reason that the best companies run sophisticated programmes for executives rather than relying on ad hoc activities.

Why do you need it?

In my own experience over the past few years, partly as a result of the increasing sophistication of procurement teams and partly through a heightened concern for corporate governance, executives have increasingly been involved in buying decisions. Indeed, they are more involved, and more of them are involved! In one of my clients, any spend over £5,000 must be signed off by an executive. In most of my clients, where consulting or some form of business change is involved, particularly leveraging technology, a wider group of executives get involved in the decision-making unit, beyond the traditional IT, finance and procurement domains and into the leaders of business units or other functions.

Engaging with the C-Suite is no longer an option for many suppliers. In a 2017 sales study by ITSMA,[1] 92 per cent of companies recognized that executive engagement was more important to their sales strategy than in the previous two years. Their reasoning included shifting from selling transactional products to integrated solutions, the need to open up new buying centres in a customer organization, the need to develop loyalty and advocates in a more competitive market, and the fact that large purchases – particularly in the digital transformation area – are increasingly board-level decisions.

Jane Hiscock at Farland Group, executive engagement specialists based in Cambridge, MA, explains three reasons why you should consider developing an executive engagement programme.

---

1 **Executives cut through the clutter that can often create delays in sales cycles.** If you bring them into what you are trying to achieve and show them how it aligns to their overall business strategy, they will very quickly become a key influencer in the sales cycle.

2 **Executives often have access to other lines of budget.** While the reason for engagement is not to be transactional, in your work with an executive leader you can often find access to budget that otherwise may not be known by those lower down in the organization. Focus on the leaders' needs and business outcomes and funding will follow.

3 **Executives are more likely to engage in co-creation.** More so than those who report to them, executives will explore a shared strategy model. This may include co-creation of new products; larger ecosystem or partnership development; even shared risk and shared upside or shared value models, depending on the work being done. Most executives can see the forest for the trees, and look to be engaged at a level that will have higher impact than just the engagement they are contracting your company to do.

Reproduced with permission from Farland Group, 2019

Who are these executives?

An executive is someone who is employed in an organization at a senior level, responsible for defining the goals and strategy of the organization, and for ensuring that the strategy is executed well and the goals are achieved. Typically, executive engagement programmes target the board of directors, executive officers and senior leaders in an organization.

The executive and non-executive directors in a public, private or third sector organization are appointed to advise the company's leadership on the organization's strategy and the way it is run, representing shareholders and owners, and taking action when standards of governance or financial management don't meet regulatory standards. Non-executive directors may advise multiple organizations, and as such are often treated as a specific peer group with targeted engagement programmes.

A particularly valuable non-executive role is that of the non-executive chairman, who takes an active leadership role in guiding the chief executive of the organization (CEO).

The CEO is the head of the company and of its leadership team, known as the C-Suite, so called because it covers all the roles that start with 'Chief'. This is the most influential group of individuals within the organization, and typically comprises the following roles:

- **Chief executive officer (CEO).** As the highest-level corporate executive, the CEO is the public face of the company, managing relationships with all of its key stakeholders, such as the board of directors and the company's investors as well as customers, the media and people working in the organization.

- **Chief financial officer (CFO).** The CFO works closely with the CEO to manage the financial performance of the organization and deliver on financial promises to shareholders, while analysing new business opportunities and their likely financial risks and benefits.

- **Chief operating officer (COO).** The COO ensures a company's operations run smoothly, working closely with the CFO on all aspects of company performance and the implications of new opportunities for its operations. In some organizations, all aspects of people and systems are within the COO's remit, while in others there is a separate chief human resource officer (CHRO) and chief information officer (CIO).

- **Chief information officer (CIO).** The CIO is responsible for the technology strategy and infrastructure upon which the company's operations run. Recent evolutions and editions to this role that reflect the importance of technology to all organizations are the chief technology officer (CTO), chief digital officer (CDO) and chief information security officer (CISO).

- **Chief marketing officer (CMO).** Sometimes known as the chief revenue officer or chief client officer, CMOs are responsible for understanding where and how to position the organization in its market to target and serve customers profitably.

The number of roles in the C-Suite will vary depending on the type or size of the organization, as will the senior leadership team representing the next level down from the C-Suite. These 'heads of' or 'senior vice president' roles are filled with a broader range of skills and held by people responsible for planning and executing programmes that bring the C-Suite's strategy for the organization to life. Some organizations include this layer of leadership in their executive engagement programmes, while others do not. If they are included, they are often targeted with different activities so that peer networking is not diluted at the C-Suite level.

Designing an executive engagement strategy

Just as with any other strategic decision, this is about deciding where to focus your resources. The first question to ask yourself is what you want to achieve.

Set your objectives

Are you trying to grow your business with your most important customers? Find and win work with new customers? Create advocates for your organization? Reposition your business in the market? Identify new sources of innovation and potential revenue streams? Create new models, frameworks and intellectual property? Win a larger share of voice in the media?

I recommend that you think about your objectives in three categories: building your organization's reputation, strengthening its relationships with customers and influencers, and growing revenues. Define what you want to achieve, over what timeframe, and decide how you will know if you've been successful. More on this in Chapter 10.

Select the executives

Next, we come to the executives you will focus on in your programme. Typically, these will be in your most important customer accounts, or prospects, with potentially some influencers added in. It may be that there is overlap between the accounts you choose for the executive engagement programme and those that are the focus of any account-based marketing (ABM) programme in your organization, such as in the case of O2 described in this chapter.

Based on the likely budget and headcount you have available, you may need to define a 'cut off' below which you aren't able to include executives in your programme. Most companies do this based on the annual revenue plus future growth opportunity of the customers they work with today, but

I have seen some organizations decide to focus purely on their best prospects, using a selection that rates each prospect company's attractiveness to them and their likely competitive ability to work with that prospect. If you are focusing on prospects, you may need to do some research to identify the right executive to invite, and understand how best to reach them. More on this in Chapter 3.

Decide how you will engage

With your executive engagement objectives defined and the executives themselves chosen, the final decision is about how you will engage. This should span the main content themes you will focus on and the ways you will reach your executives both online and offline.

The content themes should ideally stem from the issues and interests of the executives you plan to engage, married with your own strategy, brand proposition and the ways in which you can deliver value to customers. You may choose a mix of forward-looking thought leadership content on the

FIGURE 2.1 Popular elements of an executive engagement programme

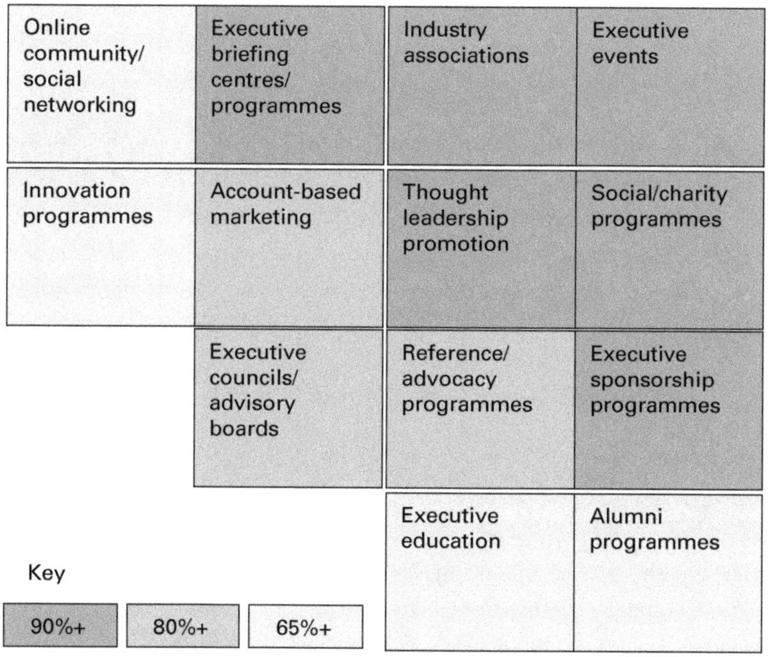

Online community/ social networking	Executive briefing centres/ programmes	Industry associations	Executive events
Innovation programmes	Account-based marketing	Thought leadership promotion	Social/charity programmes
	Executive councils/ advisory boards	Reference/ advocacy programmes	Executive sponsorship programmes
		Executive education	Alumni programmes

Key

90%+	80%+	65%+

SOURCE ITSMA 'Sales and Executive Engagement' survey, 2017

issues that matter most to your audience, with best practices and pragmatic ideas for tackling their current issues. More on this in Chapter 5.

It's critical that the ways in which you choose to engage your audience should be rooted in their own preferred contact methods combined with your culture and capabilities. The three ways to think about engaging are with networks of peers, in small groups and individually, both online and offline. These are all explored further in Chapters 7, 8 and 9 respectively, and some of the most popular techniques used are illustrated in Figure 2.1 and brought to life in the case study of O2's programme in the UK.

CASE STUDY
Designing executive engagement at O2 Business

O2 Business is the principal B2B brand of O2 in the UK, and a commercial brand of Telefónica UK Ltd, which is part of the global telecommunications group Telefónica S.A. O2 Business delivers mobile, communication and technology solutions and services to businesses of all sizes.

O2 has around 6,700 employees and over 450 retail stores in the UK, and sponsors the world's most successful entertainment venue, The O2, situated on the Greenwich peninsula in London.

Strong commitment to executive engagement

At O2, executive engagement is considered critical and taken seriously from the top down, according to Mark Larwood, Head of ABM and Advocacy Marketing. There are various engagement initiatives to get the board and senior executives in front of their customer counterparts on a regular basis, and for mutual benefit. Crucially, these programmes have strong senior sponsorship and support from throughout the business.

Increased focus on face-to-face meetings

He has seen the focus on strengthening these relationships rise significantly over the past few years – in part, he believes, because of the rise of marketing technology: 'There is so much noise now. And everyone is able to be in front of all of their customers and their competitors' customers all the time through all the different channels. So the more opportunity you have to get face-to-face with people to cut through all that noise and build strong relationships, the better.'

You really can't beat face-to-face time, he maintains: 'Much of our focus is around facilitating peer-level meetings and events to offer opportunities for executives to build relationships, get to know our customers better and really get to grips with how we as an organization can support them effectively.'

These executive engagement activities operate through two parallel programmes: ABM and customer engagement.

Aligning with ABM

O2's Lighthouse ABM programme has been running for several years. It is a true one-to-one, award-winning programme that incorporates an important emphasis on executive engagement, with multiple senior stakeholders in the business building relationships with those at the same level in customer companies. There are also executive sponsors for every account, while there will typically be a further two or three executives aligned to their appropriate counterparts in functions such as HR or CFOs.

The ABM programme recently expanded to scale across more accounts, following the typical blended ABM pyramid structure. At the top is the one-to-one Lighthouse activity, with a second tier of companies grouped into clusters of accounts with similar needs at the next level below, and this tier also includes aspects of executive engagement such as roundtable events. The bottom tier is the more general vertical marketing activity such as events, PR, online marketing and so on.

Creating customer advocacy

The second programme, established relatively recently, is a customer engagement programme centred on encouraging advocacy. Like the ABM initiative, it is run on a tiered basis.

At the top is the Customer Advisory Council, made up of senior executives from customer accounts who meet twice a year (based on Chatham House rules) along with senior executives from O2. As Larwood explains, this is the crème de la crème of customer groupings. 'These are the senior operational leaders that we ultimately need to engage to understand their strategies as an input into our strategy. The discussion isn't really about technology, but about their objectives, the challenges they face, and what is holding them back. It's then our job to take that away and convert it into opportunities to create mutual value at O2.'

The next tier down is the customer community, encompassing roughly 250 of O2's largest enterprise customers. Engagement initiatives for these companies target not just those in IT, procurement and technology but also other areas such as customer experience, marketing and finance.

It's seen as an opportunity not only to build O2's understanding of and relationships with these key executives, but also to share and get feedback on O2's strategic direction. For example:

- The company ran an imagination workshop with 90 people at the UK's 5G test-bed centre in the UK. People were given an immersive 5G experience to show 5G's potential in terms of developments with connected vehicles and the Internet of Things (IoT) and worked in teams to imagine the impact on their key business outcomes.

- The customer community is the first to receive the results of proprietary benchmarking research on the role of digital connectivity in driving business outcomes.

- O2 has set up an awards programme to reward customers applying digital connectivity to build customer satisfaction, employee engagement and supplier integration, and ultimately, deliver better business outcomes.

The third tier consists of a major annual conference called Blue Door held at The O2, which can attract up to 1,000 people from both customer and prospect organizations. It includes a range of presentations, workshops and interactive experiences on the current topics and technologies that matter most to executives in these accounts.

Compelling content

Running through all these initiatives is the crucial role of content, Larwood notes: 'High-value thinking and data-driven content is key, whether from some research we have commissioned, from an interesting spin on a burning news issue or from our own innovation group. Having content which is differentiated and provocative will always win out over product information.'

Measuring success

Success is measured through ITSMA's three Rs: revenue, reputation and relationships. As Larwood says, you have to understand the real cause and effect of increased revenues: 'If you are only measuring revenue then you are not measuring leading indicators that predict revenue. That's where understanding reputation and relationships comes in. For example, let's say we aren't engaged enough with customer experience directors. We need to open up conversations with them and position O2 as adding value in their domain, which will lead to opportunities that ultimately bring in revenue.'

Organizing an executive engagement programme

In the same way that any major programme needs a professional approach to its management and execution, so does executive engagement. There are a few foundations to get in place to maximize your chances of success.

Governance

Given the importance of this programme and the fact that it is concerned with your company's most important customers and/or prospects, it should be owned and led by one of your own executives. This person will be your programme sponsor, visibly demonstrating to the organization and to its customers the value your company places on them.

Next comes the steering group, which will be able to guide your thinking on the programme and provide further 'aircover' inside your company to help get everyone aligned behind it. Given the nature of the programme, you will likely need someone senior on it representing the account management or sales community, the business units serving customers, your delivery team and, of course, your marketing function.

Finally, you will need to establish a working group, comprising your programme manager and the people who are responsible for delivering the programme. This is likely to be marketing heavy, with people representing corporate and field marketing, plus possibly event, communications and digital specialists. Some of these people may, of course, be from your agencies or wider ecosystem. You may also include representatives from your corporate social responsibility team, depending on the objectives of your programme.

The working group will need to agree how and when it will meet and/or report to the steering group and to the programme sponsor, share progress against plans, spend against budget and success in delivering on the objectives agreed. To do this well, it's best to agree a performance dashboard upfront with both. We'll discuss this more in Chapter 10.

Internal alignment

Given the wide range of people who touch your most important clients, from marketing, through sales into delivery, finance and your own executive team, for example, you are going to need to ensure that everyone has bought fully into the drivers for the programme, the strategy you've developed, the executives you plan to engage and how you plan to operate. It may be that you will be asking for their help, such as in completing a debrief in your CRM system each time they meet an executive. Therefore, internal alignment and agreement are crucial.

This is one of the reasons for a senior programme sponsor. Ideally, they will use your internal communications platforms – staff events, videos, internal newsletters and collaboration tools, for example – to educate and excite everyone about the programme you have planned. It's fair to say that you will need to brief everyone on the programme and their role in it more often than you think before it's well understood. Take every opportunity to introduce it and update everyone on the progress being made, sharing any quick wins you've achieved to keep their attention and maintain momentum.

For those who will be central to delivering the programme, such as marketing, account management, sales, delivery teams and your own executives, you will need to be clear on the role they are expected to play. Ideally, you will co-create the roles and interdependencies you need with these people, perhaps by running workshops to agree how the programme will be delivered.

Key processes

You will have a number of key processes in your programme, which can also be co-created by working group members and other key stakeholders to help get buy-in early on. The orchestration of different teams to deliver these processes is a key part of programme management, and something illustrated well in the Microsoft case study in this chapter, with multiple teams engaging with executives throughout their lifecycle as a customer to deliver mutual value.

The first process to think about is around how you will get and maintain insight on the executives you care about. While marketing can deliver external insights through market research, analysis of your own databases and systems, and even the purchase of third-party data, much knowledge of the executives will be in the heads of your own client-facing people.

This is particularly true after they have met with the executives and learned new things from the conversations they've held. You need to agree a simple process for completing and maintaining a profile on each executive in your CRM system, not least because everyone who touches that executive needs to be fully briefed so that the executive receives a seamless experience from your company. More on this in Chapter 3.

The way you communicate with executives in your programme is a process that needs to be considered from the executive's point of view, so that they don't receive uncoordinated invitations and messages from all over your business too frequently. Usually this is something that marketing operations take the lead on, keeping track of all requests to contact the executive from anywhere in the business.

One other process to consider is the way in which you will listen to the executives in your programme, absorb feedback for your organization and act upon it. When companies claim they want to understand their customers better and build stronger relationships with them, the best way to undermine this claim and lose the confidence of customers is to ignore what they are told. It's worth agreeing the feedback loop up front and deciding how suggestions will be taken into the business, and how actions planned and taken will be communicated to the executives.

Resources and budget

You've probably gathered by now that all of this takes a lot of time and budget to do well. The good news is that many aspects of executive engagement may already be taking place across your company, but in an uncoordinated and ad hoc manner. The first thing to do is an audit of who is doing what, and where, so that you can begin coordinating existing resources and budgets into your overall programme.

It is likely that you as programme manager will be dedicated full time to the programme, and you may even have some full- or part-time support. You will also need the support of a team of specialists (such as those events managers or a research agency) as you build and execute your programme.

The companies I know that are serious about this commit sufficient budget to do it well – in the hundreds of thousands of pounds. You will need to cost out the additional budget you need, on top of what is already funded, to deliver all the elements of the programme you've designed.

Systems and technologies

Of course, you could deliver an executive engagement programme without a huge investment in systems, but there are some core systems that help. The first is a contact management or CRM system that you can use to hold profiles of the executives and the latest insights you've gleaned from speaking with them. The second is your own website and the analytics behind it.

Then come your marketing automation and content management systems, which will allow you to deliver online content to them that is both relevant and engaging, and to track how they respond.

Other technology and tools include the kind of insight platforms that track your executives on a real-time basis and deliver their latest social musings to you, or let you know which third-party websites they have visited and what they've been searching for.

With the General Data Protection Regulation (GDPR) legislation in Europe and similar privacy regulations on their way in many US states, be sure to check what information you can hold and share on your executives, and make sure they have opted-in to receive the content you would like them to engage with.

CASE STUDY
Positioning Microsoft as a digital transformation partner with account-based engagement

Beginning an ambitious journey

Five years ago, Microsoft set in place an ambitious strategy to become an acknowledged and trusted partner for customers embarking on the complexities of digital transformation. With Microsoft products moving to the cloud, adoption and consumption based on subscription models were becoming more critical than implementation of technology alone. Microsoft wanted to be seen as an expert in implementing cloud-based technology to drive its customers' business outcomes, rather than as a product-centric company.

According to Rudy Dillenseger, Microsoft Services' Director of Account-Based Engagement, this called for a reinvention of how the company engaged with its customers, with more alignment with their business strategies. That meant account teams would have to begin building relationships beyond the IT department. 'The approach was to get our sellers to have bigger conversations than just about the product or solution. So we had to look at how we could help those in the field drive this type of conversation.'

This called for some big changes in how Microsoft built customer relationships:

- a shift in mindset from technology to business processes;
- ensuring that any offerings had industry relevance;
- an emphasis on driving business outcomes;

- enabling sales with envisioning and ideas formation;
- addressing the business decision makers, not just the IT experts.

Building on business outcome selling

The resulting initiative was called business outcome selling and consisted of a number of important elements:

- Account clustering: Microsoft started small, says Dillenseger, with about 30–40 accounts in the first year. 'I think it's important for an ABM-er to start small so you can benchmark what you are doing and judge the relevance. Otherwise sellers can become disenchanted if it doesn't work.'
- Account planning sessions with the account team to determine topics that would resonate with the customers.
- Creating the stories that captured real business need.
- Encouraging broader thinking among the sales teams with ideation and envisioning.
- Enabling the accounts team with training and coaching to have conversations with customers about how Microsoft could help them achieve better business outcomes.

As Dillenseger notes, this was ABM in all but name. And the results were swift. Over the first year, deal sizes doubled, while the actual sales cycle was between six and nine months rather than the expected 18 months. Significantly, conversations with customers were being transformed into ongoing discussions rather than one-off sales activities.

Scaling up to ABM

The next question was how to scale this successful programme by formalizing the ABM process, including prioritizing customer needs, harmonizing the message across touchpoints and providing the right support for the field teams. As Dillenseger says, duplication of effort can be a problem for any company but particularly one the size of Microsoft: 'Sometimes we could end up with 10 or 20 different people at the same customer and potentially with the same person. We had to make sense of that by aligning the messages.'

The result was the ABM framework seen in Figure 2.2.

It consisted of one central account-based orchestration of all the relevant teams, including Microsoft Digital, which is the consulting team working on digital transformation. Accompanying that was a go-to-market strategy, which encompassed:

FIGURE 2.2 ABM at Microsoft

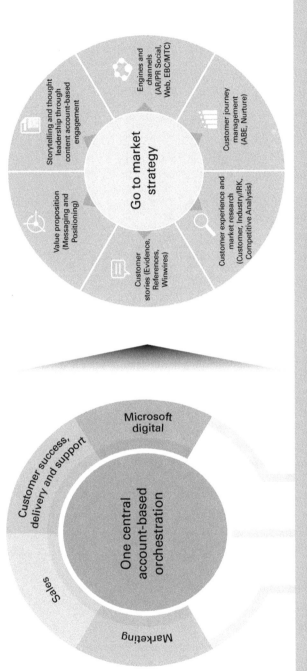

→ Account-based engagement to support our customer's entire lifecycle

FIGURE 2.3 Account-based engagement aligning digital and human touchpoints

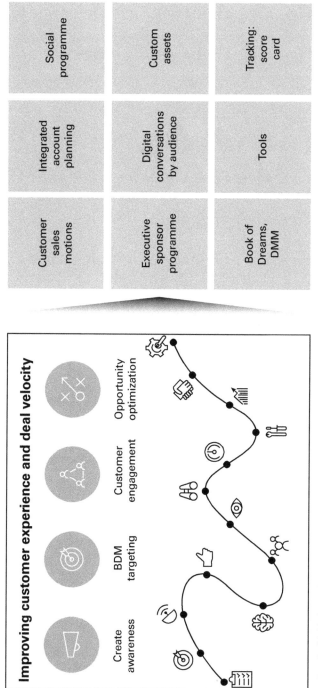

- customer journey management;
- customer experience and market research;
- customer stories;
- the value proposition;
- storytelling and thought leadership;
- digital engines and offline communications channels.

Reaching a new level of engagement

After a year of doing ABM, Microsoft decided it was time to embark on an even more ambitious programme to manage the entire digital transformation engagement cycle, including both digital and human touchpoints, as shown in Figure 2.3. So, the ABM programme was shifted up a gear to become Account-Based Engagement in order to:

- help account teams engage decision makers with a differentiated approach;
- increase share of wallet by driving more impactful projects to the business and ultimately bring in larger deals;
- position Microsoft as a key partner to transform the business;
- provide value to the customer with relevant business outcomes based on industry and horizontal solutions;
- personalize the approach by aligning marketing and sales according to customer pain points;
- coordinate content production by communicating recommendation of assets, collateral and resources.

This comprehensive programme covers the entire spectrum of customer engagement:

1 **Planning the account-based engagement.** Account planning sessions are orchestrated to define customer priorities and create a vision statement to share with the team and based on customer-specific information about the company, market position and potential opportunities. Once priorities are identified through ideation, the right contacts are identified by leveraging LinkedIn Sales Navigator, InMail and Point Drive.

2 **Creating awareness, build perception and win mindshare in the market.** Thought leadership and marketing assets are deployed through the media to position Microsoft as a leader in digital transformation. The company engages

with customers through platforms such as Twitter, Facebook, LinkedIn Sales Navigator, InMail and Point Drive.

3 **Acquiring and engaging business decision makers and IT decision makers.** The ABM team helps account teams reach new contacts by creating a platform for social selling. Through that, they can engage directly with these executives and create specific conversations aligned to customer priorities. The account teams have been trained in using these channels.

4 **Leading customer engagement.** With this step change in engagement the account teams can now qualify leads by sharing and validating with customers their vision for transformational partnership and concentrate on the priorities identified during account planning. The central team provides a set of assets and conversations that the sales people can personalize according to individual customers.

   An ideation workshop further evaluates the opportunities and qualifies them. A visual record of the ideation session is offered to each customer so they can see potential outcomes. In fact, the whole journey on the path to digital transformation is documented in a 'Book of Dreams' that contains the priorities, potential projects, benefits and possible outcomes that can be shared digitally with customers.

5 **Optimizing opportunities.** This is based on a consultative approach supported by digital tools, including a growing use of artificial intelligence (AI), to help account teams in partnership with their customers assess current digital maturity and compare it to their desired result. These, along with the Book of Dreams, are powerful inducements to have conversations about outcomes and help demonstrate value and project importance. The central team promotes activities and content to sellers geared to pipeline opportunities.

Accelerated achievements

The results have been significant. Just a few years ago, digital transformation at Microsoft didn't really exist, says Dillenseger. 'Today, Account-Based Engagement and adoption of ABM practices is driving over a billion dollars of services consulting revenue. We are delivering more value to our customers by focusing on driving business outcomes. This has led to larger opportunities and our average deal size has significantly increased, while our most senior account teams have experienced an increase of their win rate up to 57 per cent.' As Dillenseger concludes, 'This is because we are now talking to the right people about the right things.'

Summary

1 Executive engagement, at its simplest, is about having conversations and building relationships with your most senior clients and prospects.

2 Three reasons for engaging executives: they accelerate sales cycles, they have access to budget and they are more likely to co-create solutions with you.

3 Typically, executive engagement programmes target the board of directors, executive officers and senior leaders in an organization.

4 Build your strategy by selecting the executives you will target, deciding on the content you will use to engage them, and decide which online and offline channels you will use to reach them.

5 For good programme management, consider your governance structure, internal alignment, key processes and the resources, budgets and systems you need to deliver well.

Note

1 ITSMA (2017) 'Sales and Executive Engagement' survey

03

Understanding executives

Good executive engagement strategies start with a clear understanding of the executives you plan to engage. It's all too easy to focus on your own objectives for your programme and believe that these senior buyers and influencers will be as excited about what you have to say and sell as you are. But as we've said before, these are busy people who are targeted by your competitors and other suppliers who also believe they have interesting and exciting things to say.

So, what's needed here is a thorough understanding of who you are targeting, their own priorities, perception and personality, and what would make them interested in spending any of their precious time with you.

In this chapter, we'll look at the information you need to collect on the executives you want in your programme – from the most basic profile data through insights on their buyer persona to an understanding of how they like to communicate. We'll also look at how to collect those data, including the tools and technologies now available to collect them, develop useful insights and share those insights with the people who matter anytime, anywhere, so that they can put them to good use. And finally, we'll talk about privacy regulations and good practices for storing and using personal data.

What do we need to know?

There are three main categories of information that you'll need to collect on the executives in your programme. The first is basic profile information. This will tell you the facts about the executive you are targeting, such as their educational background, previous jobs, qualifications, membership of associations and networks, charity and out-of-work interests and influencers they follow. You can find out how long they've been in their current role and perhaps even details about their priority programmes in that role, including measures of success.

You may be able to find out their domestic situation – where they live, their marital status and whether they have children. All of this will give you some insight into who they are, where they've come from, what their life is like and the network of relationships they have both professionally and, sometimes, outside of work. These relationships can be particularly important when you're identifying potential influencers they turn to for advice around their buying decisions.

While this is the most basic information you'll need to start understanding your executives, you may want to look more closely at how and why they buy the type of solutions your company offers. This second type of information is their buyer persona, and is usually gathered through interview-based research. Buyer personas describe a type of buyer, not an individual, detailing the drivers for their purchase, their success metrics, the journey they take as a buyer, their decision and selection criteria, as well as basic profile information. The key differences between buyer profiles and buyer personas are summarized in Table 3.1.

Armed with your personas, you'll be able to make some initial assumptions about the executives you are targeting – matching them to a particular persona – and develop the right content and engagement techniques to interest them. As you get to know them better, you'll be able to move from general personas to specific information about them as individuals, refining your assumptions into specific insights about them and their buying behaviour.

TABLE 3.1 Buyer profiles versus buyer personas

Buyer profiles	Buyer personas
Generic: Applies across all solutions	**Solution-specific:** Applies to the buying decision for a particular solution
Role based: Describes who your buyer is, including role, responsibilities and pain points	**Buyer-behaviour based:** Describes when, how and why decisions are made
Me too: Based on publicly available secondary research, industry analyst reports and sales insights	**Differentiating:** Based on not-so-obvious insights derived from qualitative research with actual buyers of the specific solution

SOURCE ITSMA 'Crafting Buyer Personas', 2017

The third type of information you can use to understand your executives is built through psychological profiling. With the proliferation of information we willingly put out into social media these days, some firms have made it their business to analyse what we say and how we say it to develop an understanding of what drives us and how we like to communicate. They suggest whether we respond best to numbers, pictures or words, and how likely we are to think in terms of big pictures or operational details, using psychological tools such as the Myers–Briggs personality type indicator to build up a view of our personality and how best to engage with it (this is discussed in more detail further on in this chapter). While this type of information is expensive, it can be very useful to understand decision makers who are selecting suppliers for multi-million-pound, multi-year relationships.

Basic profile information

As a minimum, for any executive you plan to include in your engagement programme, think about building a profile of them that includes the following information:

1 job title, scope of current role and time in role;

2 a photograph (you want to know what the executive looks like before you meet them);

3 objectives, challenges and key performance indicators within current role;

4 previous roles held within the company;

5 previous roles held in other companies;

6 non-executive roles currently and previously held in other companies or in charities;

7 professional associations;

8 professional accolades;

9 professional contributions (speeches, articles, blogs);

10 academic qualifications and institutions;

11 personal demographic information, hobbies and interests.

A sample buyer profile is shown in Figure 3.1.

FIGURE 3.1 A sample buyer profile

Mark Williams,
IT Director

Catchphrase:
*'I want to work with
solution providers
that understand my
business.'*

Note: Content in
this **buyer profile** is
neither solution-
specific, buyer-
behaviour focused,
nor differentiating.

My background
- IT Director of transportation company
  with $3 bn in revenue
- 37 years old, married, 2 children and 2
  dogs, living in Boulder, CO
- BS in electrical engineering
- Reports to VP IT
- Worked at same company for 14 years,
  starting as a data entry clerk
- Tends to work late to directly
  communicate with offshore support staff
- Likes to learn new tools, but the ROI must
  be high
- Has a strong interest in marathon running

My pain points
- Lack of software with sufficient robustness to facilitate fleet scheduling
- Short on staff to cover graveyard shift
- Caught by surprise during implementation due to not fully understanding
  solution features

My career goal
To become a division CIO at my
current company or a different
company, or maybe start my
own consulting business

What keeps me up at night
- The never-ending quest to
  achieve >96.7% uptime
- Fear that the millennials are
  going to mutiny if we don't
  let them access social media
  behind the firewall

How I am evaluated
- Minimize cost of delays and
  disruption
- Technology ROI
- Minimize downtime
- End-user satisfaction

**My trusted information
sources**
- Peers and colleagues
- Industry analysts
- Existing solution providers
- Digital influencer blog posts
- Internet searches
- Technology conferences
- YouTube videos

SOURCE ITSMA 'Crafting Buyer Personas', 2017

Increasingly, capturing information from social networks is making it easier to build these profiles. Social listening can be automated, as we'll discuss in the technology section of this chapter, by selecting specific individuals and key words to monitor in the various conversations taking place online. But what if someone refuses to leave any sort of digital footprint? There are specialist agencies that can carry out qualitative research to help fill in the gaps using personal relationships and networks, which is particularly valuable in Asian countries where less is accessible online to non-native speakers in particular.

Use of social media can vary across cultures, like many other things. A key fact to be aware of for your executives is their cultural heritage, since this may tell you a lot about how they prefer to engage. Jon Geldart can testify to the unique challenges of engaging executives in China, for example, having spent several years developing the business of a professional service firm, Grant Thornton, in the country and having written extensively on the art of doing business in China. Some of his insights are shared in the interview in this chapter.

CASE STUDY
Engaging with executives in China

Jon Geldart, author of the Foreword to this book, is an expert on engaging with Chinese executives. Having worked regularly in China for over nine years, he has spent around 80 per cent of the last five years at Grant Thornton International focussing on the strategic development of greater China for the organization, along with acquiring experience of dealing with a number of emerging economies.

Drawing on his experience, Jon has also written a number of well-received books on China:

- *The Thoughts of Chairman Now: Wisdom from China's business leaders and entrepreneurs*, WPP Group, 2013
- *Notes from a Beijing Coffee Shop: Insights into modern China*, LID Publishing, 2015
- *Inside the Middle Kingdom*, LID Publishing, 2015.

He is currently Director General of the UK's Institute of Directors and a non-executive director for several UK and international businesses. He is also the acting Deputy Chair and Senior Advisor to the China Britain Doctoral Association (CBDA) and an advisor to the Leeds (UK) Business Confucius Institute.

Bev Burgess: *You have been successfully engaging with senior executives throughout your career and, particularly, in China. What are your general thoughts about executive engagement?*

Jon Geldart: I suppose I can sum it up by saying that my career has been spent engaging with leaders in management to get them to do things they never really wanted to do in the first place! And I have been lucky enough to do that across borders. What I've found is that humanity is actually the same wherever you are. The difference comes from culture.

Unless you are able to translate the nuances of how people respond to you in different geographical, cultural, linguistic and/or historical contexts, then you will probably never convince anyone to do anything. Convincing someone is really about encouraging a shared common purpose and an alignment around an outcome rather than agreement. The best way of getting engagement with executives is through a common and consistent alignment.

How do you distinguish between agreement and alignment?

This is a crucial distinction. Call it trying to get to a coalition of the willing. It's like climbing a mountain. You can climb it by a variety of routes but you align around the objective, the top. You don't have to get there at the same speed, agree to go in the same direction, or even use the same kind of processes. But you do have to get there. You align on the outcome but you then allow people to get there under their own steam and in their own way. This is absolutely the case in China.

What are some of the key things we need to understand about doing business in China?

The first and most important is that you have to deal with the emperor, not the mandarins of middle management. The Chinese have evolved over 5,000 years with an autocratic emperor system and structure. Seniors speak to seniors, and politicians speak to politicians. Also, never forget that China is a state-run, state-owned closed economy. As such it has a set of rules and processes that are fundamentally different from any other part of the world. The Party leader in the company is more important than the CEO.

Next is to understand the culture and the history. If you're not willing to go this far, you can't engage. You have to put the effort in, not just fly in and out. It is a labyrinthine, complicated country that has many disparate aspects but is focused around a common goal, which at the moment is driven by the president, Xi Jinping.

You don't have to be Chinese, nor do the Chinese expect you to be. But you need to grasp the concept of *guanxi*, which is the system of social networks and influential relationships that facilitate business and other dealings.

You also have to be super flexible and apply what a friend of mine calls 'the Chinese fire drill': everything is last minute, so you have to be very fast in your decision making. Rather, it *appears* to be last minute but if you read the runes you can see what's coming...

So, to be successful you have to understand the levels of seniority, the political and historical context and also the role of the Party?

Yes. And because you really can't do all that you need what I call fixers. These are people I have built close relationships with and helped over the years by doing little things that can make a big difference.

Something else to understand is that in schools the Chinese learn by rote. If students feel they don't have the right answer because you haven't told them what it is, they won't say anything because they don't want to lose face. This carries on into adulthood, but there's a twist. The Chinese are super-entrepreneurial and don't mind failing. They can turn on a sixpence!

Are they receptive to thought leadership content, such as white papers on thought-provoking issues?

Emphatically, unequivocally no – unless you are creating it from a Chinese perspective. Basically, forget all you have learned in the West. When you are engaging with Chinese leadership you have to do it from their perspective.

They take immense pride in the fact that China is taking on the world and winning. They have big brands like Haier, Alibaba, Lenovo, Air China and ICBC, the biggest bank in the world, and smaller ones like smartphone maker OnePlus and the conglomerate Tencent. So they want case studies about Chinese models of success.

In addition to surpassing the United States in terms of application numbers of patents, China has also overtaken other innovation leaders such as Japan, Germany and South Korea since the mid- to late-2000s.[1] That's why patent and copyright law is now so important in China and why Western companies can protect their intellectual property – unlike previously.

Adopting this perspective is not complicated. It's what marketers should always be doing: understanding and respecting your customer base.

How do you know when you have made a connection?

You see your suggestions being taken on, even if it's a year later. For example, I wrote branding guidelines for the Chinese accounting profession. I was amazed when they produced guidelines based on what I had done – obviously adapted for the Chinese – and when I asked how that happened they replied: well, you wrote them for us. It's about a build-up of trust and subtlety of engagement. We in the West aren't that subtle.

Stereotypes are stereotypes for a reason. If you are informed by culture and history it enables you to flex that stereotypical view of the Chinese in favour of the reality you are actually engaging with.

What are the rewards for going to such lengths in engaging with the Chinese?

Provided you accept that there is a cost of doing business whether financially, morally or emotionally, if you have a good business in the West you can scale it in China significantly and make an awful lot of money.

After all, there are 1.4 billion people. Shanghai is bigger than Australia. Some second- and third-tier cities are bigger than some Western economies. The opportunity to succeed and draw immense shareholder value from engagement with the Chinese is as big as China itself.

Can we learn any lessons from doing business with China?

The Chinese are very good at playing the long game. They take a long-term, crystal-clear view of their objective. They are also flexible and agile, which is something I admire tremendously. The benefit of agility is fast correction, which is where we can fail in the West.

The Chinese will try something, having a general direction in their head. But if that doesn't work, they will try something else. It's like taking fairy steps rather than long strides, which allows you to self-correct more quickly. You might lose a bit of money but you get back on track. And with that, we're back to the principle of aligning on the outcome while being flexible on the approach.

Creating an executive profile isn't a one-off exercise. You should be aiming to maintain an accurate profile in real time using the kinds of social listening tools – even simple Google alerts – that are available. Tracking each person's level of engagement with your company as you move into the execution phase of ABM should be a key performance metric. It will further enhance what you know about each stakeholder based on how they actually respond and behave.

Buyer personas

Buyer personas have become increasingly popular ways to identify segments of buyers with similar characteristics and drivers to purchase. ITSMA defines a persona as 'an example (archetype) of a customer who represents a group of buyers', as follows:

A persona is not an actual person; rather, it is a marketing concept. In many respects, personas are a way to segment your target audiences. However, unlike traditional segmentation, buyers cannot be assigned to a specific persona based on easily identifiable demographic characteristics. Instead, buyer personas are defined by buyer behaviors such as solution triggers, success factors, evaluation process and decision criteria. Buyer personas are used to understand what motivates buyers to choose a particular solution – and how to persuade them to choose you rather than a competitor or the status quo. In short, buyer personas are a resource that enables B2B companies to create messages and other content that resonate with the intended audience and prompt action.

You know that a marketing technique has gone mainstream when a cartoonist features it. In Figure 3.2, Tom Fishburne helps us to understand what a buyer persona is not.

The best buyer personas are built through market research interviews with people who have recently purchased a specific solution for their business (there is a vital distinction between stakeholder profiles, which are general, and buyer personas, which are solution-specific). The interview

FIGURE 3.2   What a buyer persona is not

SOURCE https://marketoonist.com/2016/12/buyerpersonas.html
Reprinted with kind permission from marketoonist

focuses on the actual buying process for the solution and the details of when and how decisions were made.

A common shortcut that marketers take is to interview their sales colleagues to build personas. But although sales may have some useful information and insights on buyers, they will not be able to accurately answer all of the questions covered in a persona interview. Technology company idio started with internally generated personas, but quickly realized that to really differentiate themselves and engage target buyers, they needed to build personas from research interviews with actual buyers of their solution, as the case study below explains.

CASE STUDY
Buyer personas in practice: the case of idio

Marketing technology provider idio, whose technology is designed to make content marketing more tailored, relevant and effective, faced a major challenge in a fast-growing and rapidly changing market: How do you stand out with a compelling message when every competitor, no matter what their technology actually does, is saying the same thing? What's the best way to articulate your value when you're competing mainly with the status quo, that is, doing nothing?

Answering these two questions required a deep understanding of customer pain points and clear value propositions to solve them. For CMO and company co-founder Andrew Davies, the key to that understanding was buyer personas. The company had used personas from the beginning, but the first iteration wasn't quite working.

As Davies is the first to admit: 'We basically made them up. We had a pretty good idea who our customers were and what problems they faced.' To really develop compelling, differentiated value propositions, the next step was to go back to the drawing board.

Developing buyer personas in earnest

In late 2014, a cross-functional team at idio, composed primarily of product development and marketing with involvement from sales and customer success, began a project to overhaul the 12 personas they started out with. The project was initially intended to generate not buyer personas but user personas.

The focus of this effort was 25 stakeholder interviews with customers and prospects. In many cases the team interviewed multiple roles within the same organization to understand their different perspectives and needs. Since there are multiple roles involved in purchasing and using idio's offerings, this range of views was particularly important.

In the course of identifying 10 user personas from the primary research, the team discovered that four of them were clearly the biggest influencers in the buying process.

While the total number of personas didn't change much as a result of the project, the substance of the personas changed significantly. Now idio's personas, which align closely to professional roles, are defined by clear pain points and priorities, straight from the mouths of actual buyers and users.

Putting personas to use

Developing value propositions

Once the new set of personas had been developed, the product development and marketing teams collaborated on another important step: developing value propositions. The primary research had yielded the pain points buyers face. Now the team included other sources of information to help with the process, including analyst views and product descriptions.

A big challenge for the sales team was getting prospects to decide they needed to do something different rather than viewing the problems they faced as intractable. With this in mind, the team concentrated on developing value propositions that directly addressed the pain points their personas faced and established the need to act. They articulated the value of idio's offerings as a means of resolving these challenges, making the status quo unacceptable.

These value propositions are an integral part of the marketing and sales process, but they aren't the only area in which idio has put its personas to use. The company is using them in just about every aspect of its business.

Product development: meeting the need

Regardless of their involvement in the buying process, all 10 of idio's personas play a central role in the way the company prioritizes the many features and functions in its product development road map.

The product development team, which along with marketing has access to persona interview transcripts and extensive notes from the development process, has used personas to develop stories. These stories are user journeys that describe why different personas are using the system and which aspects of it are most important for them. Says Davies: 'If the idea for a new feature or bit of functionality can't be placed within a story, tied back to one or more of the personas, and ultimately validated with buyer research, it doesn't make it into development.'

Thought leadership and content marketing

It's no surprise that, given the company's raison d'être, thought leadership and content marketing are a big part of idio's marketing strategy. But as for any company with a similar approach, the main challenge is determining what content to create, in what forms, and through which channels for a given audience. That's where buyer personas come in handy.

The priorities and issues of the key personas shape the story for thought leadership and determine the subjects addressed. The preferences demonstrated by these personas also dictate the form that thought leadership and other marketing content takes as well as where it is placed and how it is promoted. As a case in point, webinars have particularly good traction among the four primary buyer personas, so much of the content is distributed in this way.

To generate more interest in their outreach efforts, the marketing team uses personas to help identify potential thought leadership contributors and collaborators. Sometimes it's as straightforward as identifying a customer that has a particular pain point and getting them to contribute a blog post on their issue, resulting in something tailor-made for that persona.

Personas also guide the development of other types of marketing content, particularly use cases and webinars, the things that feed ongoing conversations. As Kevin Li, SVP of product and customer success, explains: 'Patterns begin to emerge on the user persona side.' These patterns shape use cases, such as 'improve SEO strategy'. This content feeds into later stages of the sales cycle – post-discovery, when an opportunity has been identified – to build the business case and support the need for action.

Campaigns

Persona-driven content forms a major component of the nurture campaigns that the marketing team has developed for its four primary buyer personas. Given their differing priorities and needs, each of the primary buyer personas has a dedicated nurture track. In addition to defining issues and content, buyer personas also determine the companies and job titles pursued by the lead acquisition team.

As idio's use of buyer personas to underpin its marketing efforts has matured, its marketing strategy has shifted to focus more on content development and nurture campaigns. Because most marketing content and messaging have been designed around identified pain points, it elicits feedback on the problems people are trying to solve.

This creates a sort of tacit opt-in or opt-out: if you engage with a particular type of content, it's most likely because it addresses a problem you are trying to solve. If you don't engage, you've essentially opted out of something that isn't a problem for you.

Results and lessons learned

The success of idio's persona initiative has reshaped the company's approach to marketing and selling. One measure of this success is decreasing lead cycles: that is, the duration of time from identifying a lead to qualifying it as an opportunity. The others are faster movement through the middle of the sales funnel and increasing accuracy of sales close dates from the sales team.

According to Li, perhaps the most significant benefit of using buyer personas in the marketing and sales process is: 'knowing who not to talk to or waste cycle time on. They have made it much easier to decide whether someone is a good prospect or interested but is unlikely to buy'. Personas have helped both marketing and sales decide where to focus their limited time and effort to greatest effect.

SOURCE Extract from 'Buyer Personas in Practice: The case of Idio', ITSMA, 2015
Reproduced with permission from ITSMA

What should a buyer persona cover?

The Buyer Persona Institute (buyerpersona.com) has been creating personas for clients since 2010 and accredits others to do the same (including Julie Schwartz, SVP Research and Thought Leadership at ITSMA). Its buyer persona templates cover six areas, as shown below and summarized in an example buyer persona by ITSMA in the following box:

1 **Buyer profile.** Just enough information to humanize the persona. This information can come from internal sources, secondary research and analyst reports.

2 **Priority initiatives.** The solution purchase triggers or compelling reason to act; why has the buyer decided to abandon the status quo?

3 **Success factors.** What the buyer hopes to achieve, both organizationally and professionally, by implementing the specific solution. These are the 'solution benefits' from the buyer's perspective.

4 **Perceived barriers.** What would keep the buyer from purchasing the solution?

5 **Buyer's journey.** What steps does the buyer take to research and evaluate the solution? What questions does the buyer have at each stage of the buying process? Who else is involved?

6 **Decision criteria.** What factors does the buyer evaluate when choosing between competitive solutions? How do they change at each stage of the buying process?

The value of these six areas lies in the fact that they provide a crystal-clear path from buyer insights to value proposition and content strategy development, as demonstrated in the idio case example.

A SAMPLE BUYER PERSONA

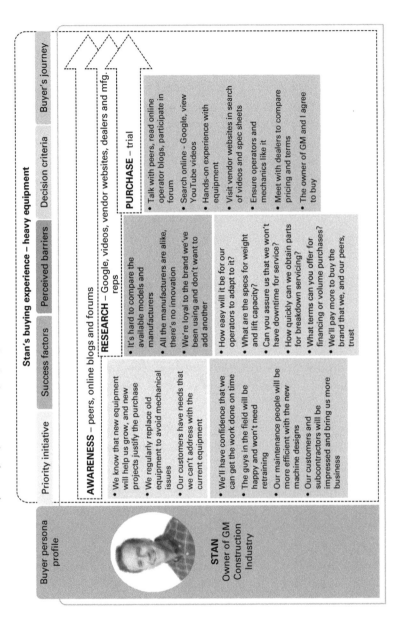

FIGURE 3.3a A sample buyer persona: Buying experience

FIGURE 3.3b A sample buyer persona: End-user-oriented IT buyer

Profile: IT/Communications Executive

Title	Senior Vice President of IT/CIO
Role	Decision Maker and Evaluator
Responsibility	Runs the technology and/or communications functions

My responsibilities

- Providing/maintaining infrastructure to execute business
- Keeping up with technology trends
  - Physical infrastructure vs cloud
  - Mobile/fixed/data options
- Minimizing risk
- Lowering costs
- Providing a good end-user experience

How I am evaluated

- Partner relationships/management
- Availability/uptime
- End-user satisfaction
- Providing functionality to support business strategy execution
- Operational excellence
- Productivity
- Performance
- Security
- Expense management

Information and sources I trust

- My own knowledge and past experiences
- Internal and external colleagues
- Strategic vendors/VARs
- Trade shows and conferences
- Analyst reports and rankings
- Industry associations

Priority initiatives	What business conditions trigger this buyer's decision to look for a solution?
Decisions are triggered when we in IT determine that legacy solutions are no longer meeting business needs; there is a need to *modernize IT*	• Our IT used to be neglected. We started a very large modernization programme for both infrastructure and business systems. We started the modernization with the basics: networks, servers and WiFi everywhere. Next was a higher-level set of tools for users to make their lives easier and help them collaborate better. • It's driven by the ongoing consumerization of client IT solutions and the expectations, particularly for field-based employees and sales reps. The last thing those guys want to do is get their laptops out.
IT supports the business units; as needs arise, we *react*	• The demands of the customers saying that they needed storage. It was really frustrating for our users so we responded with a desktop and server refreshment programme, virtualization and scalability. • It was a bad customer experience and a lot of screaming that forced us to look hard at these types of solutions.
Requests from the business users for *mobility* are a key driving force	• There was a big push from the business for mobile device management, being able to use their iPhones and iPads. It was IT's decision to select the particular product. • Typically the catalyst is that the current solution isn't being used. It's not meeting the needs of the constituents. Mobility has been a key driving force. Does it work in responsive web design? Does it have an app? Is it cloud based? • Our users want wireless everywhere. We are working on that.

Success factors	What results or outcomes does this buyer persona expect from the project?
With this solution we will be able to *deliver a dramatically improved customer experience*	• It's important for our internal customers to have a great, efficient experience. When the team experiences a slowdown, it hits everyone. Our external customers are not being served, reports are not being delivered and goods may be sitting in the port. It's going to hurt our reputation. It's also going to hurt our external customers being unable to deliver to their clients.

(continued)

Success factors	What results or outcomes does this buyer persona expect from the project?
	• We had users from all over the world connecting back to HQ for their virtual experience. Not ideal. With the new solution, we will be able to service our customers in each region through the cloud without costly infrastructure and data centres all over the world. They will get a better experience.
The new solution will help our users to share information and *collaborate better*	• We wanted to make it easier for the sales team to share data among the team and create groups. • We started to think of a higher-level set of tools for users to make their lives easier, to help them collaborate better.
We will effectively *transform IT operations* into a service organization that meets the needs of our internal clients	• That's really what our true end-game was. How are we going to better serve our customers? How are we going to make our customers feel better about our services? • For us in IT, success is putting something on their devices that lets them do what they want and is completely transparent. A very thin footprint and invisibility were very key for us. The last thing that the sales force should get is a piece of software that does something for us but not for them. • We need some central system to push distribution to the end-user side automatically to make sure things are easier for them and us.

Perceived barriers	What attitudes or concerns prevent this buyer from purchasing from you?
Price is always a factor; it has to be competitive and within our budget	• We knew that we needed this. We knew that it was going to make us much more efficient, but you know the deal. It always comes down to cost and whether the board is going to allow that budget item to go through. • Large global providers are just very expensive. We can find some local vendors that can provide cheaper services with acceptable quality. • Price is always the criterion that is weighted highest. They get eliminated when they are the highest price without offsetting value add.

(continued)

Perceived barriers	What attitudes or concerns prevent this buyer from purchasing from you?
We have doubts about your *ability to deliver* on the required functionality	• You don't appear to be completely vested in us and the solution. Show us you're keeping current and focusing on mobile. • We have a set of requirements that were created collaboratively by IT and the business. The solution has got to meet those requirements, including how it's going to be administered and the number of users.

Decision criteria	What are the top criteria used to compare alternative approaches/options to make a final decision?
First and foremost, does your solution offer the specific *mobile functionality* our end-users are looking for?	• We were looking for functionality. We wanted chat, group chat, screen sharing, easy transfer of telephone lines from one place to another, soft phones, so even if you are sitting at home, your computer is your landline. We wanted all those functionalities and integration into online conferencing. • It needed to be something that primarily met the sales team's needs, could integrate back with our CRM system, our back office CRM and could eliminate redundant activities. It had to provide mobile access, and access to real-time data. Then of course the security needs, performance and integration. • It was the maturity of the cloud environment that clinched it. It's all about the applications now, it's about accessing them on all your different devices, all the different platforms that you have. One provider's offering was just so strong. They were really thinking about everything from authentication of those applications, how we can secure our data, all those pieces.
The solution has to *integrate* well with the rest of our IT environment.	• The final two providers were more or less equivalent. One was slightly better integrated into the office suite. The other was better integrated into the telephony. Given that the unified communications is, in a way, linking the telephony to the computer systems, that's how the decision was made. • It was completely integrated with the rest of our environment. It was a no-brainer from that perspective.

(continued)

Decision criteria	What are the top criteria used to compare alternative approaches/options to make a final decision?
I *won't pay more* to get functionality we don't really need	• Do the bells and whistles from additional functionality really justify the actual spend? They didn't. So we went with the cheaper solution, which is mature thinking for an IT function. The stereotype would be we always go with the most complex technology. • The solutions architect preferred the more functionally rich solution, but he doesn't have P&L responsibility.
Functionality and cost are important, but so is the *ongoing support*	• I think for us the first thing is the service quality. Can you provide 24/7 support, what's your response time, can you do onsite support, how fast can you deliver hardware and software that we need? It's a balance between cost and quality. • It's great to talk about the function that it's going to give you from a virtual desktop perspective, but maintaining those applications that are sitting in that virtual environment, in someone else's cloud, is also challenging. We wanted to make sure we got feedback on that as well.

Buyer's journey	What are the steps this buyer persona takes to evaluate options and make a decision? What sources of information does this persona trust?
The evaluation team included stakeholders from throughout the company	• We make sure that we have all the stakeholders represented across the company. You need people from accounting and finance, security, corporate and the infrastructure team. • Running the actual evaluation was myself, our director of infrastructure, client engineering, our storage teams. We have our administrators of the virtual environments. We did branch out from a POC perspective, into the entire IT organization. • The difficult piece is changing the culture. You're adopting a new platform and new ways of thinking, managing your workload and communicating with your customers. I was very conscious about not making decisions in a silo, which is why I involved the application side of the house, infrastructure, SAP team and a non-IT person because I wanted to get the viewpoint of a non-technical person.

(continued)

Buyer's journey	What are the steps this buyer persona takes to evaluate options and make a decision? What sources of information does this persona trust?
We are familiar with most of the solution providers from current and past experience	• The research is more my knowledge of what the products out there are. I've been in IT for many years so I'm pretty familiar with what options we have out there. • One of the things we do with our strategic vendors is periodically talk to them about their wider offering. I don't see it as selling, but as part of the ongoing relationship with good vendors. • We have a bunch of guys on our team that live, breathe and die in this space. We took a lot of feedback from them on where to start looking. Then we reached out to some of our suppliers that play with multiple vendors and spoke to them to get their feedback.
We will supplement our knowledge by seeking input from industry analysts, peers at other companies, and finally an internet search to make sure we aren't missing anyone	• There's usually a Gartner quadrant or a listing of products similar to that that we can get from an analyst team. • I worked at another company for about 16 years. I obviously have a lot of contacts there. I reached out to a few folks there and some who have moved on to other companies. • Everyone in the services desk, security and compliance is familiar with solutions. Ultimately it is a mix of analyst reviews, going to trade shows (eg Interop and service desk shows, security shows), and sharing ideas with peers. We will also engage our VARs and pitch the problem to them. They will offer different solutions. You start hearing the same solutions mentioned across the different sources. Those are the ones we approach.
We put together a list of potential providers and whittled it down	• I researched the vendors who I wanted to partner with to help me with the implementation. I went through a vetting process and interviewed different vendors, looked at their experience, what vendors they did, their project management, ideology, customers they had worked with. I even got on the phone with many of their customers. • The testimonials on the respective websites were important to us because they gave us some confidence that other organizations that we respect are also using these solutions.

(continued)

Buyer's journey	What are the steps this buyer persona takes to evaluate options and make a decision? What sources of information does this persona trust?
	• I make a list of our requirements and must-haves. I use this to do some rough scoring. I will shortlist the ones that tick all the boxes. Then I schedule an introductory call to understand what the company is doing in more detail. I share our use case to see if there is a match.
	• We did two rounds of interviews for each vendor on-site. We had follow-up questions, so we really did our due diligence. Then I did one-on-one interviews with their customers. I took a lot of notes and shared my notes with the team.
We then conduct a formal RFP process to make it easy to compare proposals and pricing	• We went through each of the responses in an apples-to-apples comparison and we sent back to them a scorecard on each of their responses and how they compared without giving each other's commercial details away. We let them know where they needed to improve their proposal or where we had some concerns because either they hadn't responded fully enough or they hadn't understood our requirement fully enough etc.
	• The technical team narrowed down the list without looking at the commercial aspects of the proposals. We decided based on the technical and service aspects. The commercial subcommittee looked at the prices and finalized the shortlist based on the technical committee's recommendations. Some of our choices had very high prices, but they will negotiate it afterwards.
	• We do an IT scorecard and we expect the business to do a business scorecard. We go through the scorecards and commercials. We go to the two favourites and ask them to come back with their best and final offer.
Since these are high-profile, strategic decisions, we will usually do a proof of concept (POC)	• We set up two or three PCs with the three different applications on it. We asked the teams to actually perform testing on it, like what they do in their daily tasks.

(continued)

Buyer's journey	What are the steps this buyer persona takes to evaluate options and make a decision? What sources of information does this persona trust?
	• We asked for some trial runs of the technology. There were some mobile coverage trials, conferencing solution trials. They were also asked to show us how quickly they could spin up in a private cloud for us. And we made an evaluation on that basis in terms of capability.
	• Once we pick our shortlist we do a POC. Even if the vendor is going direct, we ask them to engage a partner because we are getting tired of the model where the partner just pushes the paper for their commission for the deal and doesn't put any effort into it. At the end of the day, once the vendor pre-sales people leave, you're stuck with no one to support you.

SOURCE ITSMA sample buyer persona, 2019
Reprinted with permission from ITSMA

Psychological profiling

Where you have the budget available, and it is important to understand fully the best way to approach and communicate with the executives you are targeting for your programme, you may wish to enlist the support of a firm that does psychological profiling.

Psychological profiles introduce the executive as a person, with some background context such as you would include in basic profiling plus some of the information on the drivers for their behaviour and likely definitions of success that you would see in a buyer persona. Psychological profiles then go on to explore their communications preferences, reviewing all of the written, photographic, video and live-presentation sources available in order to build a snapshot of the language and communication delivery mechanisms that will resonate best with that individual.

For example, my own communication preferences are very visual. This means that I prefer to see pictures and graphs such as those shown in presentations or drawn on whiteboards, rather than spreadsheets or text-based reports. It also means that I respond better to visual language, so when people want to engage me, phrases like 'we'd like to get your perspective on this opportunity' and 'you'll see results in these areas' will naturally land better than kinaesthetic language such as 'we'd like to get to grips with this opportunity' or 'let's walk through the ideas'. People with kinaesthetic preferences will respond better to interactive exercises and tools, such as virtual reality.

Other possible preferences include auditory communicators, who respond best to phrases such as 'we'd like to sound you out' or 'how does this resonate with you?' They are happy listening to seminars, podcasts or webinars, or simply discussing an issue.

In addition to communication styles, psychological profiling can provide clues as to personality types, using tools such as the Myers–Briggs personality indicator (MBTI).[2] The theory of psychological types was introduced in the 1920s by Carl G Jung and the MBTI tool itself was developed in the 1940s by Isabel Briggs Myers. Millions of people worldwide have taken the indicator each year since its first publication in 1962. It generates 16 types of personality based on a combination of preferences in four areas, summarized on Myersbriggs.org as follows:

- Extraversion (E) or Introversion (I): Do you prefer to focus on the outer world or on your own inner world?
- Sensing (S) or Intuition (N): Do you prefer to focus on the basic information you take in or do you prefer to interpret and add meaning?
- Thinking (T) or Feeling (F): When making decisions, do you prefer to first look at logic and consistency or first look at the people and special circumstances?
- Judging (J) or Perceiving (P): In dealing with the outside world, do you prefer to get things decided or do you prefer to stay open to new information and options?

Once again, using myself as an example, my profile is ENFP (Figure 3.4). I am an extravert, preferring to focus on the people and world around me, adding meaning to the information I take in and considering it in the context of people and special circumstances. And I prefer to stay open to new information and options. ENFPs are said to be future oriented, possibility focused and novelty seeking, among other things. Just these three pieces of information could help people plan how best to engage with me based on my psychological profile, using techniques such as films of how the world might look in future to get my attention.

FIGURE 3.4   ENFP: My Myers–Briggs personality type

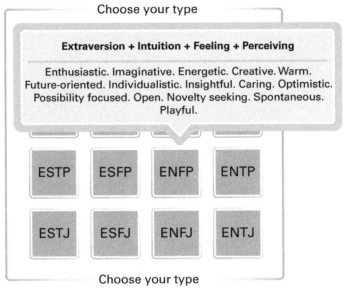

SOURCE www.myersbriggs.org/my-mbti-personality-type/mbti-basics/

Of course, there are alternative types of personality profiling tools that can be used, but the principles are the same, and the insights they deliver can make the difference between a successful first contact with an executive and one that seems irrelevant and uninteresting.

Technology that can help

The marketing technology available to help you understand executives is constantly evolving, so it takes an expert to really provide advice on what you should consider using, and when. Kathy Macchi, a senior associate of ITSMA and Vice President, Consulting Services at Inverta, is more expert than most. Based in Austin, Texas, Kathy keeps a close eye on how the martech landscape is changing and making it easier for companies to identify and understand the executives that are most important to them.

CASE STUDY

Bev Burgess: *How far can technology really help us with an executive audience?*

Kathy Macchi: Modern marketing is an interesting dichotomy. On one side, we have more tools than ever to support data-informed, highly coordinated, omnichannel marketing. The technology has just exploded in popularity in the past five to seven years, so the ability to create impact with brand experiences at scale has never been more of a reality. But our audience is more sophisticated now, too, and they're looking for 1:1 personalization. B2B executives expect the same level of customization that they experience as a consumer, so what we end up with is a bunch of high-powered technology that's missing the mark when it comes to what truly engages audiences, and a group of savvy executive-level buyers who are craving relevant engagement from the solutions they research.

How does it help us build an understanding of our target executives?

Technology can generate the insights that help us create that high level of personalization and relevance that executives want. Those insights allow you to create a thought-provoking viewpoint that can pique an executive's interest, to tee up a 'conversation of value'.

A 'conversation of value' is a give-to-get proposition. An executive will never share their challenges, their concerns or confidential information with you unless you have something valuable to bring to the table. Being able to create and have those two-way conversations is a distinct advantage over your competition.

To achieve this true insight-driven marketing requires knowledge of the dynamics of what's happening inside an organization within the context of their market: how are their strategic priorities playing out in real life, who has the power and how do things get done?

However, having the right strategy, technology and tools can help with the research, value creation and message activation that makes true engagement happen. And executive engagement is the key to creating an information-value exchange that strengthens relationships to a competitive advantage.

Let's dig into the beginning of that list. What goes into the research phase?

The process for researching executives may seem self-explanatory, but you can waste a lot of time chasing down dead ends and collecting data that isn't important. Three key tool categories can help support you in your effort.

Information harvesting. This is the least sophisticated of automated research tools, and they'll crawl the internet and scrape publishing information, social media profile information and other areas where your executive has appeared and deliver to you a readout of unstructured information.

Information aggregation. This is a close cousin to information harvesting. This tool takes a similar approach of crawling the internet for published information, but deduplicates, structures and organizes the information into a readout. It arranges all the information into logical groupings to allow for easier consumption and understanding.

Information analysis. This uses computer-based machine learning or artificial intelligence (AI) to add context through patterns. For example, tools may recommend word choice, tone and style based on the way the executive speaks and writes. This technology is in its infancy for B2B and the personality profiles generated can seems almost like a horoscope where there is always some aspect you could find true in the right circumstance. But with the field of machine learning and AI growing rapidly I expect this technology to advance significantly over the next few years.

Information contextual analysis rounds out the tools with a human perspective. Humans add the context and semantic understanding to take the analysis a step further. Many firms will produce dossiers on executives that include summaries and a list of good conversation starters. These firms will often use the other tools listed above, but then have analysts layer on their own conclusions. That ensures the executive profile is accurate and provides the context the account executive or marketing team needs to act on the data. Some firms, however, having seen too many profiles sit on a virtual shelf, have starting creating personalized, contextual narratives and materials that the marketing or account team can use to start those 'conversations of value' because the narratives are tailored for each executive's business strategies and objectives.

Are executives aware of these technologies being used by their suppliers?

Sure. Many executives are growing savvy to the marketing research process and how their online presence informs it – so they're taking things offline and tightening up the privacy settings on their social media profiles. For the same reason, event companies often gate materials presented at conferences and workshops. If this trend continues, simple information harvesting or aggregator tools won't be nearly as useful in the executive research process.

A note on privacy

Europe is now covered by the world's strongest privacy and data protection rules, the GDPR, but other countries are following fast as people become increasingly sensitive to the trade-off they are making between online convenience, such as not having to enter personal address and credit card information into the same site twice when shopping, and privacy. Europe's GDPR came into force on 25 May 2018, regulating the way that companies store and use personal information.

In terms of the impact GDPR may have for your executive engagement programme in Europe, and potentially similar regulations as they come into force around the world, here's a quick summary.

- **Gathering data.** GDPR doesn't restrict you from acquiring company data but there are strict opt-in requirements for EU individuals, before you start engaging them with marketing or sales outreach (and remember that any EU citizen residing in the United States is also covered by GDPR, so it's best to be cautious). Database security, in terms of both information storage and secure data transfer, is a key concern. Value-add landing pages are critical to your inbound contact strategy.

- **Direct mail.** Similar opt-in and opt-out rules apply to direct mail. It's fairly easy to get people to opt-in to receiving exciting mail – but managing the contact data and opt-in is key.

- **Events.** With events, it's straightforward to get oral consent for follow-up, but proving that consent isn't easy. For compliance, send out an opt-in confirmation e-mail to contacts that were generated at events, or collect written or digital opt-in onsite. You may decide to obtain an opt-in/opt-out from all attendees in advance.

- **Third-party communications.** If a third party is generating contacts on your behalf, you're still liable for their non-compliance. Make sure the forms, landing pages and consent language all conform, as well as the way they send you the data. Remember, un-encrypted Excel spreadsheets are non-compliant.

FIGURE 3.5   GDPR compliance in contacting target executives

	Opted-in	Known/opted-out
Direct source	Permission to contact	No permission, cannot contact directly use social media
Third-party source	Permission to contact if data documented and managed	No permission, cannot contact directly

SOURCE ITSMA, 2018

When thinking about how to contact the target executives for your programme, Figure 3.5 gives you some guidelines based on whether they have opted in to marketing communications from you, are unknown or have opted out.

The key thing to remember is that your target executives must be opted-in to receive communications from you (or your partners) in order for you to contact them about your programme. If you have no opt-in, the best way to reach them is indirectly through social media or at a public event, where you can follow up and seek an opt-in.

When in doubt, exercise caution and seek advice from your own in-house lawyer or commercial team. This brief section is designed only to raise your awareness of the issue and not to provide legal advice.

Summary

1 Executive engagement strategies work best when they're built on a solid understanding of the executives involved, rather than on an internal focus on what your company wants to achieve.

2 Start with building basic profiles of the executives to give you some insight into who they are, where they've come from, what their life is like and their relationship networks.

3 Buyer personas describe a type of buyer, detailing the drivers for their purchase, their success metrics, the journey they take as a buyer, their decision and the selection criteria they use.

4 Psychological profiling, while expensive, can tell us a lot about how executives relate to the world, take in information and prefer to communicate.

5 Technology is available to help you understand your target executives, in four broad categories: harvesting tools scrape the internet for public information and deliver unstructured information; aggregation tools deduplicate and organize that information; analysis tools add context by looking for patterns; and contextual analysis tools allow analysts to layer on their own conclusions to create personalized, contextual narratives.

6 Be aware of data privacy regulations that apply in the country or countries your programme covers and seek legal advice on how to capture, store and use data on your target executives.

Notes

1 https://research.stlouisfed.org/publications/economic-synopses/2018/05/04/what-does-chinas-rise-in-patents-mean-a-look-at-quality-vs-quantity (archived at https://perma.cc/8QPV-9Z64)

2 https://www.myersbriggs.org/my-mbti-personality-type/mbti-basics/ (archived at https://perma.cc/W8M6-PHSQ)

04

Who should engage?

Put simply, executives like to engage with executives. Peer-to-peer networking is all-important in a business-to-business context, as buyers look to other buyers, industry influencers and SMEs to explore trends, discuss common challenges, share lessons learned and get practical advice. In fact, the quickest way to kill any executive engagement programme is to match executives with people they don't consider peers. They'll likely attend one event or meeting and then never come again, substituting one of their own team members who they believe is more of a peer for those they met around the table.

So, when thinking about who should engage with your target executives when crafting your strategy, it makes sense to start at the very top of your own organization. But although you need to start there, you can't stop there. Your executives are far too busy to be the only people involved in your programme.

In this chapter, we'll consider the range of people and roles you can leverage as part of your programme, including one or two people outside your own organization. We'll also talk about how you choose the right people for your programme, in terms of chemistry. There's a bit of matchmaking to be done here, and inevitably some of your own executives just won't be suitable for the programme.

The main players

There are a wide range of people that can play a role in your executive engagement programme, starting at the top of your organization, as mentioned. Your own executive committee, or C-Suite, are the figureheads for your programme, and this is who buyers prefer to hear from, as shown in Figure 4.1. As we explored in Chapter 2, this will include your chief

FIGURE 4.1 Executives' relationship preferences

Who at solution providers do you prefer initiates the relationship with you?		% Rank 1st	% Rank 2nd	% Rank 3rd
	Senior executives	25.9	20	13.3
	Subject matter experts	22.2	19	16
	Salesperson/account manager	16.3	13.3	15
	Service delivery manager	11.3	13.8	17.7
% of respondents (N=406)	Service delivery staff	8.9	9.9	15.3
	Product group	7.6	13.5	11.6
	Marketing	7.9	10.6	11.1

■ % Rank 1st   ■ % Rank 2nd   % Rank 3rd

Note: Respondents were asked to rank order the three most preferred decision criteria.

SOURCE ITSMA 'How Executives Engage' survey, 2019

executive officer (CEO), chief financial officer (CFO), chief operations officer (COO), chief information officer (CIO), chief human resources officer (CHRO), chief marketing officer (CMO) among others. You may even be able to involve your chairman and some of your board of directors at times, including non-executive directors.

Figure 4.1 relates to the question Who at solution providers do you prefer initiates the relationship with you? Note that respondents were asked to rank-order the three most preferred decision criteria (% of respondents (N = 406)).

Coming down the organization, others sitting on or reporting into your C-Suite will likely be more active in the programme. This group, often referred to as C-1 if they aren't on the executive committee, will include business unit directors and heads of delivery.

Heads of the account management community – or the key account managers themselves – will also have a role to play, since they know the clients best at an operational level. They will likely be those with most regular contact with the target executives in your programme and understand the services you provide for their businesses as well as the current status of your relationship with them.

More broadly, there will be SMEs within your organization whom you want to involve, since they can provide valuable insights and experience and are valued by the executives themselves. Occasionally, less obvious functional heads such as procurement, commercial, real estate or marketing can also provide insights, depending on the issues your target executives are facing. And the head of your corporate social responsibility (CSR) programme may also get involved.

Outside your own organization, you may wish to involve executives and senior people from within your partners, particularly where there is a specialism or perhaps a brand halo effect that they can bring to the programme.

And finally, there may be influencers within your wider network that you can leverage, such as industry analysts, academic experts, entrepreneurs or association members who have value to add.

A note on chemistry

We'll look at the roles that each of these groups could play in your programme. But first, I want to flag the issue of chemistry.

As we all know, chemistry is an important basis to any relationship. The ability to connect or 'click' with someone means the difference between a polite conversation (hopefully) and a really enjoyable meeting. It's the key to getting a second meeting. This applies to business relationships as much as to personal relationships, and so is worth taking into account when you are planning your engagement programme.

These connections can come from shared experiences, or from people and places you have in common. They come from interests you both pursue, from similar perspectives on the world and from shared values. They stem from a natural curiosity about other people and a general respect for their views and feelings.

Some people are more open to looking for these points of connection than others, and are generally more affable and socially oriented. Others find this hard: I've met several CEOs who really don't like networking situations and abhor making small talk, and I've learned that it's best not to put them in these situations if possible. But, in their role, it is not always avoidable.

So, while you are thinking about the people you need in your programme, don't just consider their roles and job titles, but think about how comfortable they will be building relationships with your target executives.

Since you've developed an understanding of these target executives, you may be able to match people from your own organization based on their similar roles plus shared experiences, connections or interests. Or perhaps even based on their shared personality types, if you've gone to the trouble of a Myers–Briggs-type analysis. This is a great place to start and should help you decide whom to involve.

But there will be some people you need to involve even if they don't have a natural ability to build rapport. In cases like these, it's worth looking at ways to help them navigate these social situations.

At a basic level, you can make sure that your executives are well briefed on the person they are going to meet, even giving them suggested talking points that you know will resonate with the target executive. This is good practice even for your more experienced and comfortable relationship builders.

But you may wish to go further and arrange for some soft skills training around building rapport. Companies such as 'Actors in Industry' in the UK run sessions for senior professionals, helping them to build better questioning and listening skills, exploring behavioural techniques such as making and keeping eye contact and developing an understanding of the ways that our body language, voice and personal energy can impact others. All of these things are valuable life skills that can be used to build a better rapport with people we meet in both our business and personal lives.

Executive to executive

Since we know that executives prefer to meet with peers wherever possible, your own executives and the immediate team below them will play a key role in your programme. In fact, it's worth getting one of them, preferably your CEO, to sponsor the whole initiative, since it's the CEO that most of your target executives will ultimately want to meet.

Given the demands facing your CEO, your best bet is to find a way to share the responsibilities of leading the programme with other C-Suite members or C-1 executives. One company I work with asked different members of the executive committee to be the sponsor for different activities within the programme.

While the CEO is the overall figurehead of the executive engagement programme, chairing the customer advisory board for example, the COO takes the lead on an annual collaborative research project and customer summit, the CIO runs innovation days and study tours, and the CMO takes the lead on a customer awards initiative.

In a similar way, other members of the C-Suite or C-1 level in your organization may take responsibility for key customers in different sectors, so the CHRO may look after clients in the retail sector while the CFO hosts utility clients. Where business unit directors are vertically aligned, this is a natural and easy choice to make. In other cases, it will be a collaborative decision as to where your executives feel most comfortable.

Another company I know takes the approach of running customer advisory boards on a functional basis, so their CFO hosts other CFOs as a board twice a year to share challenges and experiences, while their CMO does the same with their peers and so on. Some of these boards split into different working groups between meetings to scope and run research projects that everyone can learn from, advancing their profession as well as helping solve their specific challenges.

Another company held a chairman's club, chaired by their own chairman and only open to other chairmen, with a focus on doing business in Asia since the organization was headquartered in that region. A professional service firm uses its non-executive directors to chair a network of new non-executive directors, helping them to get comfortable with and be well briefed on the responsibilities of their new role.

IBM is particularly good at running executive-level functional research, using its own executives, account directors and SMEs to engage with clients, prospects and third-party experts to run studies into the issues facing CEOs, CIOs and CMOs, among others. Their approach is shared in the case study 'IBM's Institute for Business Value'.

You may need them to occasionally go beyond one-to-one or small group meetings to deliver your strategy. For example, you may ask them to record an inspirational video to launch your programme, to deliver a keynote presentation at a customer summit or host an awards evening. Once again, it's worth considering whether they are comfortable being filmed or presenting to large groups, and whether they can communicate with impact.

Many, but not all, will have already had media training, so it's worth checking this and working with your PR or corporate communications team to organize refreshers or updates, or indeed to give your executives the skills they will need.

Briefing and debriefing

As discussed earlier, when your executives meet with their peer executives in your programme, they need to be well briefed. Whether it's a one-on-one meeting to discuss the relationship between the two companies and where it may go next, or a small group meeting like an advisory council, you will need to provide a short briefing on each target executive involved, covering:

1 their name, role and company overview;

2 their photo;

3 their objectives, challenges and pain points;

4 the status of your relationship with them, including annual revenues, services provided, project status and current opportunities;

5 possible talking points.

Once the meeting has taken place, you will need to debrief your own executive to capture any useful intelligence for the next person to meet with that target executive. No one, least of all busy executives, wants to tell the same organization the same thing twice, even when meeting with different representatives in different situations.

Personal and executive assistants

In my experience, debriefing your own executives can be one of the most challenging things about running an executive engagement programme. My advice is to work with their personal assistant (PA) or executive assistant (EA) to understand what would be their preferred way of sharing feedback post-meeting: verbally by phone or in a quick face-to-face meeting, or written in an e-mail or straight into a CRM system. Then, liaise with the PA/EA to help get the job done.

And, while we're on the subject of PAs/EAs, it's worth noting that this group of people is hugely influential in terms of working with you to schedule the engagements between your own executives and the target executives in your programme. The PAs/EAs in your own organization will reach out to their peers in your customer accounts fairly regularly, building up their own relationships, which are also important to your programme and should be supported. For example, one of my clients organizes an afternoon tea event for PAs to brief them on the executive engagement strategy and discuss the role they play in delivering it.

Key account managers and sales people

Involving key account managers and sales people in your executive engagement programme requires a careful balancing act and lots of diplomacy. On the one hand, these are the people who know the customer accounts best, albeit perhaps not at the executive level. On the other hand, they are usually responsible for selling to your customers, and many of the activities in your executive engagement programme will be designated a selling-free zone. In fact, executives expect a lot from their sales contacts, but the top expectations are not about selling! The most valuable things that sales and account managers can do is provide unique perspectives on the market and trends, put them in touch with SMEs and educate them on new technology (see Figure 4.2).

Some activities are definitely more effective when account directors and sales people do not attend, such as advisory boards and study tours, since those present feel more able to open up and speak honestly about the challenges facing them without fear of initiating an overt sales conversation. Less intimate events, such as summits and seminars, are easier to involve your account managers in, giving them roles such as hosting their client executive through the day and ensuring they get to the sessions they're interested in and spend time with the people they want to meet.

For all engagement activities, it's likely you'll need the support of the account directors and sales teams in preparing the briefing papers we discussed earlier for your own executives. They will be even keener than you are to hear the feedback from your executives following the meetings you've arranged with target executives in the client account. And, naturally, it will fall to them alongside your delivery teams to follow up with any operational issues uncovered during these meetings.

Sometimes executives invited to an advisory board meeting will be reluctant to talk about strategic issues until they've aired any operational issues around the services your organization is delivering today. These issues should always be noted, dealt with, and the action taken fed back to the executive who raised it, so that trust is built around the council and relationships strengthened. It's likely that the actions will fall to their account manager, working with operational teams, who will then need to feed back the resulting improvements to your own executive for forwarding on to the originator.

This briefing and debriefing activity is something you should think about 'contracting' with the account management and sales community as you set up your programme, making sure everyone is happy with the commitment it involves, the format it will take and the value it will deliver.

As to other involvement in your programme, that will depend on the type of activities you're running and the seniority and gravitas of your people. In reality, your target executives simply won't see all of your account directors and sales people as peers, and so won't want to engage with them. This can be difficult news for you to deliver…

FIGURE 4.2 The most important things buyers expect from sales people

Which are the three most important things an account manager or sales rep should be doing for you?
(Rank order 1st, 2nd, 3rd) % of respondents (N = 406)

	% Rank 1st	% Rank 2nd	% Rank 3rd
Provide me with unique perspectives on the market and technology solutions	10.6	10.3	10.3
Put me in touch with the solution provider's subject matter experts	12.1	10.6	7.4
Educate me on new issues in technology	8.1	10.1	10.6
Provide me with product or service information	9.1	9.4	8.9
Provide ongoing advice to help me make the right decisions and avoid land mines	11.1	8.9	7.1
Provide me with benchmarks and best practices	8.6	8.6	8.9
Educate me on issues and opportunities in my industry	7.4	9.9	7.6
Help me build the business case	9.1	7.9	7.4
Challenge my thinking	6.9	6.4	9.9
Help me navigate among alternative solutions	5.4	7.1	9.6
Tell me where on the website to find product/service information	7.6	4.7	5.9
Provide references for me to contact	3.9	6.2	6.4

Note: Respondents were asked to rank order the three most important.

SOURCE ITSMA 'How Executives Engage' survey, 2019

You can of course help them to change the way they are perceived. I've seen this done by simple acts like changing their job titles – from account manager to client executive, for example – through to helping them build up and share their own subject matter expertise, such as in a particular sector's issues or business situation. The soft skills we discussed earlier, such as communicating with impact, are worth considering here too.

Finally, there are companies that specialize in helping sales and account directors have boardroom conversations, building empathy and an outside-in mindset for the issues and challenges facing executives and how to engage around them rather than the inside-out thinking and focus on the products, services and solutions the organization sells.

CASE STUDY
IBM'S Institute of Business Value

Effective executive engagement is built on having something valuable and relevant to say to those executives with whom you want to form and/or strengthen close relationships. But it's getting much harder to cut through the sheer volume of white papers, executive briefings and expert insights landing on organizational desks.

Constantly improving the research to personalize the content is critical but no longer enough. It is also essential to make sure that those in the field are equipped to adapt and deliver the content so customers truly engage with the ideas and point of view.

Putting thought into action

A good example of best practice is IBM with its Institute of Business Value (IBV), a dedicated unit which brings thought leadership and insights to C-Suite executives and internal IBM audiences. Set up in 2001, it consists of over 60 business consultants experienced in deriving key insights from data and leveraging them across the whole of the company through a portfolio of more than 300 fact-based thought leadership studies.

Value is delivered through three programmes: thought leadership, the C-Suite programme and the Performance Data & Benchmarking programme. The output is vast, covering 14 industries, nine 'hot' topics and six roles or functions. Underpinning that is an immense database of metrics with a patented toolkit to analyse data. IBV studies are downloaded somewhere in the world every 30 seconds.

The hot topics reflect IBM's determination to stay in the vanguard of business transformation. They include areas such as AI, cloud computing, digital reinvention, global industry agendas, the IoT and quantum computing.

Spotlight on the C-Suite

The IBV has been studying the trends and priorities of the C-Suite for years. From its first global CEO study in 2002, it has built up a wealth of data about what's going on with leaders at the top of companies.

Its 2018 CMO study, for example, offered some compelling insights into what's happening with today's marketers. The IBM report predicted a much-expanded role for the profession as the custodians of the customer's needs and desires in an increasingly customer-centric and data-rich environment.

But CMOs will have to prove they have earned this expanded mandate by focusing on three key areas: offering data-driven insights that contribute greater value and measurable results throughout the organization; delivering exceptional, personalized experiences across channels and even ecosystems; and encouraging a customer-centric philosophy in the whole company through creativity, innovation, collaboration and governance.

Getting the job done with field enablement

What really sets IBM apart is how comprehensively all the content is packaged. Each of the 300+ fact-based studies comes with a full suite of materials and enablement activities used for marketing, connecting with clients, building eminence and supporting client presentations, proposals and deliverables:

- Core study materials include PowerPoint decks packaged for different uses, such as supporting client visits or presentations. They often have industry and/or regional derivatives.

- E-cards are used to disseminate information, such as key findings, links and contacts, both internally and externally.

- Social materials are created for instant messaging by both the social media teams and marketing, with relevant tweets, infographics and core blog elements.

- Study enablement equips staff for the field through training sessions, author contacts, solution links and local adaptations and translations.

- Video and event materials, including a print-on-demand facility, are readily accessible.

- From an activation standpoint, content is pushed out through four major channels: the IBV LinkedIn group, Twitter, a quarterly newsletter and a smartphone app with access to content which has been downloaded by over 30,000 people.

Building on success

There are a number of ways in which the IBV capabilities play a significant role in expanding and strengthening client relationships as well as shaping new opportunities for IBM:

- opening a door with a new client or creating an additional opening with an existing client;

- leveraging thought leadership studies in client presentations, proposals and deliverables as well as content for press releases, interviews, marketing campaigns and analyst briefings;

- inviting experts and authors to client briefings or roundtable discussions and asking clients to participate in a study as an SME or interviewee;

- co-authoring reports on topics where the IBM-ers or clients (or both) are SMEs;

- using the assets in social media to improve digital eminence;

- supporting engagement with universities for recruiting activities.

The critical point is the comprehensive framework the IBV provides to enable its executives, account teams and other staff to deal with clients and customers equipped with content that is targeted, topical and, crucially, coordinated. Significantly, tracking results is integral to the programme. IBM tracks those it touches. Rolling all this feedback across both IBV itself and on up to the highest organizational levels ensures that IBM maintains its reputation for thought leadership that makes a difference.

Subject matter experts

Outside of your own C-Suite and its direct reports, perhaps the most valuable people with whom executives in your programme will want to engage are your SMEs. These people, usually targeted with a billable-day goal rather than a sales quota, genuinely help executives think about the trends facing their industries and how to respond to them, sharing practical examples of what others have done as well as giving advice on how to improve performance in the executive's specific context.

Figure 4.3 shows five types of SMEs.

Executive SMEs are the most senior leaders in the company, up to and including the CEO, whom we have already discussed. Think of Laksmi Mittal at ArcelorMittal or Michael Dell at Dell EMC (there are lots of near-celebrity executives in the technology space – think Amazon's Jeff Bezos, Facebook's Mark Zuckerberg and Tesla's Elon Musk, for example).

FIGURE 4.3 Five types of SME

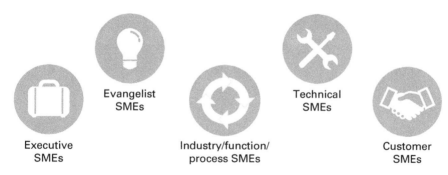

Evangelist
SMEs

Technical
SMEs

Executive
SMEs

Industry/function/
process SMEs

Customer
SMEs

SOURCE ITSMA, 2016

Evangelist or visionary SMEs are the ones who have a strong personal profile and are out talking about and advocating on important topics, typically with a view of the future. These are the people who are really helping to define and shape the conversation on a given topic, such as Sheryl Sandberg, COO at Facebook, on women in leadership or Richard Branson, CEO of the Virgin Group, on business disruption and entrepreneurship.

The workhorse SMEs are the industry/function/process SMEs. These are the people who typically come from a delivery unit of some kind – consulting, outsourcing or implementation, for example. The best of these SMEs have a mix of knowledge, such as industry, process and technology, and have practical experience as well as a broad view that allows them to advise executives.

Technical SMEs sometimes sit in a sales support function but may come from a development, engineering or technology team as well. This group also includes people whom you might not think of as being SMEs, but who play very important advisory roles – people from commercial or legal functions, for example.

The final category is what the ITSMA calls customer SMEs. These are usually account directors or sales people – the ones whose job it is to understand the customer's business and key issues or priorities – as we've already discussed.

What's interesting about these categories is that they are not mutually exclusive. Sometimes one SME might fit into several of these categories (think of the executive SMEs). Some companies have all of these varieties, others might only have two or three. The key thing is to identify your SMEs and decide whom to involve in your programme and how to leverage their time.

This is a key point, which comes back to the fact that they are usually targeted on billable days and so are less keen on spending time on marketing and sales outreach. Finding ways to leverage their time efficiently might include filming them or recording them for podcasts to circulate among your target executives, asking them to lead seminars or webinars that reach a number of executives at once, or using them in booked 'clinic' or appointment situations on a semi-regular basis. Again, IBM has started to do this online through their ExpertAdvice programme, as detailed in the case study below.

CASE STUDY
IBM ExpertAdvice programme

Business challenge

Prior to the implementation of this programme, clients and prospective clients had very few, if any, opportunities to speak with IBM SMEs. Prospective clients and most existing clients had to first go through several digital interactions with IBM, including sending e-mails and using live chat on webpages to speak to a generalist digital development representative (DDR).

These representatives were spread thinly with their various inbound and outbound marketing responsibilities, and had general knowledge of IBM products and services rather than specialized subject matter expertise. DDRs primarily interacted with prospects through a live-chat tool, which yielded a conversion rate to sales opportunity of only 8 per cent. All in all, the legacy process required prospects to overcome many layers of obstacles before speaking with someone, typically a seller, who could address their needs.

Programme objectives

The ExpertAdvice programme was implemented to eliminate layers by providing a free service to prospects where they could be directly connected with an IBM expert to discuss their business problem and technology needs. The programme aimed to:

- provide value to the prospect, whether or not they pursue a sales opportunity with IBM;
- bring IBM expertise to the forefront of the digital experience;
- introduce a human element in digital interaction; and
- generate a new business pipeline.

Execution

Over a year and a half, IBM marketing conceived, piloted and scaled ExpertAdvice – a first-of-its-kind programme that enables clients and prospects who digitally interact with IBM web pages to participate in a free, 30-minute consultation with an IBM SME on the topic of their choice. The customer journey is straightforward: a prospect exploring the IBM website in search for answers to an issue can book a consultation through an interface that allows them to directly schedule time on the calendars of distinguished IBMers, and describe the business problem they wish to discuss.

Behind this simple yet effective user experience is an elegantly designed support system, including:

- tools integrated with IBM systems to provide a seamless user experience;
- a team of digital representatives who ensure the requests are valid and would benefit from the consultation;
- a cohort of IBM experts who agree to dedicate up to two hours of their time per week to speaking with prospects; and
- a marketing team dedicated to discovering new ways to interact in an agile manner, driving traffic to prompt engagement with the programme.

The programme started as a pilot in April 2017 in the Global Technology Services unit and was scaled across IBM through 2018.

Business results

ExpertAdvice was generated first and foremost to improve the customer experience by shortening the lead time to access IBM expertise at a peer level and, in turn, to organically convert leads into opportunities. As such, the success of ExpertAdvice is assessed across three key metrics:

1 **Customer experience.** Engagement through the ExpertAdvice programme generates a much higher percentage of high-value interaction than other channels, with about 65 per cent of inquiries progressing to consultations. Those who engage in the consultation have positive feedback, most of the surveys indicating that clients had 'Great' and 'Exceptional' experiences, and that they were 'Extremely likely' to recommend the programme.

2 **Pipeline conversion.** ExpertAdvice saw high conversion rates from consultation to opportunities in pipeline, with about 30–40 per cent conversion rates, compared to other channels such as live chat that have 8 per cent conversion. Forty per cent of these opportunities came from white space clients, demonstrating the value of expertise for new IBM prospects, as noted by Steven

Dickens, zCloud Expert, at IBM Global Technology Services: 'This programme has been very well managed and has led to direct contact with three or four clients IBM would not have engaged with otherwise.'

3 **Opportunity generation.** For Global Technology Services, the longest-standing pilot, over $29 million in pipeline was generated through the programme. As the sales cycle on these opportunities progresses through close partnership with sales and the programme expands across geographies, revenue and profit will logically follow.

SOURCE ITSMA Marketing Excellence Award Winners summary booklet, 2018
Reprinted with kind permission from ITSMA

Of course, the same concerns apply to SMEs as to your C-Suite executives with regard to their ability to engage effectively on camera or in social situations. While their technical skill may be second to none, you may need to offer them support in communicating with impact or building rapport.

Delivery and customer experience teams

Your target executives will usually have time for those people in your organization who are delivering the solutions their business relies on. As the nature of B2B solutions contracting has shifted to more as-a-service model, many suppliers have moved from a licence sales mentality to one of driving usage of the solutions they sell and ensuring their customer's success.

Customer experience and success teams are popping up in many large companies, tasked with communicating with customers about the solutions they've purchased, educating them on how to get the best use out of them, providing tools to track usage and helping to monitor the overall value and ROI delivered by the solutions.

These teams, who are so close to your most important customers on a day-to-day basis, often see how those customers could improve their operations to cut costs or create new revenue streams. These pragmatic, innovative ideas are gold dust to the executives in your programme, and they will willingly meet with and listen to these delivery experts who bring an objective point of view and can add such value.

It's worth thinking about the role these delivery teams can play in helping you understand your target executives and their companies, and the mechanisms you'll use to capture their input (ideally your project management systems will link into your CRM system, but that isn't always the case).

Also, think about the content that they can help you to develop to engage your target executives, such as operational insights, 'how to' guides, ROI tools and benchmarks, and case studies. You may want to have activities in your programme such as study tours and innovation workshops, which we'll discuss in Chapter 8, led by your senior delivery and customer success executives. After all, these are the people whom your target executives will trust the most.

Except when they don't. If you've had a service delivery failure, your target executives won't want to engage with you on anything else until you've fixed it. There's no point asking them to discuss your strategy at a customer advisory board meeting if they feel you're not keeping your promises at an operational level.

Of course, one of the foundations of your executive engagement strategy may be to provide a higher level of service, or recovery focus, for the companies of the executives in your programme, and this could be one of the added-value benefits to them of participating. And remember, recovering well from an operational failure can leave your relationship with the executive in question even stronger than before the failure took place.

Marketing

In addition to being responsible for the overall design of an executive engagement strategy, marketers are often involved in planning and managing the activities within it, sometimes to the point of engaging with the target executives. For example, marketers will likely research the issues facing the target executives, manage the development of relevant content and its delivery through multiple channels, and host events such as conferences, seminars and briefings in the programme.

In some companies, marketers are also involved in sharing thought leadership research and benchmarks with target executives, acting as SMEs in these situations. And of course, senior marketers can run marketing-focused advisory boards with their peers from customer and prospect companies.

All of this depends on the gravitas and business acumen of the marketer in question: the same soft skills are needed here as for everyone else on your team, in addition to a commercial mindset that can relate to the responsibilities of running a business. You may need to support some of the marketers you select for your programme with additional training and mentoring so that they are comfortable engaging with senior executives.

Marketers do have the benefit of being customer focused and generally aware of everything your organization can deliver, while also being less 'salesy' than their sale colleagues. Plus their generally good communication skills make them easy conversationalists, which can be very useful at a social event. As such, the marketing leadership team in your company can be a good source of support for your engagement programme.

Corporate social responsibility teams

I've seen companies achieve great success through engaging important client executives on the CSR issues that matter most to them. For example, professional service firms regularly invite executives to seminars on topics such as women in leadership and sustainable finance, with smaller companies achieving great traction on topics such as these that are close to the heart of executives they seek to engage, as we'll see in the 'Source Global Research' case study in Chapter 9.

The starting point here is the insights you gathered on the executives you're targeting, which we covered in Chapter 3. Most of them will state the causes and interests they have in their public profiles, so it's then a question of mapping those to what you also care about and can talk about, and to the executives within your own company also passionate about those causes.

Your CSR leader may be the person to engage with the target executives, or they may be someone who can facilitate the topics, content and activities around the themes that matter. Some companies have used their own CSR leader to great effect as an SME, championing issues publicly on social media, while others have involved them in one-on-one meetings and briefings with CSR executives for their most important customers. The right approach for your programme will depend on the executives you are targeting, the issues they care about and your own organization's comfort and ability to engage credibly on those issues.

Partners

Most companies have an ecosystem of partners that they work with to deliver added value to their customers or reach new and different markets, and yours will be no exception. These partners can play a useful role in your programme. For example, if your business is heavily channel-reliant, like

Cisco for example, it may be that your partners have executive relationships instead of a relationship with you, and they will need to be involved in inviting and hosting those executives that you would like to include in your programme.

In this case, you'll need considerable diplomacy to complete the same due diligence on the partner representative as you would on any of your own people whom you plan to involve in the programme. Open communication will be key to ensuring that the partner's trusted relationship doesn't feel compromised or usurped, but that added value is delivered to all parties through the content and activities you provide.

If your partners are more capability based, giving your organization a greater depth and breadth of solution than you could offer alone, you may want to include your partners in activities relevant to their capabilities, such as joint innovation events. Where the partner is better known than you, this will bring a certain brand 'halo' to your events, making it more appealing for your target executives to attend. They will also be more interest if your partners are innovative start-ups, particularly when you offer access to leading-edge technologies as a benefit of your programme.

In the case of academic partners, these may be useful for collaborative thought leadership and benchmarking research, lending credibility and a certain cachet when content that your target executives have collaborated on is published in renowned journals such as the *Harvard Business Review*.

In all of these cases, be clear who owns the relationship with each target executive and tread carefully so that you don't take over that relationship, or adversely affect it in any way, with the activities you are proposing. You may wish to ring-fence the activities they get involved in to one or two within your wider programme. But remember, the same rules of briefing, supporting and debriefing around meetings apply to partners as to your own executives, just with an added layer of complexity that you need to factor in from the start.

Influencers

From your research into the executives you're targeting, you'll have a view of their wider relationship networks and the people, or types of people, who influence them. These independent, third-party voices can be great collaborators in your engagement strategy, providing extra insight and value for everyone involved.

As we saw in Figure 4.1, the kinds of influencers that senior buyers of complex business solutions listen to include management consultants, industry analysts, sourcing advisors, trade and professional association staff and the media. A representation of their networks and the people who influence their decisions is shown in Figure 4.4.

Collaborating with influencers in your programme can get you more visibility, lend weight to your content and spread the load in terms of both content creation and dissemination. In some cases you'll need to pay them for their contributions, while in others there may be a win–win situation for them in simply engaging with your target executives in a way that doesn't compete with your own objectives. They may even suggest other executives who could be part of your programme, thereby bringing you new prospects for your business.

I've seen companies run research projects with both academics and industry analysts to lend weight to their self-published studies, while others collaborate with media partners to ensure a wider impact and readership for their content and greater credibility for their engagement programme. Asking influencers to speak at executive engagement events or provide guest blogs, videos and podcasts are easy and quick ways to draw an audience in the early days when your target executives have yet to buy into the programme.

FIGURE 4.4 Executives and their wider networks

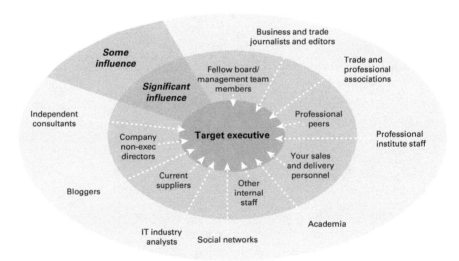

SOURCE Adapted from Burgess and Munn (2017) *A Practitioner's Guide to ABM*, Kogan Page, London, originally published by ITSMA, 2016

As with partners, it's worth setting some ground rules early on about who owns which relationships, and protecting your target executives from any influencers on their own sales mission. The briefing, supporting and debriefing approach applies equally here, too.

Summary

1 There are a wide range of people who can play a role in your executive engagement programme, starting at the top of your organization and moving out to partners and influencers.

2 The ability to connect or 'click' with someone is the key to getting a second meeting. You may need to help some of your people build rapport quickly and communicate effectively with executives.

3 Executives prefer to meet with peers wherever possible, so involve your own executives and the immediate team below them, spreading the load among them for different activities in your programme.

4 Personal or executive assistants are a hugely influential group of people in terms of working with you to schedule the engagements between your own executives and your target executives.

5 For all activities, it's likely you'll need the support of the account directors and sales teams in briefing and debriefing your executives, even if you don't actually want them to engage. Diplomacy is needed here.

6 Perhaps the most valuable people with whom executives in your programme will want to engage are your SMEs. Use these people, often working on billable hours, carefully by leveraging their time where possible through recordings or one-to-many channels.

7 Delivery and customer experience or success teams are close to your most important customers on a day-to-day basis, and can bring pragmatic, innovative ideas that target executives want to hear about.

8 In addition to being responsible for the overall design of an executive engagement strategy, marketers are often involved in planning and managing the activities within it, sometimes to the point of engaging with the target executives such as hosting events or sharing thought leadership.

9 You can achieve great success by engaging your client executives on the CSR issues that matter most to them.

10 Partners in your ecosystem can add great value, but be clear who owns the relationship with each target executive and tread carefully with the activities you are proposing.

11 Collaborating with influencers in your programme can get you more visibility, lend weight to your content and spread the load in terms of both content creation and dissemination.

05

Having something to say

So, you've identified your target executives, designed your engagement strategy, worked out who from your own organization and its ecosystem of partners and influencers will engage, and now its crunch time. What do you have to say?

The real question is 'What do your target executives want to hear?' You may have plenty to say, but it may not be relevant and timely for the executives. Or it may be too much about you and too little about them. At the heart of your executive engagement strategy is a robust content strategy. Almost all of your engagement activities will depend on it.

From your work to understand the executives you're targeting, you should have some ideas of the issues they're facing and the topics they're interested in. That's one important input to your content strategy. Your own company strategy is the other. After all, you're not going to spend your time talking about things that have no relevance to what your organization does and the ways in which it can help its customers. But at the same time, that shouldn't be your main focus.

This chapter gives you some pointers for building your content strategy, starting with a look at what executives typically want to talk about. It then explores some of the main categories of content, from updates on the value you're currently delivering to customers, through the different types of thought leadership you can bring to executives in the programme, on to the value your organization can deliver and some of the examples and case studies you can share.

What do executives want to talk about?

Executives like to talk about a range of things, but typically these boil down to the issues and opportunities facing them and their organization – in its internal operations, immediate environment or the wider world. They are also hungry for ideas about overcoming or taking advantage of them to achieve their goals. These might be concerned with specific short-term issues and goals, or as part of a hazier, long-term perspective.

When researching possible solutions for their business, along with the providers that might be able to help them, executive buyers tend to value a mix of content. This ranges from the more aspirational, long-term ideas that can be incorporated into their long-range planning, through emerging approaches that could be implemented in the next year or two, to ideas and approaches that can be implemented today (see Figure 5.1).

And don't forget the importance of the post-purchase relationship. A study shows that a third of respondents said that educational content helps them maximize the value of the solution they've bought, and almost as many say the same for best practice examples and case studies (see Figure 5.2). Next comes information about trends and research. They then rank a range of content that helps them get value directly from their purchase, including tools and templates to monitor the usage of solutions and their ROI a database of common problems and their answers and recommendations for getting greater value from your solution.

FIGURE 5.1 The content buyers value

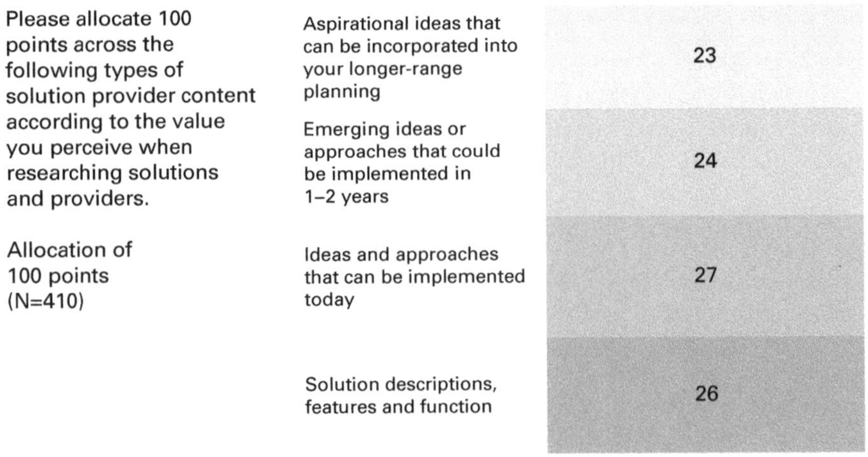

Please allocate 100 points across the following types of solution provider content according to the value you perceive when researching solutions and providers.	Aspirational ideas that can be incorporated into your longer-range planning	23
	Emerging ideas or approaches that could be implemented in 1–2 years	24
Allocation of 100 points (N=410)	Ideas and approaches that can be implemented today	27
	Solution descriptions, features and function	26

SOURCE ITSMA 'How Executives Engage' survey, 2018

FIGURE 5.2 Even post-purchase, buyers value a wide range of content

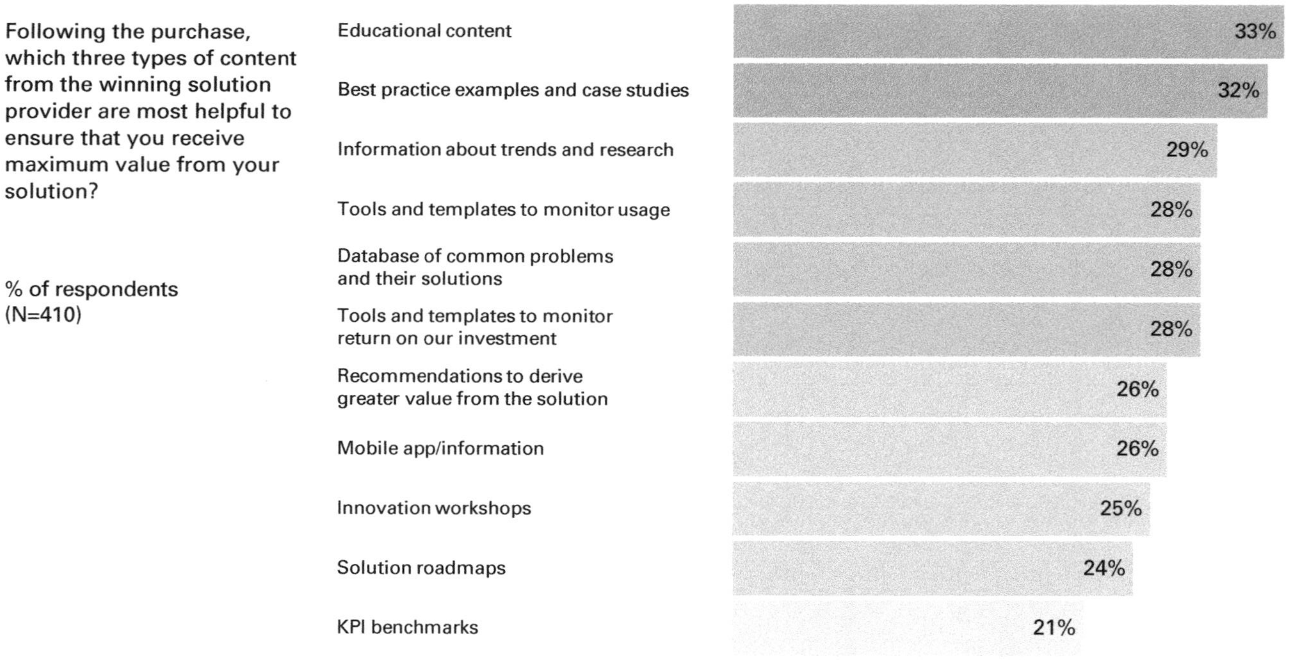

Following the purchase,
which three types of content
from the winning solution
provider are most helpful to
ensure that you receive
maximum value from your
solution?

% of respondents
(N=410)

Content type	%
Educational content	33%
Best practice examples and case studies	32%
Information about trends and research	29%
Tools and templates to monitor usage	28%
Database of common problems and their solutions	28%
Tools and templates to monitor return on our investment	28%
Recommendations to derive greater value from the solution	26%
Mobile app/information	26%
Innovation workshops	25%
Solution roadmaps	24%
KPI benchmarks	21%

SOURCE ITSMA 'How Executives Engage' survey, 2018

Personalize!

As we saw in Chapter 1, as consumers we've come to expect a personalized experience from our chosen suppliers, including personalized content. Executives expect you to make your content relevant to their unique business issues and their industry, as well as their role, company size and country (Figure 5.3). This is no mean feat! It's one reason why programmes such as the one delivered by IBM's Institute for Business Value (IBV) are so successful – they achieve this level of personalization.

Figure 5.4 indicates that, in the main, executive buyers find that the content they receive from their solution providers gives valuable guidance and recommendations and is of excellent quality. However, be on guard: they also say that it can be more sales oriented than educational, and can be difficult for them to find. Even more concerning is that they say the sheer volume of content can be overwhelming, with inconsistencies and conflicting information a problem – as well as being downright boring. These are all traps to avoid.

FIGURE 5.3 The value of personalization

Which one type of content personalization is most valuable to you?

% of respondents (N=406)

	%
Your organization's specific business issues	31
Your industry	28
Your specific role/ job function	22
Companies about the same size as yours	11
Your region/ country	8

SOURCE ITSMA 'How Executives Engage' survey, 2019

FIGURE 5.4 Buyer's experience with solution provider content

Thinking about your experience during the solution purchase process, to what extent do you agree with the following statements?

Mean rating (N=410)

Statement	Mean rating
The solution provider content gave valuable guidance and recommendations in addition to information	5.0
The majority of solution provider content we found was of excellent quality	5.0
The solution provider content was more sales oriented than educational	4.7
The solution provider could have done more to make the research process easier for us	4.7
We were overwhelmed by the volume of solution provider content available	4.5
We found a lot of inconsistencies and conflicting information in the solution provider content	4.4
We struggled with the solution provider content because it was boring	4.2

Strongly disagree — Mean rating — Strongly agree

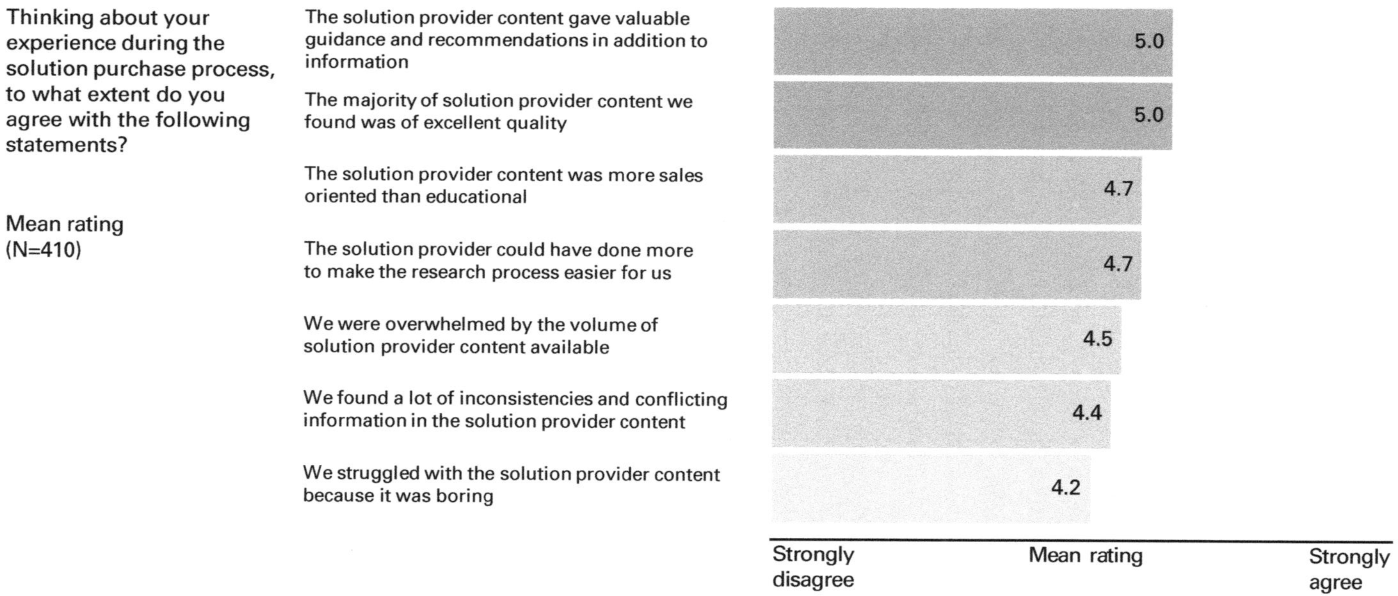

Note: Mean rating based on a 7-point scale where 1=strongly disagree and 7=strongly agree.

SOURCE ITSMA 'How Executives Engage' survey, 2018

The right format

Getting the personalization, consistency and style of your content right is one thing. But what format should it be in to engage your target executives? Buyers want it all, spending roughly equal time on short-, medium- and long-form content (see Figure 5.5).

- Short-form content includes bite-sized summaries, blog posts, infographics, white papers/articles that are three pages or less and one- to two-minute videos.

- Medium form includes white papers/articles that are more than three but less than eight pages, three- to eight-minute videos and 30-minute webinars.

- Long-form content, useful for when executives want to deep dive into a topic, includes detailed white papers/articles that are eight pages or more, videos that are nine minutes or longer and 60-minute webinars.

The Big Four professional service firms are known for the quantity and quality of their content and tend to package it well to engage the client executives who matter most to them. For example, EY's 'Insights for Executives' series demonstrates how content can be created on the issues that matter most to executives, while linking to what the firm has to sell, and delivered through a variety of formats from short to long form to meet every executive's needs. What's really clever is that the content assets in all their

FIGURE 5.5 Buyers want content in a variety of formats

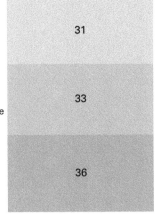

When researching solutions and providers, approximately what proportion of your time did you spend consuming content of varying lengths? Mean % of time (N=410)	Deep-dive, long-form content (eg white papers/articles that are 8 pages or more, videos that are 9 minutes or longer, 60-minute webinars)	31
	Medium-form content (eg white papers/articles that are more than 3 pages but less than 8 pages, 3-to 8-minute videos, 30-minute webinars)	33
	Short-form content (eg bite-sized summaries, blog posts, infographics, white papers/articles that are 3 pages or less, 1-to 2-minute videos)	36

SOURCE ITSMA 'How Executives Engage' survey, 2018

formats are created together, so that an executive can start with short form and work their way through to longer formats in an afternoon if the fancy takes them. Just like you or I binge watching our favourite box set on Netflix, you don't want to wait for the next episode. You want the whole series available now!

CASE STUDY

EY's 5 series: 'Insights for Executives'

Since 2011, EY's *5 series* has played a critical role in getting the Americas Advisory Services insights and perspectives into the minds of the market and the hearts of clients. It has proven incredibly successful as a fundamental component of the firm's integrated marketing programmes, including sector-led demand generation campaigns. With the *5 series* as its centrepiece, these campaigns have generated nearly $88 million in revenue, with more than $246 million in convertible sales opportunities in the sales pipeline.

In conceiving the *5 series*, EY sought a thought leadership vehicle that both captured and sustained the attention of its target audience – busy C-Suite executives looking for answers to a burning issue in the time it takes to get from one meeting to another.

The firm also wanted a template that could scale globally, so they reviewed studies on reading retention among English as a second language (ESL) populations. These suggested that 1,200 words was the threshold for effective retention and comprehension.

The *5 series* framework borrows from the fundamental five-question journalistic approach: who, what, where, why, when. Each article opens with an anecdotal or fact-based overview to grab the reader's attention, establish the situation and identify the issue. The introduction is followed by five questions that break down the issue in ways that make sense and provide unique usefulness, given the needs of the C-level executives:

1 **What's the issue?** Defines the issue clients face.

2 **Why now?** Articulates the urgency behind the issue and why clients need to act.

3 **How does it affect you?** Describes either the benefits of taking action or the consequences of not taking action.

4 **What's the fix?** Describes EY's point of view on the issue as well as how clients can act to address it.

5 **What's the bottom line?** Summarizes the issue, the need to act and the benefits that clients can realize.

In addition to a *5 series* print version, EY created a dedicated web presence, www.ey.com/5. It offers:

- a web version of the *5 series* article;
- access to the print piece in PDF format;
- a companion 90-second flash video that summarizes the issue, urgency and the fix;
- a three-minute *5 talks* video that features EY's consultants providing a more in-depth look at the issue and the fix; and
- a place to contact an EU resource to talk further about the issue.

Although results were initially difficult to quantify, qualitative results included:

- a significant increase in brand awareness;
- exponential increases in revenue and year-over-year growth; and
- reprinting of *5 series* articles by major media outlets such as *Industry Week*, Forbes.com and the *Wall Street Journal's CIO Journal*.

EY also identified a causal relationship related to its performance improvement services. Growth in this service line had been flat, so to help spur activity EY produced eight *5 series* pieces that highlighted performance issues that tied directly to business development efforts. They resulted in the biggest sales month ever, hitting 125 per cent of the business line's goal.

When they integrated the *5 series* into the sector-led demand generation campaigns, the firm used its client relationship software to measure success. Each campaign was rated using two scorecards. The first tracked whether client meetings were scheduled or held with the target accounts. The second tracked sales and pipeline. They met and exceeded goals on both scorecards.

But these sector-led campaigns did more than bolster revenue. By establishing EY's ability to ask and answer the key questions on the most relevant issues their clients face, the campaigns extended the firm's brand and reputation, and put it in position to win valuable work in the years to come.

Looking ahead, EY sees the *5 series* as much more than a marketing tool. This innovative approach to effective use of thought leadership serves as an invaluable awareness-builder, door opener and discussion starter that can activate client thinking to accelerate their business performance. And it solidifies EY's reputation as trusted advisors in the global professional services sector.

SOURCE ITSMA Marketing Excellence Award Winners summary booklet, 2014
Reproduced with permission from ITSMA

The value you are adding

If you are engaging an executive in your programme who is already a customer, the first thing they will want to understand is the value that you're adding to their business. In situations where you are one of their strategic suppliers, it's likely that your executives will meet your target executives at least annually to review the success of the products, services and solutions you deliver, and the business outcomes you are helping them to achieve.

Of course, people in both organizations will be meeting more frequently, with delivery and relationship managers meeting the client on a weekly or monthly basis to review how things are going and what else can be done to help them. In most cases today, a real-time performance dashboard will be used to communicate how a service or solution is being delivered against service levels agreed at the time when the purchase was made and the contract between your two organizations agreed, with the weekly or monthly meetings reviewing the dashboard and any trends in performance over the previous review period.

While this detailed governance is unlikely to form part of your executive engagement programme per se, it will certainly be part of the briefing you provide to anyone who is meeting a target executive from that customer account, so that they are not blindsided by any performance issues that are currently in review.

The kind of information that the senior executives in your programme will be looking for is at a higher level than in these weekly or monthly meetings, and these annual relationship reviews should potentially form part of your programme. Each organization will have its preferred way of running these meetings, but a good guideline to the topics to cover includes the following:

1 a review of the performance of the products, services and solutions against service level agreements or contract over the previous year;

2 a summary of the value delivered in terms of the business outcomes agreed at the start of the contract, such as cost savings, increased productivity, faster time to market and overall ROI;

3 in the case of reciprocal relationships, such as where a telecoms operator is buying technology solutions from an IT outsourcer, who in turn uses the communications services of the operator, a review of the 'balance of trade' between the two;

4 in the case where the two organizations also go to market together, selling technology and communications solutions to other businesses, for example, a review of the business performance of the joint venture or offering;

5 observations on the customer organization and suggestions for immediate improvements and near-term innovations, supported by case study examples from other companies or ROI calculators;

6 observations on the market in which the organization operates and its wider environment, together with thought leadership ideas on how to take advantage of the opportunities revealed and minimize the threats arising.

Ideally a natural next step from this conversation will be a more detailed innovation or design-thinking workshop to explore the ideas further and identify potential proof of concept projects and the like.

Some companies create a partnership review document, or value report, to support annual meetings like this, while others simply create a presentation or talk track. Since a key part of it will be thought leadership content, let's look at this in more detail now.

Thought leadership

In his 2013 book on thought leadership,[1] Laurie Young noted that 'thought leadership is probably one of the most influential and successful business practices that the world has seen.... At its best, [it] produces systematic, iconic work (like that in *McKinsey Quarterly*). The worst, though, has been mocked by *The Economist* as "thought followership". Some of it is not leadership and some of it isn't even clear thought.'

ITSMA defines thought leadership as 'ideas that educate customers and prospects about important business and technology issues, and help them to solve those issues – without selling'. In his book, Young defines it as the creation and dissemination of ideas that tend to result in advantage for businesses – a more generic but broadly similar definition.

The importance buyers give it has been consistently high. For instance, in ITSMA's 2017 'How buyers choose' survey, 86 per cent of executive buyers rated thought leadership as important or critical when exploring business solutions and suppliers.[2] Six months later, in ITSMA's 2018 'Thought Leadership' survey,[3] 85 per cent of marketers said thought leadership is critical or important to building relationships with executives. It's safe to assume you're going to need some thought leadership content in your executive engagement programme.

In my experience, your organization will fall into one of two categories when it comes to your thought leadership competence:

1 those that have little trouble generating thought leadership, but aren't systematically disseminating it across their organization and beyond; or

2 those with effective marketing communications engines that struggle to generate the ideas and content required for thought leadership.

The former are often consultancies and professional service firms, while the latter are often companies with a strong product or engineering heritage.

If you are in the latter category, then ITSMA's guide[4] to developing the thought leadership content you need will be helpful (see Figure 5.6).

Creating thought leadership content

STEP 1: DEVELOP A POSITIONING STATEMENT

It's not enough to simply identify a business issue that clients are facing and explain it. You need to take a strong point of view on why it is an issue, what's going to happen and how to deal with the ramifications. As we saw earlier in this chapter, professional service firm EY achieves this with its '5 Insights for Executives series'. The clear five-part structure helps the firm develop its position on a range of issues relevant to its target executives.

STEP 2: GATHER PROPRIETARY EVIDENCE

Ideas alone are not enough to convince clients and prospects to trust you. They need proof. Young[1] points out that thought leadership seldom goes through the rigorous peer review process that academic papers receive, so evidence is needed in some other form.

Companies typically gather evidence in three ways. First, by culling research from external sources and analysing it for insights that shore up their point of view. This is generally a relatively easy and inexpensive approach, increasingly being conducted with the help of data scientists who can analyse vast quantities of data such as that available via the Twitter fire hose.

Second, companies hire external research groups to carry out primary research, often on an ad hoc basis, so that their research data are exclusive and carry their brand name, such as software company SAP's research with IDC on how companies are creating new technology-based business models.

FIGURE 5.6 Four steps to thought leadership content development

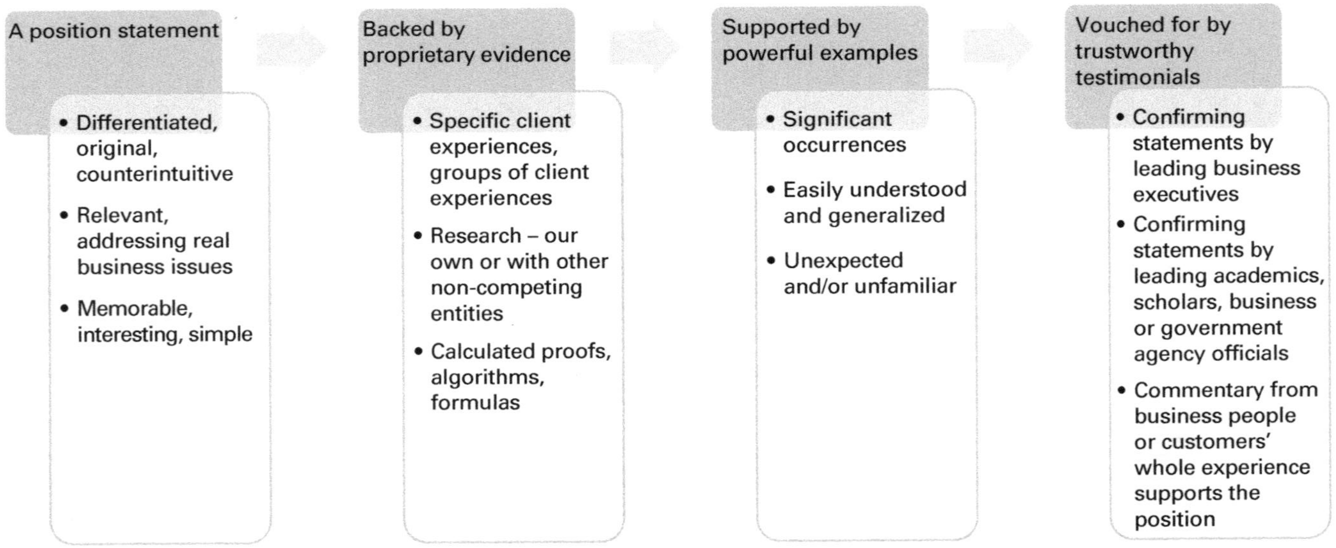

A position statement	Backed by proprietary evidence	Supported by powerful examples	Vouched for by trustworthy testimonials
• Differentiated, original, counterintuitive • Relevant, addressing real business issues • Memorable, interesting, simple	• Specific client experiences, groups of client experiences • Research – our own or with other non-competing entities • Calculated proofs, algorithms, formulas	• Significant occurrences • Easily understood and generalized • Unexpected and/or unfamiliar	• Confirming statements by leading business executives • Confirming statements by leading academics, scholars, business or government agency officials • Commentary from business people or customers' whole experience supports the position

SOURCE Adapted from ITSMA's 'How To Develop and Deliver Thought Leadership', Marketing Tool, 2007

Third, as thought leadership has become a core part of many marketing and executive engagement strategies, companies are building their own in-house research groups to put the proof behind their opinions. An example of the third approach is IBM's Institute for Business Value (IBV) (see Chapter 4), or the McKinsey Global Institute.

STEP 3: BUILD POWERFUL EXAMPLES
Examples, from named clients ideally, should be significant stories that are easily understood, and that customers can generalize across industries or markets. They should be unexpected and fresh. IBM's IBV researchers (see case study in Chapter 4) are all assigned either to a vertical (industry sector) or to a cross-industry functional area (such as AI/cognitive computing), so that they can compare their findings with each other and discuss what it means across all verticals, collecting examples that will have significant impact with multiple clients.

In McKinsey's articles and reports, there are always engaging examples, such as the story of Coca-Cola's manifesto for growth cited in 'A better way to lead large-scale change'. The article,[5] which claims that companies can double their odds of success by putting equal emphasis on the hard and soft elements of leading change, explains that 'the goal of the manifesto was to outline a path that showed not just where the company aimed to go – its strategy – but also what it would do to get there and how people would work together differently along the way'.

It posited that the 'magic of the manifesto is that it was written in detail by the top 150 managers and had input from the top 400. Therefore, it was their program for implementation'. The authors shared how Coca-Cola's approach led to quantified business outcomes. Within three years, shareholder value jumped from a negative to a 20 per cent positive return, and volume growth in units sold increased by almost 10 per cent, to 21.4 billion.

STEP 4: ELICIT TRUSTWORTHY TESTIMONIALS
Validation from outside the organization is also necessary to build credibility. Gather trustworthy testimonials from leading business executives, academics, scholars, government officials, industry analysts or customers with experience to support your position. Research shows that the most sophisticated thought leadership programmes gather ideas from a wider range of sources (see Figure 5.7) and that 75 per cent of them co-create thought leadership with their clients.

FIGURE 5.7 A range of sources for idea and issue development

| One-on-one client meetings | Client events | Client advisory boards/ councils | Industry events | Industry associations | Sales and account teams |

SOURCE ITSMA Thought Leadership survey, March 2018

FIGURE 5.8 Marketers are overly focused on the short term

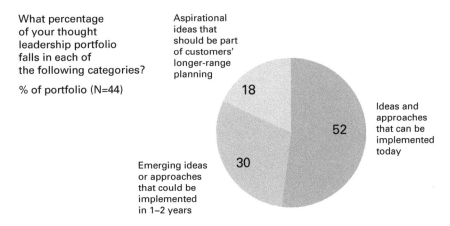

What percentage of your thought leadership portfolio falls in each of the following categories?

% of portfolio (N=44)

Aspirational ideas that should be part of customers' longer-range planning

18

52
Ideas and approaches that can be implemented today

30

Emerging ideas or approaches that could be implemented in 1–2 years

SOURCE ITSMA 'Thought Leadership' survey, March 2018

Internal 'stars' from among CEOs, senior vice presidents (SVPs) and tech-nology leaders, product managers, sales people, business unit heads and practice managers can all play a part in these co-creation projects.

A continual feedback loop is usually formed to ensure that ideas are grounded and practical, rather than simply blue-sky thinking. But it seems that marketers are perhaps under-emphasizing this blue-sky thinking today, as they focus on near-term, pragmatic ideas rather than longer-term thought leadership content – despite the fact that we know executives want content spanning short-, medium- and long-range perspectives (see Figure 5.8).

From creation to distribution

If you are in an organization where content creation is not the problem, but dissemination and distribution to the executives that matter are, then this section may help.

The key is to think about disseminating content effectively through a variety of assets and media. The current trend is to move to shorter and more dynamic formats (see Figure 5.9), but don't forget that executives also want longer-format content to binge on when they are in deep-dive mode.

Try to move from a 'publishing' mindset to one that 'enables' conversations with the executives you are targeting. 'Enablers' educate and train their people on how and when to use thought leadership in conversations, creating talking points, scripts and checklists for them to leverage. They also create benchmarking tools, self-assessments and quizzes that can be used with clients and prospects, in meetings or small events and workshops, to bring the content to life.

ITSMA's 2018 study on thought leadership showed that 89 per cent of marketers are customizing thought leadership assets, making it more relevant and personal – and we know that this is what executives want. This drives up the impact of the content, as clients can relate to it much more easily.

Let us return to IBM's Institute of Business Value. Its C-Suite studies, for instance, are role based, most recently looking at the imperatives facing CMOs, given the pace of change in markets and technology, to drive conversations and draw out implications for particular individuals.

All of this goes on in addition to the activities that a traditional 'publisher' mindset covers. For example, some IBV studies have interactive web portals where visitors can watch video content about the survey findings and access additional charts and graphics not included in the traditional pdf white paper. Studies are promoted within various social media.

For some, IBM conducts what it calls innovation jams – live online chats where IBM SMEs and buyers can discuss findings and brainstorm solutions relating to thought leadership findings. IBM has also created what it calls virtual briefing centres, built around individual verticals. The centres contain the latest industry-specific thought leadership case studies, videos and webcasts, and feature IBM SMEs discussing key topics. These virtual briefing centres are easily customizable, so they can be tailored to particular clients or sub-verticals relatively quickly and cheaply.

With all of this activity involved in creating and disseminating thought leadership, the real question many businesses are asking is: 'Is it worth it?'

FIGURE 5.9 Moving to shorter and more dynamic formats

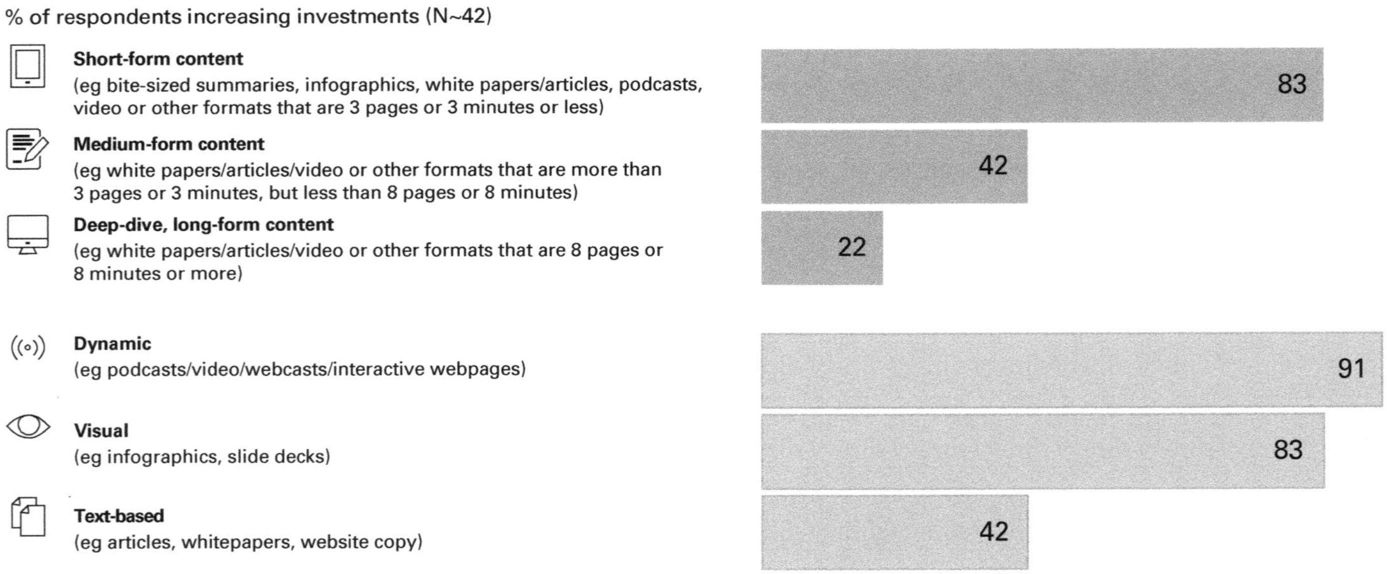

% of respondents increasing investments (N~42)

Short-form content
(eg bite-sized summaries, infographics, white papers/articles, podcasts, video or other formats that are 3 pages or 3 minutes or less)

Medium-form content
(eg white papers/articles/video or other formats that are more than 3 pages or 3 minutes, but less than 8 pages or 8 minutes)

Deep-dive, long-form content
(eg white papers/articles/video or other formats that are 8 pages or 8 minutes or more)

((∘)) **Dynamic**
(eg podcasts/video/webcasts/interactive webpages)

◊ **Visual**
(eg infographics, slide decks)

Text-based
(eg articles, whitepapers, website copy)

Short-form content: 83
Medium-form content: 42
Deep-dive, long-form content: 22

Dynamic: 91
Visual: 83
Text-based: 42

SOURCE ITSMA 'Thought Leadership' survey, March 2018

Measuring thought leadership effectiveness

While approaches to measuring success vary from company to company, most use tactical measures such as tracking how assets are accessed and used, both internally and externally. Some test perceptions, familiarity and favourability towards their brand in primary research, drawing out the impact that their thought leadership is having on all three. Others track the inbound requests or 'opportunities to meet' generated by their programmes.

Probably the best approach is to use a mix of reputation, relationships and revenue factors to evaluate your programme, which is exactly what Deloitte does to evaluate its thought leadership effectiveness.

CASE STUDY
How Deloitte upped its thought leadership game

Deloitte is a leading global provider of audit and assurance, consulting, financial advisory, tax and related services. It has approximately 286,000 people in 150 countries and territories, providing these services within a shared culture.

Deloitte recently embarked on a new chapter in its effort to become the world's leading source of distinctive business and management insight. The firm created Deloitte Insights, with a mission to deliver the very best of the firm's thinking from its professionals around the world.

How clients define quality content

Deloitte's clients told the firm they wanted content that was relevant, practical, credible and appealing. Interestingly, the fact that the ideas were coming from Deloitte was not enough. Clients wanted to know who authored the content so that they could evaluate the knowledge and experience behind the point of view and, if desired, engage that person in a conversation.

Based on feedback from clients, Deloitte established four criteria to evaluate thought leadership quality:

1 Does the thought leadership add to the conversation on a specific issue?
2 Is the thought leadership based on rigorous research, either survey based or analytical?
3 Can clients act on what they learn? If they ask for help, can Deloitte help them?
4 Does the thought leadership reflect the voice that is unique to Deloitte?

The biggest obstacle Deloitte encountered in the firm's quest for quality was its culture. There was little precedent for telling a professional that their piece was not good enough to publish. Deloitte took a carrot-and-stick approach to this obstacle. On the carrot front, it created a destination for top-quality thought leadership, with a distinct look and feel and a white-glove treatment when it came to marketing and activation.

On the stick side, the thought leadership team worked with firm and business leaders to discourage practitioners from creating one-off pieces and to eliminate any investment in marketing for these materials.

Research beyond surveys

There is a direct link between quality thought leadership and research. With research, ideas become fact based and, therefore, more credible. However, research does not start and end with surveys. For example, data science tools can sift through millions of pages of text and detect patterns within a matter of months; it would take 30 years for a human to complete that task.

There is much to learn from the enormous amount of data that is publicly available, but tapping those resources takes time and perseverance. Deloitte created eight distinct research centres, focusing on everything from financial services to the healthcare, government and energy sectors. All employ researchers and data scientists, undertaking the kind of rigorous analysis that provides critical insights into how industries are evolving and how organizations should respond.

Focus on issues important to clients

The best thought leadership comes in two forms: responding directly to issues raised by clients and presenting solutions to problems clients haven't yet thought of. Deloitte works to do both, grounded in the philosophy that it seeks to understand the issues that matter to clients, not the issues that matter to the firm.

As such, Deloitte is very deliberate about picking its thought leadership themes. And the firm's leaders are quick to point out that their thought leadership is not self-promotional. Sales are secondary to being regarded as a trusted, authoritative voice on issues that matter to clients, which is why in the quest for utility – one of the desired hallmarks of quality – Deloitte carefully defines the topics it pursues.

There's no denying, however, the link between how thought leadership burnishes Deloitte's reputation and how that manifests in the marketplace. Indeed, it is regarded as critical that partners have a direct line of sight between the firm's thought leadership and the set of services that will help potential clients solve problems.

Big idea campaigns

Deloitte has shifted its thought leadership from multiple issues and one-off publications to multifaceted big idea campaigns that cut across industries and functions, such as additive manufacturing, the IoT and the future of mobility.

Today, Deloitte's research centres contribute to a series of big idea campaigns, conducting research and developing points of view to support SMEs in the practices. Each big idea campaign is backed by robust research, a unique Deloitte point of view and a series of perspectives on different aspects of the business theme. Deloitte starts with the fundamentals – what it is and how it applies to its clients' businesses. It then does industry-sector-level deep dives. Finally, as it learns more about a topic, Deloitte explores the recurring issues that cross sectors.

Collaborate relentlessly

Collaboration enhances the quality and credibility of thought leadership by grounding content with research and hard data. Deloitte joins forces with experts at leading universities, think tanks, start-ups, non-profits and even clients. Collaboration extends the firm's market reach and provides more opportunities to connect with clients.

Deloitte takes a long-term approach to collaborative relationship development as opposed to one that is more episodic or project based. The value in collaborative relations evolves over time and requires hands-on management for maximum return. It often takes more than a one-year commitment to reap the benefits.

Field activation

Deloitte goes to market through its client service partners. And although marketing can push thought leadership out to the market and create pull, it is the client service teams that interact with clients and prospects on a regular basis. If Deloitte wants to get its thought leadership on its client's desks, then the client service teams are the ones who must put it there.

The good news is that client service partners get calls from clients who have just read or listened to something Deloitte published and want to talk about it. Client service teams need to thoroughly understand the topics and be prepared to communicate with clients in a tailored way.

Measure what matters

By measuring what matters, Deloitte marketing has proven the ROI in thought leadership. Deloitte ties thought leadership measurement to its business objectives with the three Rs:

- Reputation: Building brand eminence
- Relationships: Enhancing the value of client connections
- Revenue: Putting the firm in contention for more work.

The actual metrics themselves are numerous and varied, with an emphasis on quality rather than volume. Perhaps the most important thought leadership metric is share of voice. Deloitte wants to own and drive the conversation around its big idea campaigns, not just be a participant.

SOURCE Adapted from 'How Deloitte upped its Thought Leadership Game', ITSMA, 2018
Reproduced with permission from ITSMA

Value propositions

There is very little value in raising issues with executives if you have no idea how you can help to solve them. You'll need to develop compelling value propositions that communicate what you can do and differentiate you so that your solution is more relevant than any other supplier they can work with.

> ITSMA defines a value proposition as a clear and simple statement that reflects the essence of the unique value a business will provide to a client or target market, through a combination of benefits and price.

The most successful value proposition starts with an executive's business issue, in *their* words and from *their* perspective, and we've already discussed how critical it is to understand these issues, both in Chapter 3 and in our discussion on developing thought leadership content. It describes *your* solution to their issue, the particular benefits *your* solution provides over competitor solutions and the business outcomes they should expect by implementing your offering through a combination of benefits and price.

Value propositions should be simple, clear, easy-to-absorb statements, adaptable to specific executives and backed up by proof points. Wherever possible, they should be financially quantified. They encapsulate the reason that your potential buyers should purchase your company's product, service or solution rather than anyone else's.

A note on value

All of us make subjective judgements about value every day. It is a personal calculation of the benefits of anything we buy against the cost to purchase it. For executives, the benefits may be tangible, such as a percentage reduction in travel costs by using online collaboration tools, or intangible, such as minimizing the risk of changing your telecoms supplier by staying with the incumbent. Wherever possible, if your value proposition offers tangible benefits to a client, you should try to quantify those benefits and show where other clients have received them from you in the past – if you can.

Executives take a broad view of costs beyond the price they actually pay for a solution. There are costs to consider about the time involved in taking on a new supplier, for example, or relating to potential risks to reputation to be considered, such as if a supplier has questionable sourcing strategies or sustainability policies.

Ultimately, executives will choose the proposition they perceive to have the greatest value for them relative to the available alternatives. For examples of both tangible and intangible benefits you could include in your propositions, see Table 5.1.

TABLE 5.1   Examples of tangible and intangible benefits

Tangible benefits (can be quantified)	Intangible benefits (difficult to quantify)
• Increased efficiency • Increased revenues • Increased sales • Market share growth • Reduced time to market • Reduced costs • Increased customer loyalty • Increased differentiation from competitors	• Reduced risk and worry • Ability to set new trends or be a market leader • Ability to be a hero in his/her own company • Recognition, praise, esteem by industry, peers or community • Ability to join a prestigious group of companies that use your services

SOURCE ITSMA, 2019

To be effective, value propositions must uncover *unique* differentiation and quantify superior *value*. Furthermore, value propositions have to be more than words: they must be based on tangible, proven and repeatable results. Otherwise the executives you are targeting will see right through them.

Five elements in a strong value proposition

Usually, you won't be creating your organization's value propositions for the target executives in your programme – ideally your product marketers will be doing that – but it's worth knowing what a strong value proposition includes. And you may need to create a value proposition for your executive engagement programme to get both internal and external executives to participate, so this section will explain how to do that.

There are five elements to include in the value propositions you write for your executives. Table 5.2 shows each one and the questions you can ask your colleagues to help you get to the answers.

Crafting the value propositions is a multi-step process. First, fill in the blanks on the template. This ensures that all the elements of a good value proposition are present. Next, write the story in prose, eliminating clichés and fillers, and then adapt it for the intended use, whether it is online content, an executive-to-executive meeting, a presentation or part of an annual account relationship review.

Let's work through this template step by step.

TABLE 5.2 A value proposition template

Who is your target market?	Which individuals will buy or influence the purchase?
What are their needs or problems?	What is their life like? What keeps them up at night? Where are their pain points and what language do they use to describe them?
What will your product or service do for them?	How will they define value? What language will they use?
Why should they prefer your offer over the competition?	Why can't they do it another way – or do it themselves? What differentiates your approach?
How does the value of your offering outweigh the price?	How will you deliver value through your engagement and underpin it with a sound commercial contract?

Reproduced with permission from Dr Paul Fifield

STEP 1. DEFINE YOUR TARGET MARKET

Many value propositions are generic, talking to 'large enterprises' or 'government organizations'. This is poor even at a segment or role-based level. You should ensure that your propositions are for a specific executive buyer or group of buyers. So, use language like 'as a CMO in one of the world's largest banks' or 'as the management team tasked with transforming the way your people work'.

Once you've identified them, connect with them by showing that you understand their main priority or concern. And again, use the language they would use themselves, not your own.

STEP 2. DEFINE THEIR NEEDS OR PROBLEMS

From your initial work to understand your executives, you will have identified the issues, opportunities and challenges facing them today. By including a statement about their needs in your value proposition, you are demonstrating your understanding of their situation. In addition, by using the language that they are using about their problems (perhaps in their statements to shareholders, for example), you are starting to build a rapport with these executives, so don't talk about cutting operational costs if they are talking about driving efficiencies in operations, for example.

If you are in the position of having identified a business issue facing the executive through your thought leadership, which they themselves are as yet unaware of, you will need to educate your buyers on the route to action before you begin to sell your solution. You may want to describe how others in their situation are approaching the issue. Your target executives may be aware they are behind the curve in terms of responding and will be interested to see how their peers are faring, particularly if they are traditionally a 'follower' rather than an 'innovator'.

However, if what you are recommending is completely innovative and new, and you are appealing to buyers who traditionally break moulds and lead the pack, the very fact that no one else is running a similar initiative will appeal. With CEOs around the world most worried about disruptions to their industries coming from new digital entrants such as Uber and Airbnb, you will get their attention if you can recommend an innovative approach they could be taking to a common business issue facing companies in their sector – particularly if it brings competitive advantage and a whole new revenue stream they hadn't considered.

STEP 3. DESCRIBE WHAT YOUR PRODUCT OR SERVICE WILL DO FOR THEM

This step is about describing the benefits that your offer, or solution, will give the executive. It shouldn't be a description of your solution comprising a list of features, but a summary of the business outcomes you'll provide, written in their language. The key here is to understand how they are measured and how they define success, linking the benefits you are offering with those things.

The more you can quantify the value of the tangible benefits on offer, the greater the interest generated. People like to see numbers – credible, hard numbers. However, even relative or qualitative numbers (eg improved efficiency and higher satisfaction), if backed up with proof, are acceptable. It is better not to use adjectives but to use stories that demonstrate your claims. Value propositions should be underpinned with real-life testimonials, success stories and references.

Four main areas of quantification you might want to consider are:

1 efficiency;

2 quality;

3 profitable revenue growth;

4 value creation.

It is easiest to quantify the efficiency benefits such as impact on productivity, headcount and turnaround time. However, the more valuable benefits are the impact on revenue, especially profitable revenue, and actual value creation (eg new revenue streams, access to capital, attainment of a leadership position). Solutions that address these areas are likely to be most relevant to senior manager, C-level executives and board-level executives and to command a greater price premium.

STEP 4. EXPLAIN WHY THEY SHOULD PREFER YOU OVER OTHERS

To be successful, your value proposition must explain why your solutions are superior to your competitors'. What makes your offer unique? Most marketers find this question hard to answer. In many cases an inside-out focus is to blame. You need to start with the executive's point of view and examine what your competitors are saying to them in order to focus on the things you know are important to your executives and where you have a distinct advantage.

Review competitor materials to help you identify and prioritize your differentiators and build a case as to why the client should work with you and not them. What do they offer in the same area as you? What are their value propositions? What assets do they have in terms of client references, intellectual property or SMEs? What do they claim to be their key differentiators?

STEP 5. EMPHASIZE HOW THE VALUE THEY'LL RECEIVE OUTWEIGHS THE PRICE THEY'LL PAY

This is a difficult step, partly because of the subjective nature of value that we discussed earlier on. But you need to help your target executives understand how all the benefits they'll get from working with you will outweigh the costs – both financial and others such as time, risk or reputation – to deliver real value. These sources of value may not be part of the technical solution they're buying, but perhaps more about the commercial contract, or even access to a community of peers through your executive engagement programme.

Here are some sources of value you might like to consider at this point (some of which may relate directly to the benefits on offer through your executive engagement activities):

1 access to leading-edge technologies and innovations;
2 training (product, application, sales, quality) and professional development;
3 competitive intelligence;
4 leverageable relationships including political, regulatory or non-executive;
5 joint research;
6 intellectual property, including market benchmarks, reports, studies, industry trends, research, best practices;
7 access to areas of corporate expertise such as CSR or diversity programmes;
8 advertising, promotions, co-branding;
9 community recognition/visibility/public relations.

Test, test, test

Once you have developed your proposition, it's time to get feedback, both internally and externally. Your value propositions should be tested with a select group of relevant internal executives and possibly external advisors, such as industry analysts or individual consultants or professionals from your network who understand the executives you are focused on. If your programme is international, your value proposition should be tested in multiple geographies owing to language and cultural issues.

Some questions to consider using when you test include:

1 Based on the wording, is it clear to you what I am describing? If not, what is unclear?

2 Is this something you would be interested in learning more about after reading this proposition? Why or why not?

3 Do you think this solution is valuable to executives like those we are focused on? How so? Would the value outweigh the costs?

4 Is it clear what is different or better about our proposition compared to similar propositions from other companies? How is that difference of value to the executives we're focused on?

Since a range of people from your organization will engage with your target executives, you also need to validate your proposition with them. Are the statements believable? Are they comfortable with the words and concepts conveyed? Can they communicate the gist of the value proposition using their own words?

Through a series of structured conversations your value proposition should be tested, revised and tested again. The validation process does not need to be onerous but it should be thorough. Value propositions are too important to be based on assumptions, and executives will quickly dismiss any that appear irrelevant or without substance.

Creating an elevator pitch

Any sales person will tell you that when they're trying to get the attention and interest of an executive in the hope of booking some time with them for a more in-depth discussion, they have less than a minute to make an impression. Even your value proposition will be too long for this type of meeting.

A classic example of this is when meeting a target executive in an elevator. You have 20–30 seconds to make an impression – hence the term 'elevator pitch'. What you choose to say during that elevator ride will make the difference between the executive asking for a follow-up meeting as they leave the elevator, and one who can't get out of the elevator fast enough!

We can learn a lot from our consumer marketing colleagues here, who have had to put their value proposition across in 10-, 20- or 30-second commercials that get the consumer's attention and persuade them to buy.

Here's a great example from Apple for their new Apple Card, targeting people who love Apple Pay, leveraging the values Apple stands for and emphasizing the overarching benefit that it encourages you to pay less interest.

- Apple Card completely rethinks everything about the credit card.
- It represents all the things Apple stands for. Like simplicity, transparency and privacy.
- It builds on the incredible ease and security that millions of people love about Apple Pay.
- And it's the first card that actually encourages you to pay less interest.
- Whether you buy things with Apple Pay or with the laser-etched titanium card, Apple Card can do things no other credit card can do.

So, once you have developed your value proposition statement, it's worth going the extra mile and distilling it down into a short, powerful phrase that your own people can use when they meet the executives in your programme. And the best way to test the power of these statements is through role-play. If you can't make your pitch convincingly, you need to work on it until you can.

Examples and case studies

One of the most compelling types of content that executives like to hear about is best practice examples and case studies from other organizations. These are reassuring in that they show that others have similar issues to deal with, and inspiring in that they share the approaches others took and the lessons they learned. And where these proof points reinforce the thought leadership issues you've put forward, and substantiate the value propositions you're offering, so much the better.

Most case studies cover the following information:

1 a description of the specific issues, opportunities or threats facing the client and the business implications if not addressed;

2 a description of the approach taken, including challenges overcome;

3 the (quantified) business outcomes achieved as a result;

4 lessons learned and next steps.

However, most of the marketers I meet say that getting clients to agree to tell their stories, especially in the form of case studies demonstrating how suppliers have helped them achieve their business outcomes, can be very difficult. Some dismiss it out of hand, having a central policy of providing no references for any supplier. Some are asked before the solution they have bought is even working, and are understandably reluctant. Others find it so difficult to track the outcomes they've achieved that the story is less compelling owing to this lack of tangible results. And some are never asked, since the sales person takes the 'reference clause' out of the contract as part of their negotiating tactics for the deal. So, building interesting and compelling case stories and best practice examples to engage executives can be hard.

A guide to the process behind identifying and generating great case study stories from among your clients is shown in Figure 5.10.

FIGURE 5.10 The process behind creating case study stories

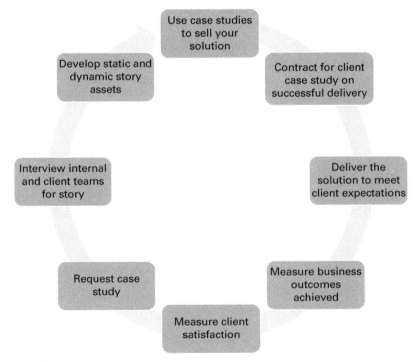

SOURCE ITSMA, 2019

One thing to bear in mind is that you'll need to be clear on the proposition for the client whose story you want to tell. They'll be asking 'What's in it for me?' If you get this right, this will be one of the most powerful ways you can engage an executive, by helping them tell their story to great personal benefit.

A wonderful example comes from Fujitsu's approach to encouraging the CIO at London's Heathrow airport to tell the story of how they used technology to transform the traveller's journey at Terminal 2.

In a key account of Fujitsu's, this executive was not engaging with Fujitsu at all, and had unsubscribed from marketing communications. In order to re-engage, Fujitsu did some work to understand the executive and the account's context, uncovering the fact that Heathrow was in competition with London Gatwick airport to expand, since the UK needs an additional runway.

The marketing team at Fujitsu took the approach of helping the CIO to tell their transformation story (enabled by Fujitsu's solutions), thereby helping Heathrow's bid to host the additional runway. They developed both static assets (non-live assets, including a written case study, video case and article interview in their iCIO magazine, *iCIO Magz*) and dynamic assets, essentially live activities, including a PR tour at the terminal to showcase the great job the CIO had done.

As a result, they achieved 19 pieces of press coverage for the CIO and Heathrow, supporting its successful bid for the extra runway. Perhaps more importantly, the CIO asked for communications to be switched back on and became a Fujitsu advocate.

We're back to value propositions in a way; you'll need to consider what value the storyteller, your client, will get from becoming a case study. Some possible benefits are:

1 free advertising or PR for them and their company;

2 bragging rights for them and their colleagues;

3 company brand lift;

4 internal morale boost;

5 a recruitment support tool;

6 access to your senior leadership;

7 personal career enhancement; and

8 personal brand lift for the storyteller.

The range of static and dynamic ways in which you might ask your client to tell their story is illustrated in Table 5.3.

TABLE 5.3 Static and dynamic ways to tell case study stories

Static	Dynamic
Company name/logo usage	Media or influencer interview
Client quote	Client reference call
PowerPoint summary slide	Study tour/site visit host
Media release	Conference presentation or panel member
Social post or blog	Seminar/briefing centre participation
Article (2–3 pages)	Live webinar or online session participation
Industry award submission	Advisory council discussion
Full case study (4–8 pages)	
Advertisement copy	
Video/film	
Recorded podcast interview	

SOURCE ITSMA, 2019

Tell me a story

As you've probably realized by now, case studies are essentially stories, and luckily the human brain is wired to listen for stories. If you use storytelling techniques in your examples, you increase the chances that they will be seen or heard by your target executives. Stories reach three distinct parts of the human brain and directly connect to our instincts, our emotions and our higher-order, rational thinking. Over thousands of years of evolution, our brains have been wired to communicate in this way. Stories resonate with us.

How should you present your case studies as stories? Simply put, stories have three components:

1 **A plot or storyline.** This is the essence of the story, which, according to experts, can be articulated in as few as six words.

2 **A story, or narrative, arc.** Starting with an opening scene, following various crises including a point of no-return, reaching a climax and finishing with the *dénouement*, the arc is the journey you are taking the audience on.

3 **A cast of characters with predetermined roles.** Having a hero and a villain is a good start. When they are joined by other archetypes, the story becomes more engaging.

However, just as when cooking from a recipe, the ingredients on their own are not usually enough. How you mix them together matters hugely. There are three dimensions to get the 'special sauce' of storytelling to set:

- First, there must be coherence between the business and the story.
- Second, the story itself should be credible, authentic and ambitious.
- Finally, the audience need to identify with the story and be thrilled by it.

It is up to you to let your imagination loose. Because storytelling allows (arguably demands) the use of humour, surprise or suspense, it is an outlet for you to exercise your creative skills. And that's what you'll need to do to engage time-poor, easily bored executives.

Summary

1 Executives like to talk about a range of things, but typically these boil down to the issues and opportunities facing them and their organization – in both its internal operations, immediate environment or the wider world – and ideas for how to overcome or take advantage of them to achieve their goals.

2 If you are engaging an executive in your programme who is already a customer, the first thing they will want to understand is the value that you're adding to their business.

3 Executives rate thought leadership – ideas that educate customers and prospects about important business and technology issues and help them to solve those issues, without selling – as important when exploring business solutions and suppliers. You will need thought leadership content in your executive engagement programme.

4 Executives want thought leadership to help them think about the immediate, medium-term and long-range issues facing their business.

5 There is very little value in raising issues with executives if you have no idea how you can help to solve them, so you'll need to develop compelling value propositions that communicate what you can do and differentiate you so that your solution is more relevant than any other supplier they can work with.

6 Value propositions should be simple, clear, easy-to-absorb statements, adaptable to specific executives and backed up by proof points. Wherever possible, they should be financially quantified. They should encapsulate the reason that executives should prefer your solution rather than anyone else's.

7 One of the most compelling types of content that executives like to hear about is best practice examples and case studies from other organizations. These are reassuring in that they show that others have similar issues to deal with, and inspiring in that they share the approaches others took and the lessons they learned. And where these proof points reinforce the thought leadership issues you've put forward, and substantiate the value propositions you're offering, so much the better.

8 Present your case studies as stories creating a clear plot, a narrative arc and a cast of characters so your cases become more engaging.

Notes

1 Young, L D (2013) 'Thought Leadership: Prompting Businesses to Think and Learn', Kogan Page, London
2 ITSMA (September 2017) 'How buyers choose' survey
3 ITSMA (March 2018) 'Thought Leadership' survey
4 ITSMA (2007) How To Develop and Deliver Thought Leadership, Marketing Tool, http://www.itsma.com/research/how-to-develop-and-deliver-thought-leadership (archived at https://perma.cc/U7VD-EASR)
5 Keller, S and Shaninger, B (July 2019) 'A better way to lead large-scale change', extracted from the book by McKinsey partners Keller, S and Shaninger, B (2019) *Beyond Performance 2.0*, John Wiley & Sons, Hoboken, NJ

06

Knowing when to engage

It's not enough to know which executives you want to engage and understand what they want to hear. You'll also need an idea of when to engage them, too, and how. In the long-term relationships that underpin the sale and purchase of complex business solutions, there are progressive stages that executive buyers move through. And at each stage they are looking for different things.

Before the buying process and relationships begin in earnest, executives have to recognize that they have an issue, or need. This recognition may be prompted by the kind of thought leadership content we discussed in Chapter 5, or it may simply come from within their own organization or peer network. Once recognized, executives must decide what to do about it, beginning their own research process to help their thinking.

From there, they will evaluate different solutions and suppliers until they, and their organization, are convinced of the right route they should take. Once an initial purchase is made, they'll be questioning whether they made the right decision and looking for proof that the business outcomes they sought are being delivered. Once this is proven and their trust and loyalty secured, they will (hopefully) recommend their supplier across their own organization and beyond.

In this chapter, we'll explore this purchase process and look at what information and types of engagement executives are looking for at each stage to help you plan your engagement strategy to meet their needs.

Engagement along the buying process

Executive buyers move through stages as they make decisions to purchase high-value, complex business solutions. There is some debate about the impact of purchasing moving online, and about the buying process collapsing and becoming more chaotic with no clear sequential stages. While this may be true for lower-value purchases, the high-consideration decisions we're talking about are still very process driven, even if buyers do move backwards and forwards through the process a bit less predictably than in the past.

The buyer process is described well in Figure 6.1, using the model developed by ITSMA. It travels from the early stages of building relevancy as executives explore the different suppliers they could work with, to the role of client intimacy once the deal is done. Historically, most marketing and sales resources have been spent on the first part of this process, demonstrating relevancy to secure a sale. But recent research shows[1] that 55 per cent of B2B companies are increasing their spend on the second half of this process, post-purchase, in order the strengthen relationships with their clients and encourage them to become advocates who will help to grow their business.

The buying stages

Executives are constantly scanning their organization and its external environment for issues and trends that can represent either opportunities or threats to their future success. At the point that they recognize an issue and identify a new need or opportunity, a potential buying process begins. The ITSMA model calls this the 'Epiphany' stage, where you as the potential seller should be ensuring that the buying executive recognizes the opportunity and thinks of your company.

The potential buyer then starts searching for possible solutions and alternative ways of meeting their newly recognized need. They begin to clarify what it is they are trying to achieve and what help they may need, and then explore alternative ways of achieving their goals. At this stage, you will be focusing on demonstrating your relevancy for their front-of-mind challenge.

If you do this well, the executive will want to know more about your company as they begin to create a shortlist of people who could help them. They'll be comparing what you can do with others on the list, so it's time to raise your game and really demonstrate how what you offer stands out compared to the alternatives they're considering. Your goal is to get them to prefer you above anyone else.

As Figure 6.2 shows, throughout these first three stages in the relationship buying process, executives spend almost as much of their time offline as online, tipping over to more time offline as they reach the interested stage.

FIGURE 6.1 The B2B buying process

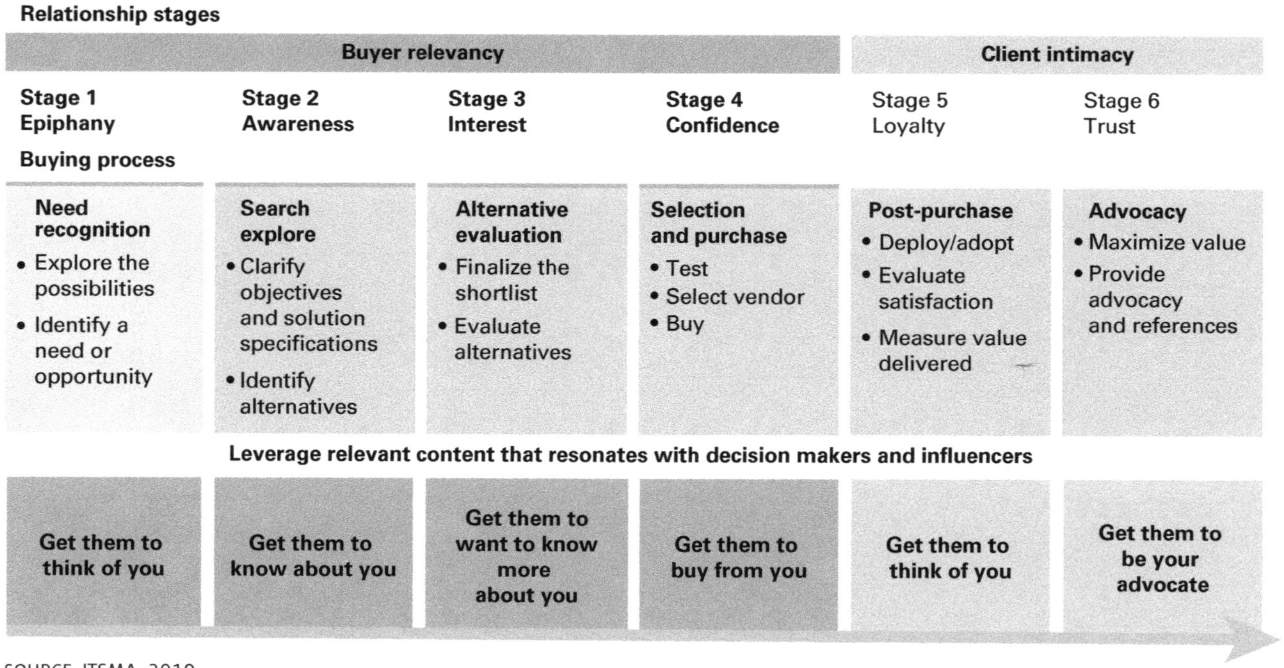

	Relationship stages					
	Buyer relevancy				**Client intimacy**	
	Stage 1 **Epiphany**	**Stage 2** **Awareness**	**Stage 3** **Interest**	**Stage 4** **Confidence**	**Stage 5** Loyalty	**Stage 6** Trust
Buying process	**Need recognition** • Explore the possibilities • Identify a need or opportunity	**Search explore** • Clarify objectives and solution specifications • Identify alternatives	**Alternative evaluation** • Finalize the shortlist • Evaluate alternatives	**Selection and purchase** • Test • Select vendor • Buy	**Post-purchase** • Deploy/adopt • Evaluate satisfaction • Measure value delivered	**Advocacy** • Maximize value • Provide advocacy and references
			Leverage relevant content that resonates with decision makers and influencers			
	Get them to think of you	**Get them to know about you**	**Get them to want to know more about you**	**Get them to buy from you**	**Get them to think of you**	**Get them to be your advocate**

SOURCE ITSMA, 2019

FIGURE 6.2 Buyers spend nearly as much time offline as online

During the different phases of the purchase process, approximately what percentage of the time did you spend online vs offline? Mean % of time (N=410)

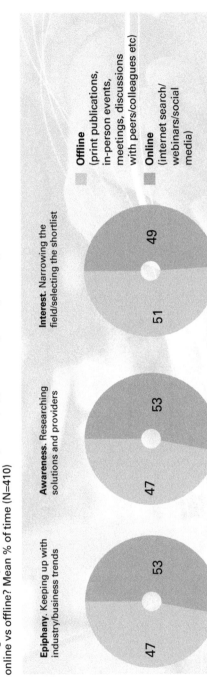

Epiphany. Keeping up with industry/business trends

53

47

Awareness. Researching solutions and providers

53

47

Interest. Narrowing the field/selecting the shortlist

49

51

■ **Offline**
(print publications, in-person events, meetings, discussions with peers/colleagues etc)

■ **Online**
(internet search/ webinars/social media)

SOURCE ITSMA, 'How Executives Engage' survey, 2018

You as the seller must make sure that your engagement activities meet them where they are, synchronizing among your online and offline channels.

The fourth stage is about giving them the confidence to make the decision to buy from you. This confidence will come from many sources, including proof points that you'll deliver on your promises, testimonials from other clients and the qualifications and expertise of your team. And that confidence has to be extended to all the decision makers and influencers involved, which demands a multifaceted approach to engagement.

Once they have bought from you, loyalty will grow as you deliver the value you promised. Ensure from the start that you're supporting the adoption and use of whatever it is you've sold their organization. Is it working? Do people know how to use it and get the best from it? This is not just a delivery issue, but one of communication too. You may be doing everything you agreed to do, but it may be invisible, such as via remote sensors and maintenance. Ongoing engagement to communicate the value you're delivering and capture feedback is essential.

Once you're delivering on your promise, you should focus on making an advocate of the buying executive. By this point, executives are almost back at the beginning of the process again, watching trends and looking for innovative ideas, best practices and ongoing education on how to get the best value from the solutions they've bought and the solutions they could buy next. Some of your engagement activities here should continue to support and challenge their thinking, while others may be about encouraging them to educate others and speak on your behalf. It's a fine balance.

For many companies, especially in the professional services sector, the ultimate goal is to become a trusted advisor to the executives in their client accounts. Research in 2019[2] into how executives engage has revealed that most rely on just two to four suppliers to be their trusted advisors, with the most common number being three. So the competitive stakes for any company wanting to make sure they're in that exclusive group are high.

We will now take a more detailed look at what works best to engage executives at each stage of this buying process.

Epiphany

The epiphany stage is all about getting your target executives to have you top of mind. When executive buyers are doing their research to keep up with industry trends and find potential solutions, as Figure 6.3 underlines,

FIGURE 6.3 The sources of information buyers rely on most when doing research

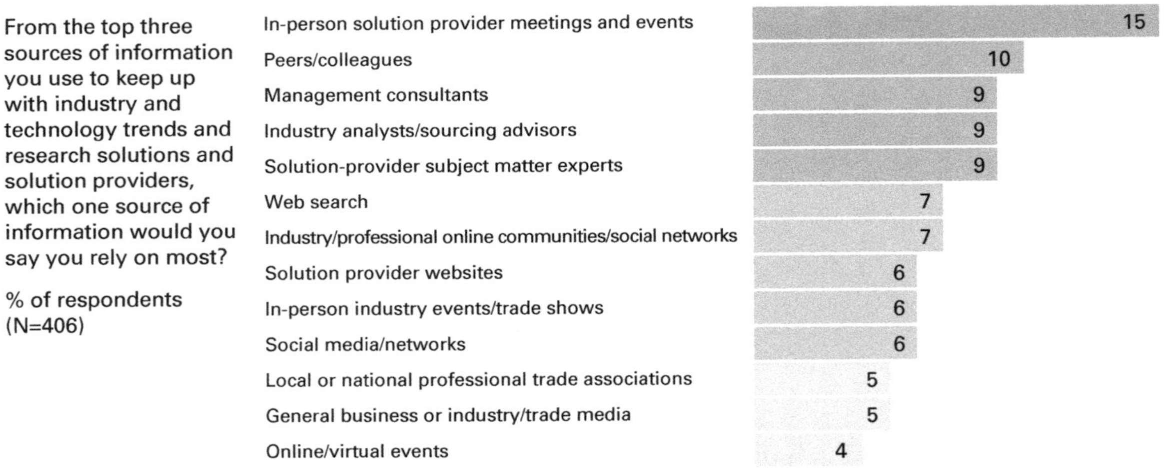

From the top three sources of information you use to keep up with industry and technology trends and research solutions and solution providers, which one source of information would you say you rely on most?

% of respondents (N=406)

Source	%
In-person solution provider meetings and events	15
Peers/colleagues	10
Management consultants	9
Industry analysts/sourcing advisors	9
Solution-provider subject matter experts	9
Web search	7
Industry/professional online communities/social networks	7
Solution provider websites	6
In-person industry events/trade shows	6
Social media/networks	6
Local or national professional trade associations	5
General business or industry/trade media	5
Online/virtual events	4

SOURCE ITSMA, 'How Executives Engage' survey, 2019

they place great importance on in-person meetings or events with solution providers, followed by using their own peers and colleagues as sources of insight.

The most compelling kinds of events or meetings are business seminars presented by your SMEs or by industry analysts, innovation workshops or in-person executive briefings. These content-rich events are just right for executives doing their research (more detail on this in Chapter 8). However, bear this in mind: the solution provider meetings they rely on are very likely to be run by their own strategic partners or other providers that they currently do business with. This can make it challenging for new potential suppliers to find a way in, unless you manage to make your proactive outreach stand out as relevant and engaging.

Next on their priority list come meetings with other individuals such as management consultants, industry analysts or sourcing advisors. This is where your own SMEs as reliable sources of knowledge and insight are equally well placed.

Together, all of these personal touchpoints represent most of the offline channels that executives spend their time on in the early stages, which, as we have seen, accounts for just under half of their research time.

Online channels are less relied upon but still important at this stage, including web searches about issues or solutions, online professional communities or social networks and, of course, your website. Larger industry events and trade associations or media come near the bottom of the list, while at the very bottom are online or virtual events, which many suppliers offer but which few executives rate as helpful.

IBM is an excellent example of how a company can position itself as a strategic supplier and use its account teams and experts to engage its clients' executives. We've already heard about the company's comprehensive approach to thought leadership content through its Institute for Business Value in Chapter 4, and the systematic way it leverages its experts.

In addition to these initiatives, IBM has recognized the importance of the epiphany stage of an executive's buyer journey by developing a digital tool to give sales teams the ability to collaborate, discover content that sparks new ideas for a client and access its experts to build that relevant and engaging outreach that executives respond to.

CASE STUDY
IBM Engage!

Business challenge

IBM's global markets sales enablement and innovation team had a challenge: scale its face-to-face (F2F) enablement methods to a broader audience in a cost-effective manner. Its F2F enablement methods were highly impactful; however, they were resource intensive and constrained by location and time. Sales teams desired access to the most relevant content and the ability to collaborate on new client ideas on a regular and just-in-time basis, at speed and at scale: for example, at the beginning of each quarter, prior to a client meeting or in response to shifts in market trends and strategic priorities.

Business objective

The goal was to create a digital AI-based platform to scale client-centric business development enablement at significantly reduced cost. This would enable account teams to mobilize quickly and more regularly, regardless of location and without waiting for an F2F event, as well as codifying the work that sellers and sales teams already did to provide future insights and enhanced enablement.

The result was IBM Engage!, a digital collaboration platform that helps IBM's sales teams build new, client-relevant opportunities and prepare for client engagement. Imagine sales teams having the ability to collaborate, discover content that sparks new ideas, access SMEs and build the most compelling opportunities to engage client executives – all in a digital environment. Imagine a digital tool having the power to continuously learn from all the input to provide sellers with more relevant content and enablement in the future.

Programme execution

Account teams are able to launch a digital workspace in IBM Engage!, where all team members are served up multimedia content to quickly gain insights and spark new ideas for their specific client. Teammates are able to digitally collaborate in the location and time zone most convenient for them. They can share their ideas, build on each other's ideas, then vote on and prioritize the most relevant and feasible ideas to address their client's unique business challenges. They are pointed to the relevant IBM solutions and offerings to enable these ideas.

The tool also guides the team to digitally build on their prioritized ideas with a compelling, client-relevant value proposition, which can be downloaded in different formats and shared with client buyers; additionally, opportunities can be launched directly to IBM's CRM system.

IBM Engage! is an easy-to-use tool that includes a dashboard and four key steps:

1 **Understand.** Surfaces insights to determine a client's most pressing challenges and needs.

2 **Ideate.** Grounded in a shared understanding of the client goals and needs, team members explore new ideas and possibilities that would be enabled by IBM's strategic capabilities.

3 **Prioritize.** The team digitally collaborates to rank ideas by feasibility and importance to the client.

4 **Build.** The best ideas are built into 'opportunity briefs' describing the new capabilities and benefits of the idea for the client.

Business results

IBM Engage! inspires sellers to be client-centric while focusing on business development. It enables account teams to envision and build on new opportunities to address their client's most pressing business challenges and align IBM solutions and offerings to help clients achieve their goals. The tool's key differentiator is the ability for sales teams and SMEs to collaborate digitally at any time and location most convenient to them.

The work that account teams do can now be codified; therefore, the more teams use Engage! the more valuable it becomes, as IBM Watson, the question–answering computer system capable of answering questions posed in natural language, is able to create insights and recommendations.

IBM Engage! provides sellers and account teams with the ability to:

- turn insights into real opportunities;
- consistently generate high-quality, client-relevant opportunities to ensure an ongoing, robust pipeline;
- quickly mobilize around new initiatives or market trends;
- increase productivity in envisioning, developing and managing new client opportunities.

With a digital ideation platform now in place, the sales enablement and innovation team has the flexibility to engage any number of account teams digitally to drive enablement around new IBM initiatives or when there are shifts in the market environment or business priorities. In addition, the team can leverage analytics from the IBM Engage! tool to learn where to focus enablement efforts.

SOURCE ITSMA, Marketing Excellence Award Winners summary booklet, 2018
Reproduced with permission from ITSMA

The type of content that works hard for you at the epiphany stage in a relation-ship is business-issue-led thought leadership and trend analysis, demonstrating that you understand the situation facing executives and can help them think it through. Research and benchmarking data can also be useful at this stage to illustrate what others think about an issue or how they are beginning to tackle it in their own organization.

Awareness

At the awareness stage, your goal is to get executives to think of you as a potential solution to their problem. The sources they rely upon to find out about you remain broadly the same in these two 'research' phases at the beginning of the process.

However, the content you will be using here begins to bring your own point of view and proposition to the fore as executives focus less on the general trends impacting their business and more on your company and how it could help. At this stage you'll be putting forward your SMEs' points of view on how to solve the issues facing your target executives, and sharing case study stories of where you have helped other, similar companies.

You will need to provide an overview of your company for those unfamil-iar with it – or indeed to help existing clients understand the breadth and depth of what you do beyond what they buy from you today. While it's tempting to provide a longlist of the facts and figures about your organiza-tion (business scope, number of employees, revenue, profit, capitalization, geographic spread, offerings, research and development (R&D) spend, industries served, top clients, sustainability focus etc), don't forget to high-light the most relevant facts to both the executive and the issues they face.

In fact, your best bet is to couch all of these facts and figures as proof points backing up your recommended solution. We talked about value propositions in Chapter 5, and this is where your initial value proposition comes into play, demonstrating that you do have a solution to their particular problems.

Interest

The interest stage is where executive buyers finalize their shortlist of alterna-tive suppliers who could help them meet their business goals. Your aim is to get them to add you to the shortlist and then prefer you from among those they are considering. This is no mean feat, since 9 times out of 10, buyers develop a shortlist of just three companies, with existing suppliers usually on it. Research from 2018[3] into how executives engage showed that existing suppliers win the deal 55 per cent of the time.

At this point, offline contact becomes more important than online, and interactive and experiential engagements that allow potential solutions to be brought to life are the most powerful. This includes high-touch experiences such as innovation centre visits, with buyers typically making one such visit to each of the suppliers they're shortlisting. We'll talk more about how to run these in Chapter 8.

As shown in Figure 6.4, executives will be making side-by-side comparisons of the solutions and companies they're considering, so meeting with them to take them through solution demonstrations and details is critical. Different executives in the decision-making unit will want different information, of course, so save the deep-dive technical specification for the technical buyers, while taking financial buyers through ROI benchmarks and painting a picture of the business outcomes achievable for the business buyers. These should all form part of your targeted value proposition for the buyers.

Examples of best practice are also important now, potentially drawn from companies like their own or from among their peer group, along with case study examples of where solutions have been implemented. Remember that the executive's peer group is hugely influential and their referral or support for your company at this stage will shape your buyer's understanding and perception of you, leading to that all-important preference for your company over others on the shortlist.

Meetings and events with your SMEs remain important, especially if they can paint a picture of the future and provide strong points of view to engage the executives. Meeting the people who will deliver the solution can also make a difference, as service delivery managers are another group of people in your own company with the ability to ultimately become trusted advisors to your target executives.

Confidence

At the confidence stage, buyers are looking to test their preference and make a final decision on whom to buy from, getting the contractual agreement in place. You want them to choose you.

FIGURE 6.4 Selecting the shortlist

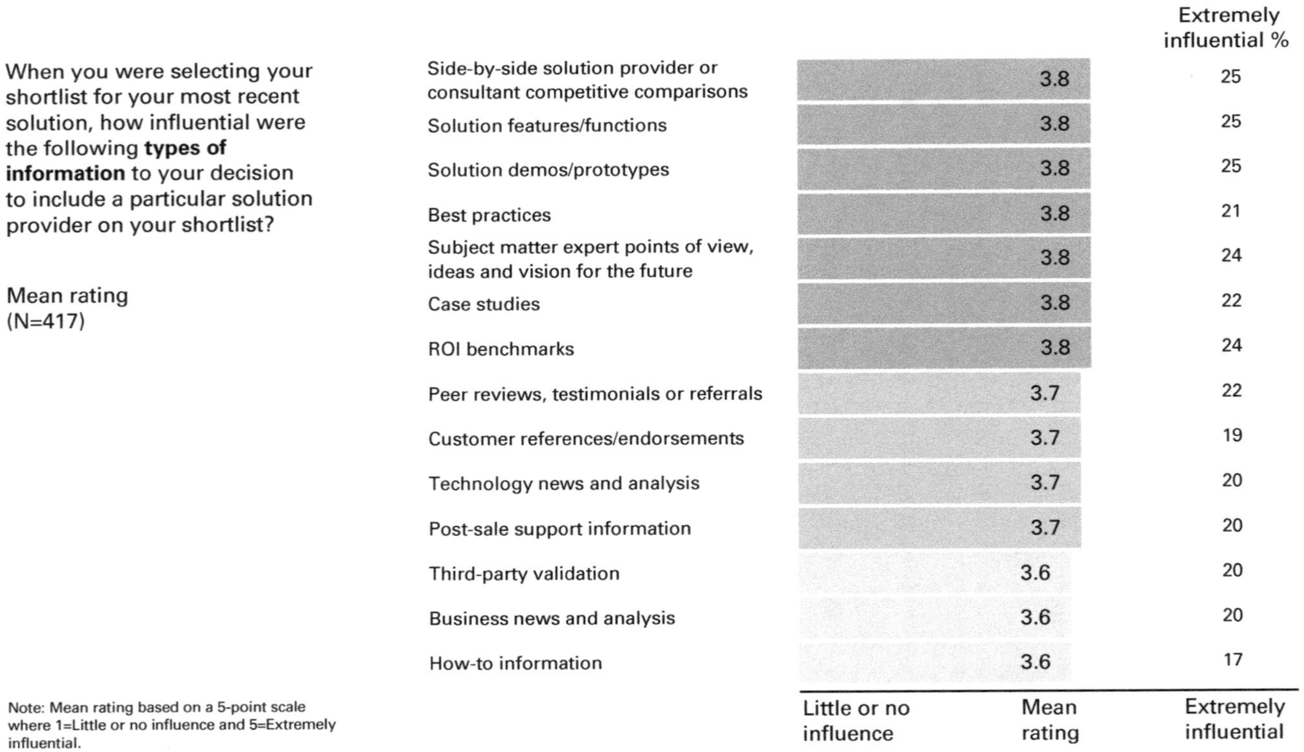

When you were selecting your shortlist for your most recent solution, how influential were the following **types of information** to your decision to include a particular solution provider on your shortlist?	Mean rating	Extremely influential %
Side-by-side solution provider or consultant competitive comparisons	3.8	25
Solution features/functions	3.8	25
Solution demos/prototypes	3.8	25
Best practices	3.8	21
Subject matter expert points of view, ideas and vision for the future	3.8	24
Case studies	3.8	22
ROI benchmarks	3.8	24
Peer reviews, testimonials or referrals	3.7	22
Customer references/endorsements	3.7	19
Technology news and analysis	3.7	20
Post-sale support information	3.7	20
Third-party validation	3.6	20
Business news and analysis	3.6	20
How-to information	3.6	17

Mean rating (N=417)

Little or no influence	Mean rating	Extremely influential

Note: Mean rating based on a 5-point scale where 1=Little or no influence and 5=Extremely influential.

SOURCE ITSMA 'How Buyers Choose' survey, 2017

What they need at this stage includes the proposal documents and presentations detailing your solution. I've seen countless suppliers focus so much on pulling together a detailed technical proposal and contract that the overall value proposition to the executive is lost. Neither the document nor the presentation hangs together as a story with a compelling narrative. It's almost as though all the earlier stages of the relationship you've worked through are forgotten.

Too little focus remains on emphasizing your understanding of the trends and unique issues facing the buyer, the collaborative way you have shaped the right solution with the client, your vision for the future, the value that you will deliver and the reasons why they should prefer you. Instead, the document is full of technical specifications and legal clauses. No wonder that the final proposal presentation often leaves everyone uninspired. With too little preparation and a lack of charisma from the pitching team, these events can too easily become lacklustre.

But these presentations are an unrivalled opportunity to excite executives once again about the art of the possible for their business. The best companies use these opportunities to surprise their audience. I've seen games used, virtual reality deployed, filmed testimonials and even a carpet rolled out to represent the journey supplier and buyer were embarking on together.

As we saw in Chapter 1, yes, price is a crucial factor. But so is your ability to demonstrate your understanding of the executives' industry and the business issues. Important, too, is your evident experience with the solution (where have you done this before?), as is your overall trustworthiness. Other factors include the relationships you've built along the way and your overall chemistry and cultural fit.

Loyalty

Once you've been selected as a supplier, your work really begins to build that long-term, mutually beneficial relationship with your buyer, and specifically with the particular executives who have bought from you. Like any relationship, you may find you uncover things you didn't know about each other, so there may be unexpected issues to deal with.

But if you can make it through these, you're on the way to a loyal and trusting relationship. Get the executives at your new client to think of you, both in terms of appreciating what you are delivering for them and considering what you could do for them next.

In ITSMA's 2019 survey on executive engagement, respondents reported that the most common ways they had engaged with suppliers in the preceding three months were by opening and reading an e-mail, having a phone conversation or conference call and having a one-on-one meeting with a solution expert, specialist or sales person. Other ways mentioned by more than one-third of executives were having one-on-one meetings with senior executives, watching a video, using the solution provider's website to access content or attending an online event (see Figure 6.5).

Less popular but still mentioned by more than a quarter of executives were reading a white paper or case study, attending a customer advisory council meeting, using the provider's app to access content, communicating via social media, accessing the provider's online community, listening to a podcast or clicking on an online ad.

But which do they most value? Figure 6.6 indicates that when it comes to valuing relationship-building activities run by suppliers, private customer events are top of the list, followed by private executive-level briefings and executive-level business events and one-on-one executive-to-executive relationships. These should be the cornerstones of an executive relationship programme.

Slightly less popular are public customer events, satisfaction monitoring, dedicated microsites and online public communities and social networks. These are followed by customer advisory councils, small peer-networking events, custom newsletters and recreational activities.

In many ways this hierarchy of what executives find valuable makes sense, if you consider why executives participate in relationship programmes, as shown in Figure 6.7. They are keen to build closer relationships with the senior management executives at their supplier companies while at the same time learning and continuing their own professional development. They also want to influence their supplier's offerings and strategic direction, and participating in advisory councils in particular is a great way to do that. They appreciate that taking part in these programmes will give them access to key people in the company, such as SMEs, and the opportunity to network with their own peers.

Lower down the list but still valid is their drive to take on a leadership role and promote themselves, thereby advancing their own career prospects and potentially even finding their next job.

They want content that helps them get the best from their purchase, such as information on how to use the solution that's just been bought and usage monitors to track people using the solution. Satisfaction surveys that report

FIGURE 6.5 The ways executives have recently engaged with suppliers

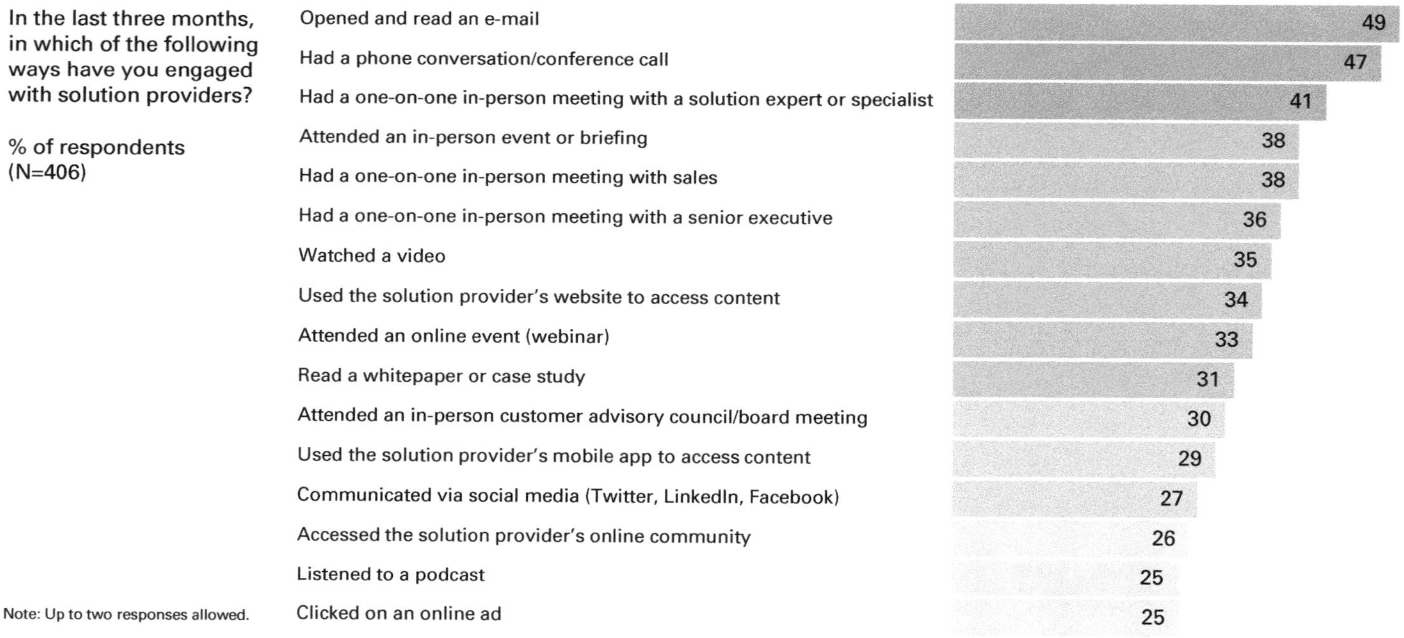

In the last three months, in which of the following ways have you engaged with solution providers?

% of respondents (N=406)

Engagement method	%
Opened and read an e-mail	49
Had a phone conversation/conference call	47
Had a one-on-one in-person meeting with a solution expert or specialist	41
Attended an in-person event or briefing	38
Had a one-on-one in-person meeting with sales	38
Had a one-on-one in-person meeting with a senior executive	36
Watched a video	35
Used the solution provider's website to access content	34
Attended an online event (webinar)	33
Read a whitepaper or case study	31
Attended an in-person customer advisory council/board meeting	30
Used the solution provider's mobile app to access content	29
Communicated via social media (Twitter, LinkedIn, Facebook)	27
Accessed the solution provider's online community	26
Listened to a podcast	25
Clicked on an online ad	25

Note: Up to two responses allowed.

SOURCE ITSMA 'How Executives Engage' survey, 2019

FIGURE 6.6 Most valuable relationship-building programmes

Thinking about the
programs in which you
participate, which two
would you say provide
the most value to you
and your organization?

% of respondents
(N=406)

Programme	%
Private customer events	16
Private executive-level briefings	15
Executive-level business events	14
One-on-one executive-to-executive relationships	14
Public customer events	11
Satisfaction/feedback/loyalty/net promoter initiatives	10
Dedicated 'microsite' or portal for your company with information about their project work and thought leadership	9
Public online communities or social networks	8
Customer advisory councils or boards	7
Small, intimate, local peer-networking events	7
Custom-developed newsletters tailored just for you and your company	7
Social or recreational activities	7
Customer reference programs	6
Joint in-kind charity work/joint corporate social responsibility programs	6
Private online communities or social networks the solution provider facilitates	5
Joint PR/advertising/co-branding	4

Note: Up to two responses allowed.

SOURCE ITSMA 'How Executives Engage' survey, 2019

FIGURE 6.7 Primary reason for participating in relationship programmes

What is your primary reason for participating in these solution provider relationship programmes?
% of respondents (N=406)

19	19	18	13	12	10	9
Enables me to establish relationships with the solution provider's senior management executives	Enables me to learn	Enables me to provide input and influence the solution provider's offerings and strategic direction	Provides access to developers/ engineers/ subject matter experts	Facilitates networking with my peers	Allows me to take on a leader-ship role	Enables me to promote myself and advance my career

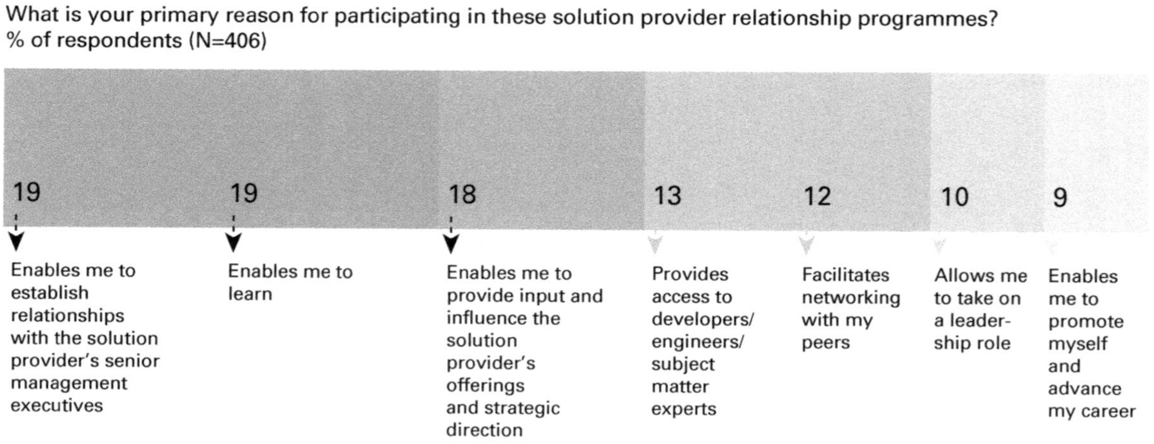

SOURCE ITSMA 'How Executives Engage' survey, 2019

how people are finding the solution give executives further insight into what needs to be done to drive adoption (if well done) and the business outcomes they wanted from the solution.

ROI calculators and value reports are usually welcomed, since many executives find it difficult to prove that the value they promised in the business case for a solution has, in fact, been delivered. Any support you can provide at this stage will help to build loyalty.

And of course, once you've been delivering the solution for a while, executives like to hear about your observations and recommendations on how to change and improve things. Even minor operational innovations are valuable, since you often bring a different perspective that can identify new ways of working that the client's teams just don't see.

One company that has been working hard at this post-purchase engagement with its clients is the global enterprise software company SAP. It has mapped out the journey that its buyers and users travel once the solution has been bought, and identified integrated ways to help clients get the maximum value from their purchase and hopefully remain loyal customers.

CASE STUDY
SAP: Moments that matter

Business challenge

Over the past 45 years, SAP has been on a journey with customers to help them create value for their organizations by applying technology to solve some of their most complex challenges. As SAP continues to derive more of its revenue from its cloud solutions, it needed to develop a greater customer-centric marketing approach for the post-purchase (pre-renewal) journey.

This business-to-business customer lifecycle journey approach needed also to align with the sales, operations and services areas, which required a cultural shift to not only focus on the entire journey, but also to drive collaboration across the organization and provide the resources necessary to effect such a change.

Business objective

The customer marketing loyalty and advocacy team developed an initiative called 'moments that matter'. The goal was to harmonize the post-purchase journey across the various business units and solutions so that all customers would receive a consistent, and foundational, level of content to enable their success.

The initiative, based on industry best practices and the best practices of SAP's cloud business units, identified seven key moments in the post-purchase journey that would enable the customers' success with their acquired solution and build a solid relationship with the company. By engaging and supporting customers throughout these moments to drive their usage, adoption and success, SAP would achieve its business objective of customer loyalty, goodwill, renewals and expanded revenue.

Programme execution

The customer marketing loyalty and advocacy team drove the initiative, working closely with the cloud customer operations team as the company embraced this post-purchase customer experience approach. Significant cross-organization collaboration, albeit somewhat novel, not only with the cloud operations team, but also across the regions and the many lines of business and their own customer success teams, enabled a comprehensive customer-centric programme to be developed.

This collaboration required new methodologies not just for the marketing efforts, but also for operating processes and technology efforts. The company's global footprint and vast portfolio of business solutions, especially from many acquired companies, increased the complexity of pulling this together.

The 'moments that matter' initiative, harmonized across all SAP cloud solutions with a templated approach, ensures that a consistent experience and a foundational level of information are provided to all customers, independent of their size, segment or solution. Starting with the 'Welcome programme' when the contract is signed, it continues with 54 touchpoints through the customer journey aligned with the seven programmes within the initiative. The other six programs are 'Go-live', 'Show value', 'Emergencies', 'Renewals', 'Anniversary' and 'Advocate' (see Figure 6.8):

- **Welcome.** The welcome content helps customers get ready for delivery and adoption. The programme packages all the available resources, tools and training for customers as they start their journey. SAP created unprecedented consistency by using the same look and feel as well as content templates across all of its business units and solutions.

- **Go-live.** Customers often face major change management when they install new systems. SAP helps with company-wide adoption. SAP's goal is to celebrate the customer's success and make them feel good about using a new system.

- **Show value.** SAP carries out an annual (or more frequently, if necessary) health check to reinforce the value the customer receives from the product and illuminate any areas for improvement or underutilization.

FIGURE 6.8 The moments that matter initiative

Welcome   Go-live   Show value   Emergencies   Renewals   Anniversary   Advocate

SOURCE ITSMA Update 'How Marketing Should Lead Client Experience in the Digital Age',
August 2019

- **Emergencies.** Dealing quickly and effectively with unforeseen events gives customers confidence that problems will be solved. SAP surveys customers post-support to ensure satisfaction.

- **Renewals.** During these moments, SAP shows a vision of continued success. SAP views winning a renewal as the outcome of demonstrating to customers the value they have received.

- **Anniversary.** SAP celebrates relevant dates to strengthen customer engagement and generate goodwill.

- **Advocate.** SAP has developed a framework called the advocacy spectrum covering a variety of low, medium and high efforts of advocacy that work with the type of advocates customers choose to be. This advocacy can have a positive impact in several ways:

    - customer engagement;

    - market buzz;

    - reduced sales and acquisition costs;

    - reduced support costs;

    - retention, renewals and expanded revenue.

Additionally, creating an always-on communications approach to ensure continued engagement between the 'moments' was important to the post-purchase journey. This four-pillar, always-on strategy consists of:

- **Always in touch.** This includes communications such as newsletters, updates and anything else that is relevant to appropriate touchpoints.

- **Always engaged.** The company is active in digital engagement, including webinars and other electronic media from appropriate sources, such as marketing support or useful third parties.

- **Always connecting.** SAP encourages peer-to-peer connections via the SAP community or through live events.

- **Always inspiring.** Customers are keen to learn about how others have implemented SAP solutions through relevant case studies.

The team ensures that there is consistent messaging and therefore a consistent experience across all business units. Within the SAP brand of 'The Best Run SAP', this programme emphasizes that SAP is on the journey with the customer in terms of both co-creating and ensuring that their needs are met on their journey to be best run and successful. All messaging is based on three pillars:

1 **Commit to customer success.** SAP collaborates with customers throughout their journey to ensure their success.

2 **Maximize value.** The company provides the resources customers need to adopt, use and gain value from the SAP software.

3 **Enable the intelligent enterprise.** SAP helps customers understand trends and address a new generation of intelligent business processes that will impact their business.

Business results

The moments that matter initiative has:

- established a formal, harmonized programme of solution-specific touchpoints providing customers with a consistent experience across varied solutions and regions;

- provided customers with the relevant guidance and information they need, when they need it, to get started and move through their journey successfully;

- generated on average more than 30 per cent open rates among executives;

- resulted in content usage that aligned to SAP's objectives and confirmed the customers' need for assistance at these critical stages (eg the top content in the 'Welcome' moment includes 'Getting Started', 'Planning Your Journey' and 'Tips for Project Success');

- increased post-purchase participation within the line of business and solutions teams with the templated approach.

SAP plans to continue to evolve post-purchase efforts for enhanced customer success, illustrating to its customers that it is running together with them on their journey.

SOURCE ITSMA Marketing Excellence Award Winners summary booklet, 2018 and ITSMA Update 'How Marketing Should Lead Client Experience in the Digital Age', August 2019
Reproduced with permission from ITSMA

Trust

The 'Trusted Advisor' model for client relationships, originally created in 2000 by Robert Galford (and published in the book by Galford, Charles Green and David Maister[4] in 2012, aimed at professional services firms), claimed that 'the key to professional success goes well beyond technical mastery or expertise. Today, it's all about the vital ability to earn the client's trust and thereby win the ability to influence them. In these high risk times, trust is more valuable than gold'.

Although this statement was first made nearly a decade ago, it still rings true today. With the political, economic and environmental uncertainty facing the world, and the digital disruption facing most industries, it's no surprise that executives look for a trusted advisor to help them think through their most pressing dilemmas.

What's interesting is that they typically limit themselves to just three such advisors (see Figure 6.9). And when asked with whom they have the most trusted relationships, senior executives are the most popular response, according to 34 per cent of those polled, followed by SMEs, mentioned by 26 per cent. With another 11 per cent prioritizing service delivery managers, that's nearly three-quarters of executives who haven't mentioned an account director, sales person or product specialist.

This is not surprising when you realize what executives think contributes most to their suppliers becoming trusted advisors. As Figure 6.10 illustrates,

FIGURE 6.9 Trusted advisor relationships

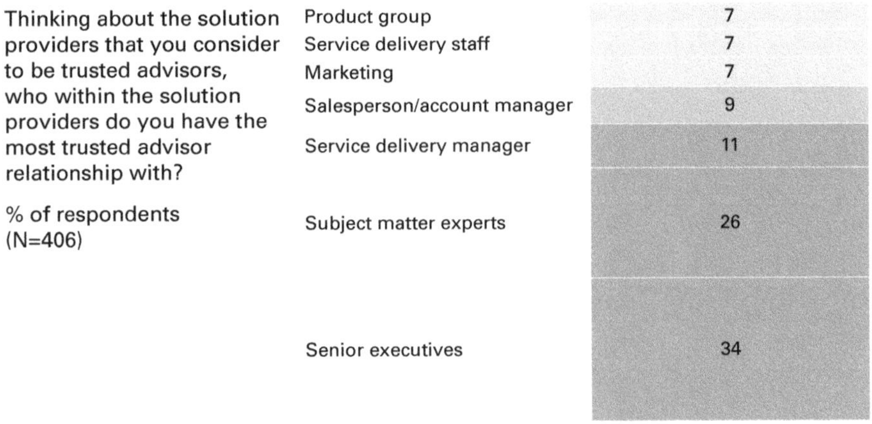

Thinking about the solution providers that you consider to be trusted advisors, who within the solution providers do you have the most trusted advisor relationship with?	Product group	7
	Service delivery staff	7
	Marketing	7
	Salesperson/account manager	9
	Service delivery manager	11
% of respondents (N=406)	Subject matter experts	26
	Senior executives	34

SOURCE ITSMA 'How Executives Engage' survey, 2019

FIGURE 6.10 Actions that lead to trusted advisor status

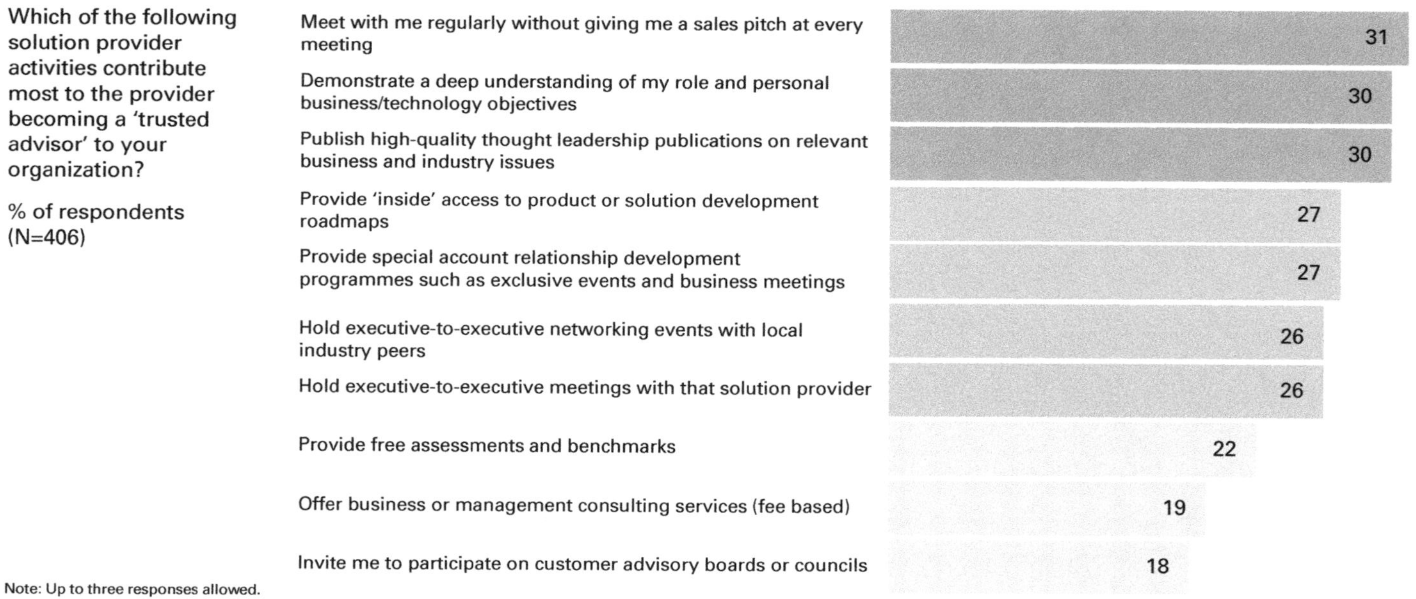

Which of the following solution provider activities contribute most to the provider becoming a 'trusted advisor' to your organization?

% of respondents (N=406)

Activity	%
Meet with me regularly without giving me a sales pitch at every meeting	31
Demonstrate a deep understanding of my role and personal business/technology objectives	30
Publish high-quality thought leadership publications on relevant business and industry issues	30
Provide 'inside' access to product or solution development roadmaps	27
Provide special account relationship development programmes such as exclusive events and business meetings	27
Hold executive-to-executive networking events with local industry peers	26
Hold executive-to-executive meetings with that solution provider	26
Provide free assessments and benchmarks	22
Offer business or management consulting services (fee based)	19
Invite me to participate on customer advisory boards or councils	18

Note: Up to three responses allowed.

SOURCE ITSMA 'How Executives Engage' survey, 2019

top of the list is their ability to 'meet with me regularly without giving me a sales pitch at every meeting'. This demands a sophisticated, detached mentality on the part of the supplier, and a long-term perspective rather than a quarterly, quota-driven focus.

The trusted advisor is a more subtle idea than the 'challenger sales' person,[5] defined by research and advisory services firm CEB (2011) as 'the ability to do three things: teach, tailor and take control'. Rated as the most successful sales people, ahead of the relationship builders, the challenger is 'focused on pushing the customer out of their comfort zone, while the relationship builder is focused on being accepted into it'. While both the trusted advisor and the challenger sales person bring the client executives ideas and possible solutions, the latter is inevitably focused on the immediate sales pitch while the former has the long-term relationship with the client in mind.

The second most significant activity that executives rate in trusted advisors is for them to 'demonstrate a deep understanding of my role and personal objectives' and to 'publish high-quality thought leadership on relevant business and industry issues'. We've talked about both of these things already, but here is where they really start to pay off as you focus your research efforts and your thought leadership investment around your most important clients.

There are other activities important for gaining this desired status:

- Executives rate having 'inside access to product or solution development roadmaps'. Briefing executives on your development plans is one thing, but involving them in early trials and giving them access to leading-edge technologies can become a valuable benefit and differentiator when they are making a choice between you and a competitor. Getting their input on your roadmap like this makes all the difference, as does inviting them to participate in an advisory board or council.

- Offering the account relationship programmes that we saw in Figure 6.6 is another important contribution to achieving trusted advisor status, including executive-to-executive meetings and events, which we will look at in more detail in the next three chapters.

- Finally, trusted advisors work hard at helping their client executives continually improve their performance, with free assessments, benchmarks and consulting services seen as significant contributions to achieving this goal.

Summary

1 Executive buyers move through stages as they make decisions to purchase high-value, complex business solutions. Your job is to build relevancy as executives explore the different suppliers they could work with, and then build client intimacy once they have decided to buy from you.

2 Executives are constantly scanning their organization and its external environment for issues and trends that can represent either opportunities or threats to their future success. At the point that they recognize an issue and identify a new need or opportunity, a potential buying process begins.

3 At the epiphany stage, you as a potential buyer should be getting your target executives to think of you. They rely most on in-person meetings or events with solution providers, and then on their own peers and colleagues as sources of insight.

4 At the awareness stage, your goal is to get executives to see you as a potential solution to their problem, bringing your point of view and proposition to the fore as executives focus less on the general trends impacting their business and more on your company and how it could help.

5 The interest stage is where executive buyers finalize their shortlist of alternative suppliers who could help them meet their business goals. At this stage, interactive and experiential engagements that allow potential solutions to be brought to life are most powerful.

6 At the confidence stage, buyers are looking to test their preference and make a final decision on whom to buy from, and get the contractual agreement in place. Your job is to get them to choose you. The best companies use pitch situations to engage and surprise their audience rather than merely reciting proposal documents.

7 Once you've been selected as a supplier, your work really begins to build that long-term, mutually beneficial relationship with your buyer. Ensure that the executives at your new client appreciate what you are delivering for them and are considering what you could do for them next.

8 To be selected as one of the three trusted advisors that executives have on average, field your own executives, SMEs and delivery managers, demonstrate real understanding of their business and objectives and avoid making a sales pitch at every meeting.

Notes

1 ITSMA (2019) Service Marketing Budget Allocation and Trends study
2 ITSMA (2019) 'How Executives Engage' survey
3 ITSMA (2018) 'How Executives Engage' survey
4 Maister, D H, Galford, R and Green, C (2012) *The Trusted Advisor*, Simon and Schuster, New York
5 Dixon, M and Adamson, B (2011) *The Challenger Sale: How to Take Control of the Customer Conversation*, Portfolio Penguin

07

Engaging with peer networks

Peer networks are powerful. Executives trust their peers to tell them the truth about suppliers and their solutions, and to share ideas, challenges and lessons learned in a way that they simply won't do with those they don't consider as peers.

But the way that people define and access their peer networks is changing. Where executives at the top of their organizations today have traditionally built their networks face-to-face over time, millennials in the workforce (who are increasingly becoming the executives you want to engage) rely much more on social networks and the peers they have never met in person.

As the way that peer networks operate continues to change, you need to reflect this in the way you engage with them. This chapter looks at four different techniques you can use to reach and engage with your target networks, either separately or in combination: collaborating through research, running engaging events, building new communities and working with alumni.

How are peer networks changing?

Traditionally, executives have built their networks through face-to-face meetings and events; in other words, by spending time together. They may have been to the same college or university, started off in the same company or belonged to the same professional or trade association. And gradually, over time, their network has continued to expand as they meet new peers through their career. For these executives, the face-to-face exchange of information remains important, although some – the digital migrants – also engage with their peers online through social networks.

FIGURE 7.1 Millennials rely on social networks

<40 years old (N=161)		Age 40 or older (N=245)
Social media/networks*	**1**	In-person solution provider meetings and events*
Industry analysts/ sourcing advisors	**2**	Peers/colleagues*
Local or national professional trade associations*	**3**	Solution provider subject matter experts
Web search	**4**	Management consultants
In-person solution provider meetings and events*	**5**	Solution provider websites

Top five sources of information used.
*Indicates a statistically significant difference.

SOURCE ITSMA 'How Executives Engage' survey, 2019

But what about the new executives in the workforce – the millennials? These digital natives build their peer networks online as much as offline, and rely on social media to keep themselves up to date on issues and trends that may affect them (see Figure 7.1).

These millennials are increasingly taking up executive roles in the organizations that matter to you, so when you are planning how to engage with networks of millennials, make sure you focus on the online collaboration that's so important to them. With research, that means collecting, collaboratively analysing and disseminating data online as well as offline. For large events, live streaming may be a way to engage the millennials not attending in person, or ensuring highlights are fed out through social media channels. If you're building a community, it's important to have an online place for the network to collaborate, even if it's just a closed LinkedIn group. And the same is true for any alumni networks you create and run. Let's look at each of these engagement techniques in turn.

Collaborating through research

The very fact that peers network to keep up with trends, share challenges and learn from each other means that research, both in terms of the process and the data generated, is a powerful tool for engaging with them. Companies such as IBM and PwC have understood this for years. We learned all about the IBM Institute for Business Value and its extensive research methods among C-Suite executives in Chapter 4.

Leading professional services firm PwC uses a similar approach to engage with CEOs around the world. Since 1997, it has interviewed the world's chief executives to understand their perspective on the business environment, their priorities for the year ahead and the challenges facing them. In 2019, the firm looked back over the 22 years of its research among this powerful network of business leaders and found a correlation between the CEOs' expectations for their own organization's growth and actual growth in GDP during the following year.[1]

This correlation means that the views they are collecting from this network each year act as predictors for the health of the global economy. As you can see in Figure 7.2, the proportion of CEOs who expect growth to decline increased in every region, which doesn't bode well for the global economy as we enter a new decade in 2020.

To gather this kind of data is no mean feat. In 2019, PwC conducted 1,378 confidential quantitative interviews with CEOs in organizations with revenues of $10 million or above across 91 territories and all major industry sectors. Ten per cent of the interviews were by phone, 73 per cent online and 17 per cent by post or face-to-face. They also conducted face-to-face, in-depth interviews with CEOs from five continents to provide anecdotal evidence and bring the data they had gathered to life with quotes and opinions.

So why go to all this trouble? Well, in addition to providing invaluable insights into your target executives that will advise both your own strategy and solutions development, this kind of research delivers great value to the executives involved. We already know that they want to meet you without receiving a sales pitch and that they value the insights you can bring them about their industry, company and role. With this kind of research in hand, your insights are evidence-based rather than simply being points of view, and this evidence can help your target executives shape their own strategy and operations.

Put simply, conducting research among peers will help you start conversations and build relationships. I've been amazed at how willing even the busiest executives are to help out with a research initiative if they're doing it on a give-to-get basis – that is, they give you an interview or some data and, in return, they get a summary of your findings. They may even get a debrief and discussion of the implications for their organization. This is useful stuff.

So, we know it's worth doing. Now, how do you get it done?

FIGURE 7.2 CEO optimism for growth in 2019

EXHIBIT 2

In every region, the share of CEOs who
belive global growth will 'decline' grew
significantly

QUESTION

Do you believe global economic
growth will improve, stay the same,
or decline over the next 12 months?

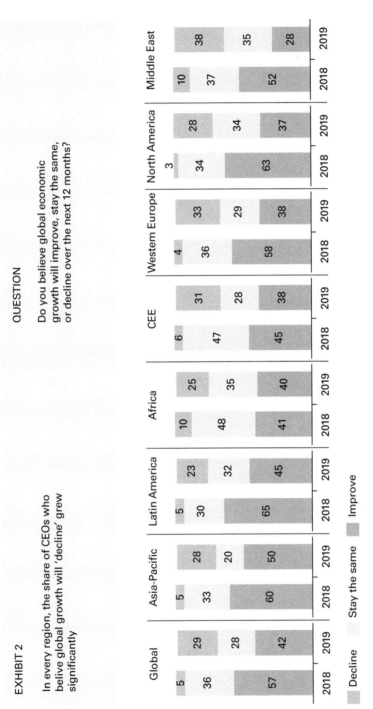

■ Decline   ■ Stay the same   ■ Improve

SOURCE PwC 22nd Annual CEO Survey, p 8
Reproduced with permission from PwC

Deciding what to research

The first thing to do is decide what topic or themes you will research. There are a few things to keep in mind here. The first links to your own strategy and brand. What business are you trying to build? What do you want to be known for? This has to be your first decision criterion, since there's no point researching something that is outside the scope of what you can confidently talk about as an organization.

A great example is Interbrand, a global brand consultancy and division of Omnicom, based in New York, which has been running research on the best global brands for 20 years. This brand valuation ranking provides a useful index to those companies featured in the ranking, which can track their brand's value going up and down relative to their peers, while showcasing Interbrand's area of expertise and opening up conversations on how the company can help increase their client's brand value, and hence company value. In 2019, the top three most valuable brands were once again Apple (#1 at US $234 billion), Google (#2 at US $168 billion) and Amazon (#3 at US $125 billion),[2] while new entrants include Uber (#87 at US $5.7 billion) and LinkedIn (#98 at US $4.8 billion).

The second criterion has to be what matters to the executives you want to engage. Just as we discussed in Chapter 5, when discussing how to decide what themes to focus your thought leadership on, the same applies to your research topics. In fact, the research you do will usually support one or more of your thought leadership themes.

A few years ago I was lucky enough to work on the EMC Privacy Index.[3] EMC – now a combined organization with Dell (Dell EMC) – understood that privacy was an increasingly hot topic for executives who bought its storage and security solutions, and wanted to demonstrate that it understood the trade-offs that people around the world made between privacy and convenience online.

We created a research project that asked 15,000 people around the world (1,000 in each of 15 countries) how they felt about that trade-off overall, and in the different areas of their lives, such as when shopping, dealing with their bank, using government or health services and socializing with friends. The online survey delivered an index of how willing people in each country were to trade privacy for convenience. The people of India were ranked most willing, while those in Germany were least. Across the areas of their lives, people globally were happiest to trade privacy for convenience when dealing with their government or health provider, and least comfortable when shopping online or socializing.

This research was used to drive headlines globally and in each of the countries participating, as well as to engage executives online through an interactive tool that made it possible to play with the data. EMC events – from the global EMC World through to country-specific roadshows – also used the data, and reports were created for the main industries featured (government, health, finance and retail). Crucially, it was also used to start conversations with executives about one of their most pressing issues, which then led into discussion about how EMC could help.

Perhaps a lesser but still important criterion to apply when deciding on your research themes is whether you want to do a timely, one-off piece of research or develop a multi-year index, such as in the two previous examples. One way to look at this is in terms of 'waves' and 'migrations', as a former boss of mine used to say. Waves are things that come and go. They matter today and may drive behaviour for a while, but they won't last. A classic example of this is Y2K (for those who can remember it), when everyone was focused on what would happen to their computer systems on 1 January 2000. There was much consulting and research around this topic at the time, but it's completely irrelevant now.

A migration is a long-term shift in the way that we do things, and a current example would be how we use AI to improve performance across all areas of our life and work. This features in both the current PwC and IBM surveys, and I suspect will remain a part of those surveys for the foreseeable future. As such, it could easily be the subject of an 'AI adoption index' or similar, delivering value to both the researcher and the respondents as they plan their investments over the coming years.

Running a successful research project

Back in 1988, I started my professional career in the market research department of British Gas. The team there were kind enough to sponsor my final year at university and accept me back as a graduate trainee in 1990. During my time with them, I worked on the largest UK survey: The National Domestic Equipment Survey, or NDES. With 45,000 respondents across the UK, collected through a team of five research agencies, the survey revealed the number of homes with gas appliances and where they were in the country, providing a sales map for boilers, fires and other systems.

At the time, there were no computers on our desks, and a massive computer readout was delivered for us to work through and create charts from, which in turn would be made into slides for presenting across the business. It was a very successful annual and then biannual survey, but it required a huge amount of management and coordination.

Today's research projects are more digital and can be done in a fraction of the time that the NDES took, but the principles behind running a successful research project remain the same. Let's take a look at them now.

Every research project needs clear objectives and scope, and these are best pulled together in a research brief (even if you don't plan to use an agency partner to help you run your project).

THE RESEARCH BRIEF

Your research brief should contain everything that anyone working on the project needs to know, as follows:

1 **Research objectives.** This section describes why you are doing the research, such as to help build your awareness and credibility around a particular issue among a network of executives, as PwC has done with its CEO surveys.

2 **Context.** This describes the market or environment in which the research will take place, and any defining factors, such as the changing way in which brands are built in today's online world for Interbrand.

3 **Research problem and desired output.** This section defines the issue or problem you are looking to explore: for example, identifying the trade-off between privacy and convenience that people around the world are willing to make. You may frame it in terms of your current hypothesis that you wish to test, such as your belief that most people are willing to trade privacy for convenience in all areas of their lives, or leave it as exploratory. The desired output will help to shape the research approach and how the questions are asked, such as EMC's wish to create an index with the data that can be updated periodically by repeating the research.

4 **Existing knowledge and previous research.** This section details the information already available to researchers to inform the development of any hypotheses and the research instrument to be used. It may also be used to ensure the research you do is differentiated from that already in the market (yet another digital transformation survey anyone?).

5 **Sample and quotas.** This section details the number of people you wish to be in your research sample, or how statistically significant or representative

of the universe of possible respondents you want your data to be. This decision will depend on both your objectives for the research and the budget you have available. For example, if you're aiming to see your results featured in broadcast media you will need a statistically significant sample size. Within your sample, you may wish to call out comparisons between elements such as different company sizes, industries, respondent job roles or performance levels, among others. If so, you'll need to set a quota so that enough people in each category participate in your research project.

6 **Budget and timescales.** This gives clarity as to the funds available for the research and the timescales for completing the project and making results available. Your budget may influence the research method(s) you use, since face-to-face interviews are more expensive than telephone interviews, which in turn are more expensive than online surveys. And surveys that you create and conduct for a specific purpose are more expensive than omnibus surveys that run regularly and in which you can pay for a few questions to be asked just for your purposes.

A RESEARCH PARTNER

You may decide to work on your project with an agency or research partner. Specialist agencies are available for all kinds of research, and you may choose one based on their familiarity with your industry and your audience, their geographic reach and language abilities, their interpretation of your brief and proposed approach, and how easy and enjoyable you think it will be to work with them.

You may also wish to use a partner that can promote your research to the network of executives you are trying to engage. I once collaborated with the British Institute of Facilities Management to reach facilities managers across the country in a benchmarking survey. This allowed me to leverage their expertise in shaping the survey instrument, their regular communications with the executives to drive responses, and their conference platform to share results. For their part, they benefited from the relevant content that they could share with their audience, both online and at their conference.

Many companies also partner with third parties such as industry analysts or associations to add credibility to their research if they themselves don't yet have the brand power to drive participation.

RESEARCH METHODS

There are a range of research methods available, depending on the type of results you want to achieve. The most credible for generating headlines and building indexes or benchmarks that peers can engage with is quantitative surveys, such as in the PwC and EMC examples quoted earlier. The survey instruments (questionnaires) can be created, presented and answered online, using research systems such as Survey Monkey, or via telephone and face-to-face interviews, although the former is by far the cheapest method.

In my experience, it is usually a struggle to keep the survey questions succinct and easy enough to answer in 15 minutes, so that those completing the survey make it all the way to the end, but a research partner will guide you on that.

Having said that online surveys are the cheapest method of collecting quantitative data, companies such as PwC and IBM usually do some telephone and face-to-face interviews too, since these are, of course, more engaging. These may either follow the quantitative survey, where people are asked to rank possible answers, state how much they agree with statements, select from a list of options and so on, or they may include more qualitative discussion to elicit quotes and anecdotes that bring the data to life.

These more qualitative interviews help to provide depth behind the numbers, and are usually run alongside a quantitative study to make the data more engaging. Where individual interviews aren't possible, a focus group discussion of peers can be facilitated to provide the same outputs, and this can easily be arranged around events where peers are already networking, such as in a private breakfast meeting before a conference begins.

Other research methods include observational research (where subjects are observed going about their day or completing their tasks to generate insights), mystery shopping (where researchers behave like a customer or client to gauge performance), and even public data analysis (where companies use a data feed from a social media platform and analyse it for trends, behaviours or sentiment).

For a major piece of research designed to engage peers with ideas and data, it's likely you'll want to combine several of these methods. And you may even choose to take your research one step further and model the data you collect to generate new insights and implications. O2 (see the case study in Chapter 2) has recently done exactly this in a truly collaborative exercise, using development economics to model out data collected by YouGov in a survey designed by consultants Manasian & Co. This ecosystem of partners helped O2 explore a hypothesis based on digital connectivity and working practices, which led to national headlines and secured a TV interview for its head of business about the £34 billion increased productivity which better connectivity could create for the UK.[4]

A NOTE ON CONFIDENTIALITY

All of the professional research initiatives I've referred to have been conducted with integrity, and individual responses have been anonymized and treated confidentially. This is critical for any research designed to engage executives, and something to take very seriously in your own research projects. Capturing and storing data has regulatory implications in Europe, in particular, and if you're in any doubt, it's worth checking with your research agency or your internal legal counsel.

For example, ITSMA runs several research exercises each year, with one of the most popular providing benchmark data for marketing executives on the priorities and budget allocation of their peers over the coming year,[5] as shown in Figures 7.3 and 7.4. These studies help marketing executives justify their budgets internally and plan how best to allocate them to compete in the market.

In addition to providing information on absolute budget size and allocation, the data explore where spending is increasing or decreasing: for instance, in 2019, 55 per cent of companies were planning to increase their investment in engagement and advocacy programmes, while 3 per cent planned to decrease their spend in this area (Figure 7.4).

Each executive in this global study is asked to complete an online survey, and their data are aggregated to provide insight into the trends in marketing priorities and spending plans for the year. Those that complete the survey can ask to have their own data benchmarked against five other named companies, whose data are aggregated up to provide a benchmark, keeping each individual's responses anonymous.

FIGURE 7.3 Changes in the marketing budget

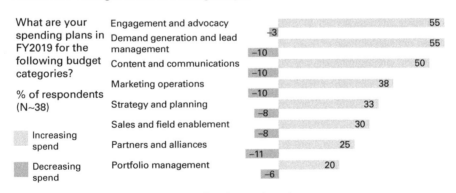

SOURCE ITSMA Services Marketing Budget Allocations and Trends, 2019

FIGURE 7.4 Engagement and advocacy budget allocations

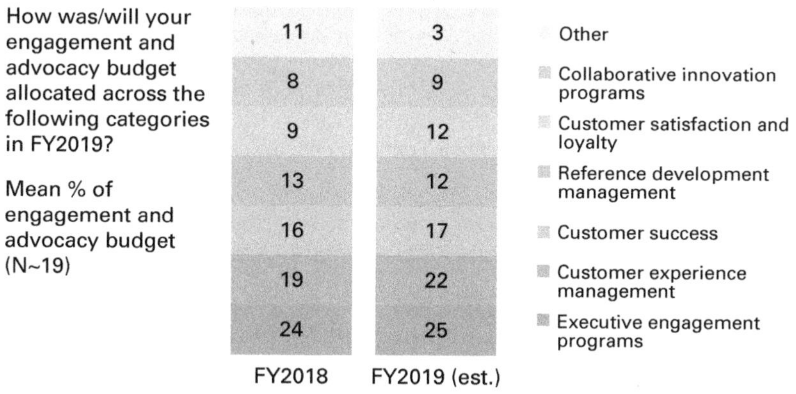

How was/will your engagement and advocacy budget allocated across the following categories in FY2019? Mean % of engagement and advocacy budget (N~19)	FY2018	FY2019 (est.)	
	11	3	Other
	8	9	Collaborative innovation programs
	9	12	Customer satisfaction and loyalty
	13	12	Reference development management
	16	17	Customer success
	19	22	Customer experience management
	24	25	Executive engagement programs

SOURCE ITSMA Services Marketing Budget Allocations and Trends, 2019

It's this balance of confidentiality and value that makes studies like those ITSMA, PwC and IBM have been running endure over the decades, as executives build trust in the data and the source.

Collaborating throughout the research process

There are many ways to engage with executives as you work through the research process. You may start by involving a small group in defining and scoping the research project and brief. O2 and ITSMA do this through their advisory boards, while others engage advisors and partners to work with them on the project, perhaps from the media or academia.

Advisory boards or steering groups made up of representatives from the peer group you are targeting can also be a great source of qualitative interviews, helping you to prioritize the most important questions for a survey instrument while giving you the anecdotes and examples you need to bring your data to life.

The quantitative phase of your research is another opportunity to collaborate and engage with your targets, particularly if you adopt the blend of telephone and face-to-face interviews alongside online survey responses, as PwC does. During these conversations with the peers you would most like to engage, you can offer personalized debriefs of the data and start a conversation about their own issues and challenges.

Once the data have been collected and you've begun your analysis, your advisory board, steering group or the interviewees that are considered a priority can help you interpret what you're seeing. In the case of ITSMA, we regularly do research into ABM best practices and benchmarks, and build models and frameworks based on the data in collaboration with our Global ABM Council, including executives from companies such as Adobe, BT, EY, Panasonic, Red Hat and SAP. The collaborative analysis and development of a narrative based on the research findings keeps the study relevant and punchy, and presented in language these executives understand.

Those same people will usually happily test any online benchmarking or diagnostic tools you've built with the data, providing valuable feedback before you launch it to a wider market. Those who have been involved all the way through can also welcome the opportunity to co-present the data and implications at conferences of their peers, on webinars or via video or podcast recordings shared through social media. As we know, peer-to-peer conversations are all-important, so facilitating this kind of storytelling through your research initiative is a powerful approach.

Running engaging events

One of the ways that O2 has leveraged its data on the business gains that come from better digital connectivity is to use it at its annual customer event, the Blue Door Conference, at The O2 arena in London. Over 1,000 executives are invited to this event, from companies of all sizes. Like many other companies, O2 runs its event to bring peers together to discuss the issues facing them, be inspired by case study examples of how others have tackled those issues, hear about the latest trends and emerging solutions and build their own networks.

When asked what helps them decide which events to attend, executives rate the quality of the speakers or thought leaders presenting at the event at the top of their list of criteria, followed by the relevance of the topic to their unique business issues, industry and role, and the cost of attending. Their relationship with the solution provider whose event it is, and the quality of the peers who will also attend, are other important factors (see Figure 7.5).

The large events and conferences that suppliers attend or put on for executives are now high-quality experiences, with personalized agendas and white-glove treatment for the most important clients or prospects. Some are even events within events, as smaller groups of executives are streamed into boardrooms around the main event to discuss priority issues for them. The approach taken depends on the type of event and who is running it, so let's break this down a bit further.

FIGURE 7.5 Event decision criteria

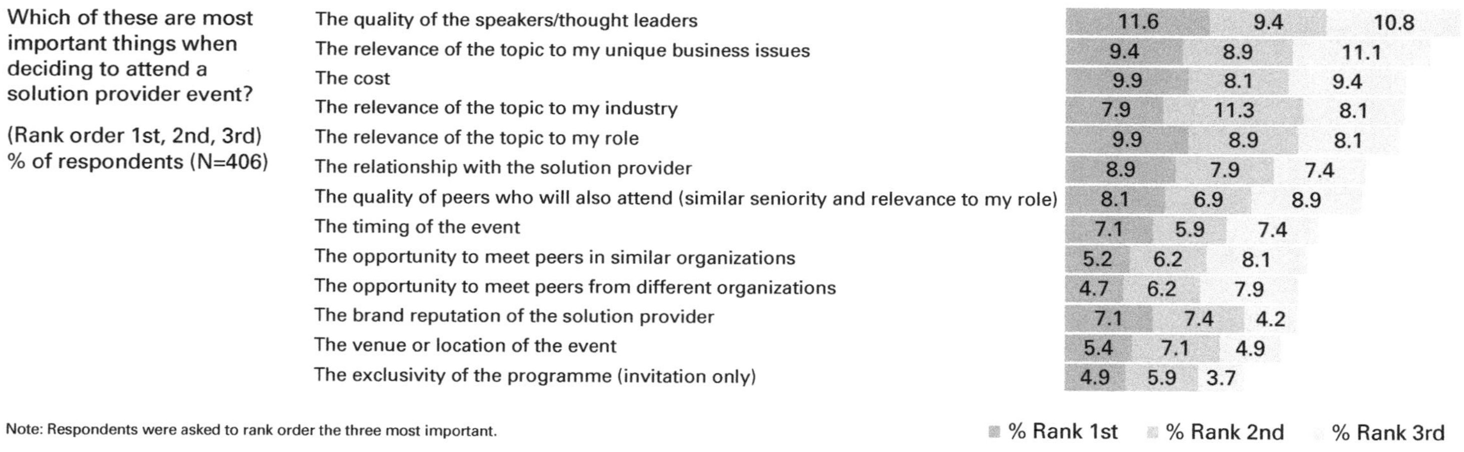

Which of these are most important things when deciding to attend a solution provider event?

(Rank order 1st, 2nd, 3rd)
% of respondents (N=406)

Criteria	% Rank 1st	% Rank 2nd	% Rank 3rd
The quality of the speakers/thought leaders	11.6	9.4	10.8
The relevance of the topic to my unique business issues	9.4	8.9	11.1
The cost	9.9	8.1	9.4
The relevance of the topic to my industry	7.9	11.3	8.1
The relevance of the topic to my role	9.9	8.9	8.1
The relationship with the solution provider	8.9	7.9	7.4
The quality of peers who will also attend (similar seniority and relevance to my role)	8.1	6.9	8.9
The timing of the event	7.1	5.9	7.4
The opportunity to meet peers in similar organizations	5.2	6.2	8.1
The opportunity to meet peers from different organizations	4.7	6.2	7.9
The brand reputation of the solution provider	7.1	7.4	4.2
The venue or location of the event	5.4	7.1	4.9
The exclusivity of the programme (invitation only)	4.9	5.9	3.7

Note: Respondents were asked to rank order the three most important.

SOURCE ITSMA 'How Executives Engage' survey, 2019

Trade shows and exhibitions

You may believe that executives don't typically attend trade shows and exhibitions, but there are a few around the world that are so critical to their industry that they draw a senior audience. Two examples are the National Retail Federation (NRF) run every January in New York and the Mobile World Congress (MWC) in Barcelona every February.

NRF is billed as the retail industry's biggest show, and is the centrepiece of the NRF Retail Week each year where 'the entire industry unites to get a whole new perspective' (nrfbigshow.nrf.com). An amazing 38,000 attendees from 16,000 retailers across 99 countries come to hear visionary speakers set out the future of retail and see solutions from 800 exhibitors. Those who can't attend in person can follow the conversation online and on social media using the hashtag #NRF2020.

MWC bills itself as the largest mobile event in the world, bringing together the latest innovations and leading-edge technology alongside today's most influential visionaries. It incorporates a thought leadership conference featuring prominent executives representing global mobile operators, device manufacturers, technology providers, vendors and content owners.

Suppliers wishing to engage some of the senior executives attending these events have a range of options. They can sponsor the event, as Accenture does for MWC and IBM does for NRF. They can also take a speaking slot at the event to demonstrate their thought leadership and expertise and start conversations, as both Nokia and Orange have done at MWC, or arrange for one of their customers to speak or enter for the awards that will be presented at these events.

Exhibition space is usually available. For instance, IBM made great use of its space at NRF one year by building a store of the future with its US client, Macy's, and making it available for other executives to come and see. It demonstrated the art of the possible through an immersive experience rather than simply telling people what could be done.

Leading companies also tend to schedule private meetings during the event well in advance, inviting target executives to breakfast briefings or roundtables around the event itself. More creative approaches include that adopted by IBM at MWC one year, where the company hired taxis to take target executives from their hotel to the event venue, doing a video interview on key issues during the journey and relaying those interviews across the world and into the event on social media. Clever.

So, there are lots of options when attending the public events and conferences where networks of your target peers will be. But one of the downsides is that you will be one of many suppliers trying to catch and hold their attention while you're there. Another option is to run your own events for these peer networks.

Your own conferences

Many technology and professional service firms run their own conferences and exhibitions to give them the exclusive attention of the executives they wish to engage. Some of these events are huge, such as SAP's annual SAPPHIRE event in Orlando or Fujitsu's biannual Fujitsu Forum in Tokyo and Munich.

A word of warning here though; creating excellent event experiences for executives on this scale is a full-time job and a specialist skill. If you're going to invest in something like this, make sure you have the budget and the expertise to do it well, since the bar rises every year in terms of the treatment executives receive when they attend events like these.

Usually these large supplier events are designed to attract different audiences, from technical users and developers through to the most senior executives, with streams of activity designed for each one. There may be a technical hall and exhibition for developers, along with the odd hackathon (a collaborative computer programming event) to crowd-source their expertise to solve a societal problem, for example. There may be a single keynote and then streams of conference speakers for different roles, including a press stream for journalists, analysts and influencers. And there will be a VIP stream for executives.

For example, at Fujitsu Forum, VIP guests from the company's most important accounts are invited to an exclusive dinner the night before the conference begins. In 2018, knowing that the stakes were getting ever higher in providing a standout experience for these guests, the Fujitsu team decided to give them something they'd never forget: a Guinness World Record.

CASE STUDY

Fujitsu: Setting a world record with peer-to-peer networking

Japanese-headquartered Fujitsu is one of the world leaders in ICT, offering a full range of technology products, solutions and services to customers in over 100 countries.

The company embraced ABM some time ago and its ABM programme is now well developed and reasonably mature. An important element of the programme is enabling executive engagement in a meaningful and memorable way. For example, every year Fujitsu holds two large customer events, the Fujitsu Forum, in Tokyo and in Munich, with executives from key accounts invited to an exclusive dinner the evening before where they are entertained by an engaging after-dinner speaker.

Promoting digital co-creation

In 2017, digital co-creation was chosen as the theme for these meetings. The pre-event dinner at the November Forum in Munich was held at the impressive BMW Museum and hosted by Duncan Tait, Corporate Executive Officer, SEVP and Head of Americas and EMEIA.

For Andrea Clatworthy, Head of Account-Based Marketing at Fujitsu, EMEIA, the challenge was to bring the digital co-creation theme alive and make it stand out among executives who attend many such dinners and hear a lot of speakers. So she decided to do something not only very different but very ambitious: 'I wanted to create an event that was experiential and memorable by involving the guests in digital co-creation with no preparation required on their part. I decided that we would digitally co-create the largest animated tablet mosaic and make an attempt to achieve a brand new Guinness World Record!'

A sophisticated set-up

The preparation for the 7 November dinner began in April. The mosaic would be comprised of 220 tablets using Fujitsu hardware. All the tablets had to be touching while a video played, seamlessly and without error, across all the tablets to make one large moving image. In other words, each tablet would play a part of the overall moving image, without replication.

The technical challenges of getting this right were significant. Not only did the video need to be chopped up into 220 distinct parts that played simultaneously at the touch of one button, but the team in charge had to devise a way for the guests to build the mosaic in true co-creation.

Each tablet would thus act as one 'tile' in the mosaic, with every guest placing at least one tablet in the purpose-built display stand housing the entire mosaic. Each tablet then had to be programmed with its location in the grid so that it could play the correct piece of the video.

The suspense builds

As Andrea recounts, 'Once all the tablets were in place, we activated the control program, which created a single large static image. This was all done wirelessly. There were definitely some tense moments as some of the tablets decided to misbehave.'

As the tension rose, all the tablets suddenly blinked into life, to be greeted by a massive cheer. To win the world record, however, it had to become a video. So after a count of five, a big red button was pushed and the video began, accompanied by rousing music.

'The crowd cheered, the Guinness World Records adjudicator declared we had achieved a brand new record, and we celebrated with bubbly, certificates, photos and much back-slapping', says Andrea.

An impressive display

More significantly, this was an impressive display of Fujitsu technology and know-how. The executives who attended will forever have a piece of Guinness World Record history to remind them of the digital co-creation experience they shared thanks to Fujitsu. And all the tablets were sold!

According to Duncan Tait:

> Co-creating a digital future with our customers is fundamental to the way Fujitsu approaches business. We highlighted this focus with the theme for this year's Fujitsu Forum, 'Human Centric Innovation – Digital Co-creation', which for us meant bringing together the latest digital technology and expertise to create new possibilities for business and society. Achieving this Guinness World Record title with our customers epitomized this approach. The final image, a stylized Japanese landscape, highlighted how each collaborator had something important to contribute, to create a whole that was greater than the sum of its parts.

Factors behind the success

Andrea believes there were a number of factors that contributed to the evening's memorable success:

- **Taking a risk.** It could have failed miserably, so the team decided not to tell customers about it beforehand. They first learned about it when she introduced the representatives from the Guinness World Records at the dinner.

- **Committing to a budget.** They spent the money they had to spend to achieve the right outcome. The tablets alone were over €1,000 each, while there were also venue hire, agency support and the people necessary for design, creation and testing to take into account.

- **Leading from the front.** Andrea took ownership and was very hands-on throughout the process. She brought in a specialist experiential event agency that subcontracted to another agency to chop up the video and get it to work across the 220 tablets. 'It was my thing and I was determined that it would be successful.'

It was hard work: 'I lost sleep and even the skin off my hands building the stand to hold the tablets. I lost days and days to testing. I even got my dad involved to make the red button that Duncan pressed to start the video', she says.

In the end, it was time and money well spent: the influenced pipeline for the event was €1.1 billion.

Clearly, running your own events allows you to showcase your own executives and thought leadership, and give platforms to the client executives who are your advocates: a powerful combination indeed. So, while there are great benefits to running your own event for networks of peers, it's useful to think beyond the event itself. How do you keep the conversation going after the event is over? And how do you make your target executives feel they belong to your network?

One option is to use an event app such as Whova, which allows those attending to network via the app before the event, posting questions to each other and scheduling meetings with peers or your own team that they want to talk to. The app has all the joining instructions, agenda and speaker details included, so that your executives can plan their time at the event. Once there, they can respond to polls during sessions and provide feedback on those sessions they've attended. And after the event, you can post the presentation materials for them to download and share, and they can keep the conversation going with both you and their fellow attendees. A natural way of working for millennials, these kinds of app are also popular with the over-forties in my experience.

This is beyond event management and all about building communities, which we'll look at next.

Building new communities

The creation of a community of peers goes one step beyond the running of a single event. One of the best examples of this is the community created by the World Economic Forum (WEF), originally the European Management Forum, formed by Klaus Schwab in 1971. Known predominantly for its annual four-day event in Davos, Switzerland, where world leaders come together to discuss some of the most pressing issues facing business and society, the Forum maintains its sense of a community of peers throughout the rest of the year with an online collaboration platform, research projects, a young leaders forum and several other topic-specific and geographically focused events around the world.

CASE STUDY
Achieving the pinnacle of success in peer-to-peer networking

When Klaus Schwab founded what was then called the European Management Forum in Switzerland in 1971, the intention of the University of Geneva business professor was to import US business practices into Europe. In 1987 he changed the name to the World Economic Forum, elevating the mission of the non-profit organization to engage the foremost political, business and other leaders of society to shape global, regional and industry agendas.

Deliberating at Davos in a secure space

The Forum annual meeting held in Davos in the Swiss mountains at the end of every January has become one of the most high-profile peer-to-peer gatherings in the world. Numerous events of global importance have been held there.

For example, in 1992 the president of South Africa, F W deKlerk, met with Nelson Mandela and Chief Mangosuthu Buthelezi for the first time outside South Africa in a seminal meeting for the country. A North Korea delegation was invited in 2015, signalling a new chance of dialogue, while in 2017 the head of state of the People's Republic of China attended to defend the country's global trade framework in the face of rising protectionist movements.

At the invitation-only four-day meeting in January 2019 there were more than 3,000 leaders from business, government, civil society, academia, arts and culture and media, as well as the foremost experts and young leaders from around the globe. They met to discuss the meeting's theme, Globalization 4.0: Shaping a Global Architecture in the Age of the Fourth Industrial Revolution.

One of the biggest inducements for these people to take time out from busy schedules to attend is the ability to engage with peers from across the globe and from diverse sectors of society in a relaxed and secure setting. As well as the formal presentations, the ability to network privately throughout the event is a rare opportunity for leaders to meet face-to-face on a neutral platform.

Having a global impact

As well as the annual January meeting, the Forum oversees a range of other meetings and initiatives:

- Four other annual meetings as well as Davos: the Annual Meeting of the New Champions, on innovation, science and technology, in China; the Annual Meeting of the Global Future Councils in the United Arab Emirates; the Sustainable Development Impact Summit in New York; and the Industry Strategy Meeting on pioneering change in Geneva. There is a new event in 2020, the Global Technology Governance Summit, in San Francisco.

- There are annual meetings for the WEF's Young Global Leaders and the Global Shapers. In addition, there are regional meetings in Middle East/North Africa, Association of Southeast Asian Nations (ASEAN), India and Latin America.

- World-class research is carried out to produce valuable insights to share at meetings on significant issues such as competitiveness, gender parity and global IT.

- Decision makers are regularly brought together from across society to work on projects that can make a sustainable difference, including a series of *Shaping the Future of...* studies into essential areas such as the digital economy and society, consumption, energy, healthcare and financial and monetary systems.

- Virtual interaction ensures that top leaders can continue their conversations in an atmosphere of trust through a proprietary platform, *TopLink*, which is a collaborative intelligence platform.

Universal engagement

As Klaus Schwab wrote prior to the 2019 Davos meeting:[6]

> The changes that are underway today are not isolated to a particular country, industry, or issue. They are universal, and thus require a global response. Failing to adopt a new cooperative approach would be a tragedy for humankind. To draft a blueprint for a shared global-governance architecture, we must avoid becoming mired in the current moment of crisis management.
>
> Specifically, this task will require two things of the international community: wider engagement and heightened imagination. The engagement of all stakeholders in sustained dialogue will be crucial, as will the imagination to think systemically, and beyond one's own short-term institutional and national considerations.

Not many companies have built communities as high profile and engaging as this one, but some are trying. If you think this is something you would like to try, here are some questions to ask yourself as you plan your own community's development:

1 **Which executives will I invite to join?** You may wish to create a community of just client executives, or invite prospects too. There are arguments for

and against mixing roles, inviting representatives from several functions to join, as opposed to building a community of one type of role, say, of CEOs. One rule to remember is that you must invite peers, and not allow substitutions. As soon as you allow people to send their deputies, this will break the peer-to-peer promise, and your target executives will not want to come. To help with this, you may decide to develop a tiered approach, with an inner circle of the most senior executives and then a wider community, where the inner circle benefits from additional meetings or insights and helps you to guide the shape of the wider community.

2 **How will I convince people to join?** For these time-poor, over-targeted executives, invitations to attend things are arriving every week. Why should they invest time in your community? You need to develop a clear value proposition and story about your community. It could be about the reciprocal learning opportunities you'll offer them, the chance to work on big issues facing business or society together, access to new innovations or events they can't buy, or even the time they get to spend with your own executives. Whatever you decide on, make sure you test your thinking with some of the executives you're hoping to get on board.

3 **How will I maintain momentum?** Just as the World Economic Forum has a combination of topic-based meetings, research projects and regional events supplemented with an online collaboration platform, you will need to plan a cadence of activities supported by regular communications. A monthly update may suffice to alert members of the community to upcoming events, whether online or offline, and to research projects that they could get involved with. Some of the activities others use include conferences and seminars, study tours, collaborative research, awards programmes, webinars, video interviews and podcasts, social media discussions and newsletters. A password-protected online collaboration area is another great tool to keep your community fresh, or if this is too difficult for you, a closed LinkedIn group can work too.

4 **How will I build trust?** This is a huge consideration and requires a non-selling mindset. While you may want to record and publish notes from meetings, your community members will not want their secrets all over the news or passed directly into the hands of their competitors, so it's important to offer a 'Chatham House rule'-style environment, where everyone knows who is in the room, discussions are only reported at a general level and no sales discussion begins as a result of the issues and ideas being shared (unless the executive asks for one).

5 **How will I know if it's a success?** This is simple. The executives you invite will keep coming back, and others will ask to join.

Creating a successful community usually relies on identifying what members have in common and allowing them to share perspectives on that while delivering insights and experiences that they value. One of the most powerful communities built and maintained predominantly by professional service firms is a network of former employees or alumni.

A note on alumni

Professional service firms – law, accountancy, consultancy – invest a lot in training their people. In fact, their people really are their greatest asset, since they have no tangible product or capital investment to base their offers on. These firms have worked out that when someone they have trained wants to leave them and move to another firm or another industry, this is an opportunity to build future value for both parties. Mostly, leavers will go on to develop their careers in organizations that could buy the firm's services. Or they may go into companies that could work as partners with the firm. Clearly, they may also join a competitor, but you can't win them all. And they may come back!

To maintain communication with leavers and keep the firm front of mind for potential services, most run an alumni programme similar to academic institutions. An alumni network is essentially a community built solely for previous employees, and delivers a range of benefits to them in exchange for their continued engagement with the firm. As an alumna of BDO in the UK (after just one year running a rebranding and communications programme for the firm), I received regular updates on its activities, interpretations of the latest financial regulations and news, and invitations to events ranging from pure networking through to content-led seminars with a high-profile speaker. Today's alumni benefit from online collaboration areas too, and social network groups, to keep the conversation going.

For the alumnus, there is huge benefit in keeping up to date with the latest professional or industry news, as well as keeping their network of contacts fresh. Future jobs may be offered and secured through such a network. For the firm, it's a very real source of opportunity, with direct requests for support coming from the alumni group as well as referrals to members of their own wider networks.

It's interesting that other B2B companies, such as those in technology and engineering, have been slow to pick up on the benefits of this kind of community. When you leave a technology firm, as I have done twice in my career, you're responsible for maintaining your own network of previous colleagues. In my view, this is a missed opportunity, and a mistake I encourage you not to make.

Summary

1 Peer networks are powerful, but the way they are built is changing. Traditionally, they were built over time through face-to-face meetings, but millennials in the workplace are redefining them to mean peers they can access through their social networks – even if they've never met.

2 The fact that peers network to keep up with trends, share challenges and learn from each other means that research, both in terms of the process and the data generated, is a powerful tool for engaging with them. Decide what topic or themes you will research by linking to your own strategy and brand, thinking about what matters to the executives you want to engage and deciding whether it's a one-off research project or an annual study or index you want to create.

3 Every research project needs clear objectives and scope, and these are best pulled together in a research brief. The brief will ensure that everyone working on the project is on the same page from the start, and will help you select an agency or research partner for your project.

4 There are a range of research methods available, depending on the type of results you want to achieve. Quantitative surveys are the most credible for generating headlines and building indexes or benchmarks that peers can engage with.

5 Professional research initiatives are conducted with integrity, with individual responses anonymized and treated confidentially. Capturing and storing data has regulatory implications in Europe, in particular, and if you're in any doubt, it's worth checking with your research agency or your internal legal counsel.

6 When asked what helps them decide which events to attend, executives rate the quality of the speakers or thought leaders presenting top in their list of criteria, followed by the relevance of the topic to their unique business issues, industry and role, and the cost of attending.

Their relationship with the solution provider whose event it is, and the quality of the peers who will also attend, are other important factors.

7   Suppliers wishing to engage executives attending large conferences and trade shows have a range of options. They can sponsor the event, take a speaking slot, arrange for one of their customers to speak or enter for event-related awards, or schedule private meetings around the main event.

8   Many technology and professional service firms run their own conferences and exhibitions to give them the exclusive attention of the executives they wish to engage. Running your own events allows you to showcase your own executives and thought leadership, and give platforms to the client executives who are your advocates: a powerful combination indeed.

9   Going one step beyond the running of a single event is the creation of a community of peers. Think about which executives to invite and why they should join, how to keep momentum going and how to build trust among the members.

10 Alumni communities have proved a great success for professional service firms. The alumni benefit by keeping up to date with the latest professional or industry news, keeping their network of contacts fresh and hearing about potential job moves. For the firm, direct requests for support come from the community as well as referrals to members of alumni's wider networks.

Notes

1   PwC, 22nd Annual CEO Survey, www.pwc.co.uk/ceosurvey (archived at https://perma.cc/SA3S-RHZV)

2   Interbrand Best Global Brands Report, 2019, www.interbrand.com/best-brands/best-global-brands/2019/ (archived at https://perma.cc/DJB3-TQ8E)

3   EMC Privacy Index, 2013, featured on infographicsagency.com (archived at https://perma.cc/3LQK-LCGZ)

4   'Business without boundaries: The role of connectivity in business growth', Development Economics with O2 Business, October 2019

5   ITSMA Services Marketing Budget Allocation and Trends, annual benchmarking survey, 2019

6   Schwab, K (5 November 2018) 'Globalization 4.0 – What does it mean?', World Economic Forum

08

Engaging small groups

The beauty of a small group is that you are able to talk to everyone. Plus, you can have a deeper discussion with peers at a seminar or workshop than you would at a conference or exhibition. Conversation is easier to facilitate across a handful of peers. It's no surprise then that most executive engagement programmes feature opportunities to engage in smaller group settings.

There are a number of small group settings you can use, and suppliers are inventing new approaches all the time, both online and offline. Offline, seminars, workshops and advisory boards are the most popular content-led events, with hospitality such as sports and cultural activities another popular choice, although hospitality is harder to run for many industries and geographies because of increasingly stringent bribery laws and corporate policies. Online, interactive webinars often appear as part of engagement programmes. This chapter will look at each of these main approaches in more detail.

The key here is to understand the executives you are trying to engage, and what their preferences are. Let's start by looking into those preferences.

What activities do executives prefer to engage in?

Executives themselves tend to prefer small group settings. They get to dig deeper into their issues, ask more questions and participate in hands-on activities to bring them to life and map out a route to solving them. They work side-by-side with their peers and your experts, with everyone benefiting.

The latest research by ITSMA into how executives engage[1] shows that the activity in which executives are most likely to participate is in-person business seminars, with either your own SMEs or industry analysts presenting (see Figure 8.1). Next come innovation workshops, facilitated by leading

FIGURE 8.1 Executives' likelihood of participating in engagement activities

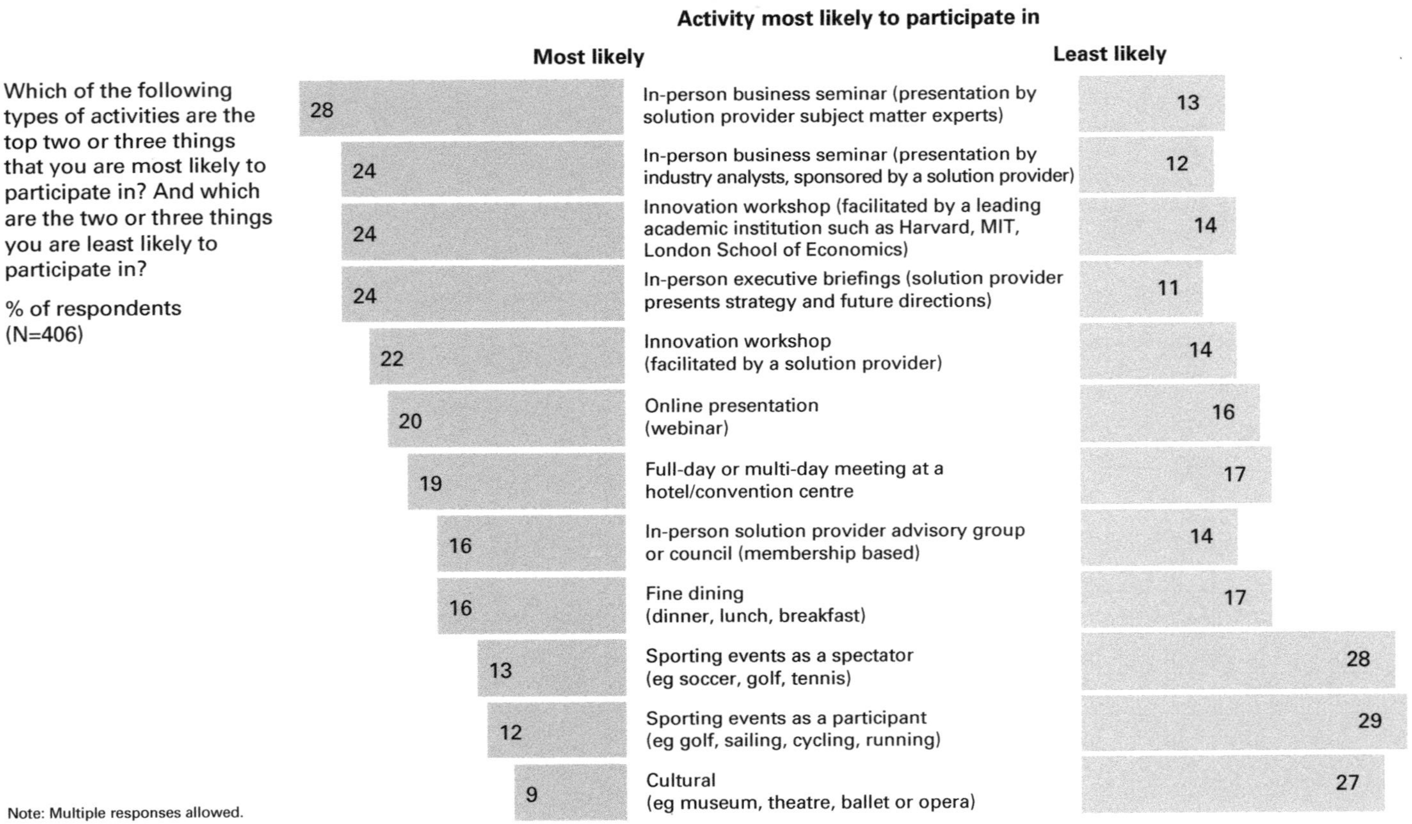

Activity most likely to participate in	Most likely	Least likely
In-person business seminar (presentation by solution provider subject matter experts)	28	13
In-person business seminar (presentation by industry analysts, sponsored by a solution provider)	24	12
Innovation workshop (facilitated by a leading academic institution such as Harvard, MIT, London School of Economics)	24	14
In-person executive briefings (solution provider presents strategy and future directions)	24	11
Innovation workshop (facilitated by a solution provider)	22	14
Online presentation (webinar)	20	16
Full-day or multi-day meeting at a hotel/convention centre	19	17
In-person solution provider advisory group or council (membership based)	16	14
Fine dining (dinner, lunch, breakfast)	16	17
Sporting events as a spectator (eg soccer, golf, tennis)	13	28
Sporting events as a participant (eg golf, sailing, cycling, running)	12	29
Cultural (eg museum, theatre, ballet or opera)	9	27

Which of the following types of activities are the top two or three things that you are most likely to participate in? And which are the two or three things you are least likely to participate in?

% of respondents (N=406)

Note: Multiple responses allowed.

SOURCE ITSMA 'How Executives Engage' survey, 2019

academic institutions (such as Harvard, MIT or the London School of Economics) or by your own team. In-person executive briefings, where you share your company's strategy and future direction are also popular, as are online webinars, full-day meetings and advisory boards.

At the bottom of the list come the hospitality events, whether sporting, cultural or fine-dining, and this may be due to the difficulties in some firms and countries of executives attending these types of activities. It's worth adding that if an executive is going through a procurement process with you that is in the final stages of selection, they may not be able to attend any event that you invite them to outside of the formal procurement process.

Let's now look at each of these main types of small group event in turn.

Seminars and webinars

Every engagement programme I have seen includes in-person business seminars, since these are not only the most preferred activity of the executives themselves, but are perhaps one of the most cost-effective, easy-to-run elements of a programme. Webinars are equally well used, but less preferred by executives. This varies by country (they are twice as popular in the UK, for example, as in Germany) and by demographics (millennials are more comfortable participating online, as we've seen before). Most people use a combination of both to reach a wider audience, depending on their experience with that audience.

Whether you are running a face-to-face or an online version, content and speakers are key for your event to be successful. This is what draws executives in, as we saw in Chapter 7. But there are a few critical success factors to take into account when planning and running your seminar or webinar. Here's a checklist to help you think about your approach:

1   **Define your objectives.** Your reasons for running a seminar or webinar are likely to be a subset of the objectives for your engagement programme as a whole. If we think about the buyer process, for example, it's unlikely that you will use a seminar or webinar to increase awareness of your company and its solutions, but more likely that you will use them from the interest stage onwards through purchase and into post-purchase. To spend a half or full day with you, the executives in your programme are likely to be already aware of and interested your organization. So, your

objectives for these events are likely to be about positioning your company as having expertise or a point of view on issues that matter to them, increasing their consideration for you as a potential supplier and building relationships with them as individuals to the point where they become your advocates.

2   **Decide on the theme and content.** You may decide to run a series of webinars or seminars on a particular theme, with the content varying each time. For example, I work with brand consultancy Manasian & Co, whose Little Bird Talks are run on the theme of great storytelling. They've featured James Kerr telling the story of the New Zealand rugby team, the All Blacks, and Dr Kevin Fong telling the story of the lunar landing in 1969. While the speaker and the content of each talk have nothing in common with the other talks, the theme is consistent. We've talked a lot about anchoring your thought leadership themes and research initiatives around the things that matter to your target executives, and the same is true for these events. In fact, it's likely that these events will be one of the main vehicles for you to share your thought leadership and research.

3   **Recruit great speakers.** The quality of your speakers is the number one decision criterion for executives deciding whether to attend your event. They may be academic partners, analysts, influencers, client executives, other business leaders, sports personalities or your own executives and SMEs. If you can, watch or listen to them speak before you recruit them, since public speaking is not everyone's forte. Most speakers will have some video clips online, either as a TED talk or via YouTube for you to check that they're a good fit for your audience.

4   **Plan the experience.** Event management is a specific skill, as I've said before, and you'd be well advised either to find someone on your team with the right skills to manage your events, recruit someone, or outsource it to a specialist agency. As we've seen, the bar is being raised ever higher in terms of what gives executives a great experience. The right content and speaker are your foundations, because they can make or break your event, but the experience you provide for your executives is the icing on the cake, and makes a good event into a great one. The experience begins from the first invitation to attend, through the regular reminders about the event, any pre-event polls, questions around dietary preferences and the necessary joining instructions. It continues through the event itself, from the ease with which people find the venue and how they are

welcomed on arrival, to the comfort of the venue, the quality of the refreshments and the degree of interaction and engagement during the event. (The latter is particularly important in a webinar, where it can be all too easy to speak at the audience for an hour rather than use polling or Q&A sessions to get the audience talking.) And it carries on after the event, from the ease with which executives can leave the event, to the follow-up communications afterwards.

5   **Brief your team.** For a seminar in particular, and to a lesser extent for a webinar, your team need to be briefed on the objectives of the event, the content and speakers, the flow of the event, and crucially on their role in the event. How would you like them to behave? It can be things as simple as not talking to each other but always mingling with the invitees, making sure that everyone is warmly welcomed and never left standing alone. You may wish to go further by providing a photo and short summary of all attendees and agreeing who will host whom from among your own team. Finally, brief and rehearse your speakers. This will make the difference between an OK event and a great one, as they know what you expect from them and you can check that they are delivering what you need.

6   **Seek feedback and review against your objectives.** While you gain experience over time in terms of what does and doesn't work for your audience, every event is different and, in my experience, there is always something that can be improved at each one. Capturing feedback from your own team and the executives attending helps you to continually improve, so it's important to check how the experience was for them, whether online (very suitable at the end of a webinar) or offline (which some executives still prefer at the end of an in-person seminar). As well as checking on the executive's experience, you may also wish to check if their perception of your company has shifted through their experience, or if they would like to know more about the topics discussed, or have ideas for other topics in future events.

One of the benefits of webinars is that you can have speakers and executives from all over the world participating (time zones permitting), and they can still take place when companies put travel freezes in place, preventing their executives from making all but the most necessary business trips. Having delivered webinars for nearly 20 years now, I can tell you that one of these benefits also presents one of the greatest challenges: speakers in separate locations.

Audiences respond to natural conversation much better than presenters reading their speeches (trust me, I've done both in my time), and the three ways that this is easiest to achieve are by being in the same room, working with someone on a regular basis so you can anticipate each other, or rehearsing in full. Ideally, you'd have all three! Plus, planning interaction every 10 minutes at a minimum is important, since it's all too easy for executives to listen to a webinar on a muted line while doing the hundred other things they need to get through if you're not keeping their attention and asking them to interact via polls and questions.

Interaction in seminars is just as important. We're told that we can only focus our attention for 20 minutes, so plan to have some form of interaction every 20 minutes at least, whether that's an audience poll, Q&A or table exercise. Some sessions could be all about interaction, as in breakout workshops. You might even want to extend that interaction during the breaks, giving people Q&A walls to post questions and advice, for example.

Interactivity and audience engagement are key, and really drive a great event. And the executives who are in your programme have lots to offer. Perhaps that's why innovation and design workshops have become increasingly popular in recent years.

Innovation workshops

The second most likely small group event for executives to participate in, innovation workshops, are all the rage right now. Suppliers are increasingly developing purpose-built innovation or briefing centres, with staff recruited to ensure their smooth running and deliver memorable experiences to the executives that visit.

ITSMA's 2018 research into how executives engage[2] revealed that 89 per cent of executives visit a supplier's innovation centre either during their purchase process or post-purchase, with 77 per cent of those visiting up to four centres. The majority of those visits happen when the executives are either keeping up with trends or researching potential solutions and suppliers (71 per cent for both), while only slightly fewer attend when making a final purchase decision (67 per cent) or after the purchase is made (68 per cent). More than three-quarters (77 per cent) describe the visits as valuable, claiming that their impression of the supplier improved as a result of the visit, they developed a stronger relationship and came away with a better understanding of the latest trends and developments relevant to their business and role.

FIGURE 8.2   Content delivered during an innovation centre visit

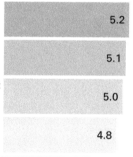

During your most recent visit to an innovation/briefing centre, how would you characterize the content covered during the visit? Mean rating (N=366)	Problem solving (collaboration to solve your most challenging business issues and opportunities)	5.2
	Solution provider focused (corporate information, roadmaps, strategic direction)	5.1
	Thought leading (informed on latest trends, expert points of view, ideas and vision for the future)	5.0
	Sales oriented (product, service and solution information)	4.8

Note: Includes respondents who have visited an innovation/briefing centre. Mean rating based on a 7-point scale where 1=not at all and 7=to a great extent.

Not at all   Mean rating   To a great extent

SOURCE ITSMA 'How Executives Engage' survey, 2018

When planning an innovation centre visit, which may be for executives from different companies but is more usually for a group of executives in the same company, the same checklist applies as for a seminar, with a few nuances. Most suppliers put problem solving at the heart of the content they share during a visit, with collaborative exercises run to solve the most challenging opportunities and issues facing the executives attending. Often this will leverage research completed in advance, such as benchmarking research that highlights where the client company could focus its innovation to improve operations or build future revenue streams (see Figure 8.2).

Other content includes relevant information from the supplier themselves, such as future technology roadmaps or strategic investments, or expert opinion and points of view on some of the trends and issues facing the executives. Least likely to take centre stage is sales content, and it may even be that no sales people are invited to attend.

The degree of interactivity increases significantly in an innovation centre visit. This is about collaborative problem solving, after all, and techniques such as design thinking are commonly used to define a context, explore alternative ideas, develop ideas and prototypes and agree action plans. ITSMA's 2018 research showed that just under a third of the time during a visit is spent listening to formal presentations about the latest trends and developments. Another quarter is spent engaging in interactive discussions, while the remaining time is split equally between watching live demonstrations and collaborating to create new ideas (see Figure 8.3).

FIGURE 8.3 Time spent at innovation centres

During your most recent visit to an innovation/briefing centre, approximately what percentage of the time was spent in the following activities?
% of time (N=366)

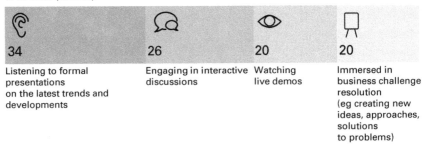

34	26	20	20
Listening to formal presentations on the latest trends and developments	Engaging in interactive discussions	Watching live demos	Immersed in business challenge resolution (eg creating new ideas, approaches, solutions to problems)

SOURCE ITSMA 'How Executives Engage' survey, 2018

One of the companies most skilled in running these workshops for clients is Capgemini, whose Accelerated Solutions Environments methodology engages executives in client and prospect organizations around the world to help them solve the most pressing business issues facing each of their companies.

CASE STUDY
CAPGEMINI: Accelerating the power of group dynamics

Capgemini is a global leader in consulting, technology services and digital transformation. One of the ways they bring a client's opportunity for digital transformation to life is through an interactive workshop approach called the Accelerated Solutions Environment (ASE). This aligns diverse stakeholders – business, IT, customers, vendors and subject matter specialists – to define and tackle complex business challenges within days rather than months or even years.

Creativity and change through collaboration

According to ASE Facilitator Wim Wensink, Capgemini has been successfully using this approach to effective collaboration for almost 20 years with many FTSE 100 and *Fortune* 500 clients. It is based on the MG Taylor methodology originally set out by Matt and Gail Taylor in the 1970s, which emphasizes the integration of the physical environment, work processes and technology augmentation to facilitate human creativity for large-scale change.

Central to the service is a carefully designed event co-created by the ASE facilitation team with the client, underpinned by a rigorous method and process. A lead time of at least four to six weeks for preparation ensures that the business challenge is defined specifically enough so it can be tackled with the right objectives, participants, inputs and outputs to achieve the best results.

These meetings run from one to three or more days and/or consist of multiple events over a project lifecycle, while Capgemini can also develop an Acceleration Zone at the client's site to act as a custom-built collaborative workspace.

Getting the right people involved

Generally, the meetings involve three main types of people: the people who make decisions, SMEs and those who will be in charge of making change happen. A lot of thought is put into who should attend, with members strictly vetted (for example, the account teams which deal with clients will only be invited if there is a specific role for them).

At the beginning of an event, some of the people might be cautious about speaking openly in front of senior management. But that changes quickly, Wensink says: 'The way we design our programmes means that people soon feel they are on the same level and even the most senior executive is seen as one of the colleagues by the event's end. And that's a great result.'

Because these events are geared to making large-scale change sustainable, developing an effective agenda makes all the difference, notes Wensink:

> When we design the agenda we are focused on two main things: transformation on the one hand and transaction on the other. Transformation means getting everyone in the room on the same page, getting the energy and the mindset moving in the same direction. The transactional part is about setting steps, timelines, deliverables, milestones and whatever is necessary to make the agreed change happen. We have to get the balance of that right, and that is specifically addressed in the co-creation preparatory work we do with clients.

Nor are these events always run solely within the client company. Occasionally customers will be asked to participate, probably in the early stages, to demonstrate the client's commitment to change. Wensink has also facilitated groups consisting of several suppliers and a client to jumpstart improvements in the way they work together.

Tracking progress

The relationship doesn't end once the event is over. The Capgemini team returns to the client to evaluate progress six to eight weeks later, whether the event has been run as part of a larger consulting contract or as a one-off. As Wensink explains, 'Many clients come back to us after months and even years to talk about their progress so there is a rich cycle of feedback. We want to make sure they keep the energy high once they leave.'

Another, much smaller company has used the same approach with executives from different companies within the same industry. US firm GLMV Architecture created its ECHO workshops as part of a programme to grow its zoos and aquariums practice.

CASE STUDY
GLMV Architecture's ECHO workshops

The Wichita-based 120-person firm wanted to take a creative approach to becoming a trusted advisor in a niche market: its zoos and aquariums practice. 'In many industries, we become insular in the way that we think', says organizational development consultant and self-proclaimed zoo nerd Michael Clifford, GLMV's Curator of Innovation and Partnerships, who runs the firm's ECHO Initiative. 'Zoos are established organizations, often run by municipalities and private 503(c)3s, and are not necessarily set up for solving ecological, social and environmental challenges in the way that the for-profit sector can.'

Creating space for ideas

GLMV saw an opportunity to spark new thinking by bringing zoo professionals together with innovators from outside their world to talk about how they are solving big challenges. They created ECHO, an annual think tank workshop for mid- and senior-level professionals in accredited zoos and aquariums, named for the 'resonance' of the ideas they wanted to present.

During the two-and-a-half-day invitation-only event, 35 zoo leaders come together to focus on ideas, innovations and dialogue. Past speakers, called Thought Partners, have included NASA's award-winning scientist Dr Vikram Shyam, Joel Sartore of National Geographic Photo Ark, specialists in behavioural and community health and authors such as Duke University Professor Dan Heath and inclusion specialist Nina Simon.

The event – a mix of facilitation, presentation and small group conversation – is designed for engagement. No presentations are scheduled during meals so that participants can focus on conversation. The goal? To put smart people in a room with time and space for ideas to collide.

Logistics are taken care of by the ECHO team – from flight arrangements to airport transfers, shuttles, hotel accommodations and meals. 'We try to take care of all the details so that our attendees can focus on the content and collaboration', says Clifford.

Multiple years of sold-out events has confirmed the value of GLMV's approach.

Participants say they value what it provides for those at the top of an organization and report that their time at ECHO pays off. 'We hear that it is so wonderful to have the space and time to actually think', says Clifford. 'It can be hard for them to carve out time to be reflective during their regular routine.'

Building on success

One senior vice president credited ECHO's LEGO Serious Play session with changing his approach to executive meetings. He started convening each meeting in a new location, from the animal keepers' kitchen to the education offices. 'Now those executives are seeing things they would never see, and it breaks down the sense of ivory tower that can exist around the executive team', says Clifford.

For Palm Springs' Living Desert Zoo and Gardens, ECHO sparked the addition of rocking chairs in an older part of its zoo to encourage visitors to spend time with species that are not always a top attraction. Those rocking chairs are often in use, providing opportunities for more empathetic connections between humans and animals. Another zoo has used the ECHO model itself as inspiration to create more collaboration in their own organization.

After the first successful event in 2016, participants asked for more. The result is ECHO Digital, a series of online conversations about big ideas and zoological challenges (recent ones tackled conservation impact and diversity and engagement). GLMV maintains a list of 400+ zoo leaders and sends out invites to register for the live calls. Attendance is limited to 12–25 people to allow for idea sharing, but after the call, the whole list receives a written summary of top takeaways.

'I've had several zoo directors tell me, "please make sure that we keep getting those summaries"', says Clifford, adding that the briefs are widely read by those who aren't able to attend.

The ROI of commitment

Since ECHO began, GLMV has seen its zoo work rise by 400 per cent. The zoo studio has grown from 2 specialists to 10, and they are winning more complex, higher-quality projects. One project on the boards (and presented at a recent industry conference) aims to be the most complex African habitat in the country, solving the design challenges of cohabitating species. Another created safety innovations that allow animal care staff to move top predators without being in the same space.

'We want to improve innovation across the whole industry, not just with our clients', says Clifford, adding that today's highly educated zoo professionals expect a collaborative process, not a predetermined solution. 'When we get hired, (clients) know that we are going to ask the tough questions, challenge the way they do things and foster innovative thinking.'

Clifford believes that his non-architecture background has been an asset to ECHO's success. 'I don't have the answers', he says. 'My job is to bring people together to identify their own problems and their own solutions. But I've also been in their shoes and that goes a long way, too.'

As GLMV develops its position as a trusted advisor for zoo master planning and architectural design, they've leveraged Clifford's organizational design background to add services. Consulting projects have included assisting with organizational restructures, streamlining conservation missions and establishing a collaborative input process for endangered species recovery projects with United States Fish and Wildlife and the Smithsonian.

Of course, creating ECHO was not simple or stress-free. While the effort was championed by senior zoo designer Craig Rhodes and a handful of senior directors with a vision, GLMV interviewed Clifford eight times before moving forward. In its first two years, the tension of overhead expense and the pressure to show ROI by winning work was real, even as they took the long view.

'That has now flipped', says Clifford. 'Now we think every studio should be doing this. Of course, you can't just copy a model. It needs to be context-specific to that market.' GLMV is now experimenting with ways to apply what they've learned to their other market sectors, including education, healthcare and a new aviation market programme called *Elevate*.

SOURCE Adapted from 'Curating conversations: how one firm took a non-traditional approach to market positioning', Friedman & Partners, October 2019
Reproduced with permission from Friedman & Partners

Whether you run these workshops for one company at a time or for executives from multiple companies, they should be a key feature of your engagement programme.

Advisory councils

Another powerful way of engaging your target executives is through advisory boards and councils. These are strictly non-selling environments where executives can share their own views on the trends, issues and opportunities facing them while providing you with a greater understanding of the challenges plus suggestions and feedback for your own strategy.

Back in 2009, when co-authoring *Marketing Technology as a Service* with Laurie Young, I interviewed Orange Business Services for a case study on their approach to advisory boards. Even then, they were ahead of the pack in the way that they planned and organized their boards, and in structuring multiple boards for different levels of executive and different regions of the world. As far as I'm aware, their corporate advisory board is still running, and just this year was quoted to me by a client executive as one that he received great value from attending.

Also in 2009, Jane Hiscock set up the Farland Group in Boston, MA, offering to run executive councils on companies' behalf in recognition of both their importance to any executive engagement programme and the complexity of running them well. Hiscock's advice to you is to focus on designing a shared experience that delivers value to everyone involved.

CASE STUDY
Designing valuable shared experiences at Farland Group

US-based Farland Group is a management consulting firm recognized for designing valuable shared experiences between its clients, such as IBM, France Telecom/ Orange, Fidelity and Huawei, and their most valued customers. Set up in 2009, it has developed proven methodologies to bring the voice of customers into the strategic decision-making process. This includes developing strategies to enable a more client-centric approach, building and overseeing customer advisory boards and councils and organizing executive events and forums.

Founder Jane Hiscock has more than 20 years of experience in building marketing and communications strategies for leading technology, healthcare and financial services brands. Her early work was with business-to-consumer (B2C) companies like Perrier, Rollerblade and Black & Decker. She took her market-testing B2C expertise to the business-to-business sector, helping large enterprise brands to transform their client experience.

Bev Burgess: *Let's look at one of your key offerings, executive customer advisory boards. How do they operate?*

Jane Hiscock: We describe it as a trusted ecosystem of C-level customers, partners and prospects who can feed into your organization's strategy and create an ongoing, iterative process to help you make the best bets you can with your strategy and investments. These boards create reciprocal value for your clients and their most important stakeholders because customers, influencers and key prospects gain so much from the opportunity to learn from their peers and exchange perspectives on emerging trends with the hosting company.

The most successful boards are those where the customers are committed to helping your company succeed, and offer unvarnished, trusted advice to you and your team to help you improve, whether through validation and evolution of your strategy, new product ideas, investment prioritization or establishing new markets and lines of business. We have seen advisory boards run for ten years and some that have run their course in two.

They flourish when customers recognize that they are actually being listened to, and their advice is acted on – or if advice is not acted on, they are helped to understand the reason why. They then consider their valuable time worth investing and you, in turn, have created something super-sticky which can often turn into something else even more valuable. Time is such a precious commodity to executives that the time invested in these programmes must be well spent.

The critical success factor is to have a long-term mindset. These are not short-term meetings. It can take at least a couple of meetings to get relationships comfortable enough to yield the full benefits.

What was the thinking behind the concept?

When I started to work with technology companies after being in B2C I found that engineers just weren't that interested in what customers thought. That has now changed dramatically, of course, but back then it wasn't the case. The early thinking of setting up Farland Group in 2009 was to try to take B2B to the place B2C had been for some time in terms of engaging customers in the way services and products were designed.

Senior executives who were usually not deep technical users needed to be communicated with in a different way for our B2B vendors to be successful. You couldn't engage with them as you would an engineer. They had limited time and wanted to feel as if they were having some input over their vendors' strategies. We were very fortunate to have IBM as an early client because IBM had been doing this sort of executive engagement and education at senior levels for some time. So we were able to access and test out our thinking about successful approaches.

What value can these boards create?

Over the course of each board lifecycle, clients see tangible results such as the identification of new markets and buyers, the co-creation and development of new lines of business and the deepening of client relationships leading to greater revenues.

For example, some years ago many of IBM's clients began to have increasing concerns about security issues. Early inklings of that came from these board meetings and it was a testament to IBM executives that they actually listened to their customers and did something about it by investing heavily in a line of business to serve those needs.

Another of our clients, a supply chain company, has developed a much more rigorous roadmap system for their product team because of advisory board discussions. The CEO has said that that the advisory board is the most important strategy-setting mechanism he has.

We have found that while boards of directors are helpful to CEOs on fiduciary issues, customer advisory boards act as a market-testing, non-fiduciary sounding board and enable them to test out ideas in a relatively safe environment while hearing about any problems or issues customers are having. It is, if you like, a sort of Petri dish of their client base. There is often a good chance that if their biggest customers are facing a specific problem, it exists on a wider scale outside that room.

What happens if companies fail to act on these concerns heard in the meetings?

If you don't take action in some way and communicate that back, customers will feel you aren't listening and the board quickly loses its value. It's not as if people purposefully ignore advice, but they have day jobs and it can be hard to make necessary changes.

That is something we work very hard on: helping our clients remain focused on what we have heard in the meetings and figure out how to act on it. It helps to have senior executives in the room who have the influence and ability to push for change inside the company.

What does setting them up involve?

Customer advisory boards take a huge amount of commitment and energy, particularly at the start. You have to recruit the members, educate each participant about how to get the most value from the meetings and create content that resonates with them all. Then the meetings have to be properly facilitated so that everyone feels they received something from investing their time.

While we have a carefully designed process and structure for every teleconference and every meeting, we need to allow the discussion to go where it goes to a certain point to ensure that everyone is heard. That can be hard to facilitate, but if there isn't that flexibility it can leave a bad taste in the customer's mouth.

How have you seen the concept of executive engagement evolve over the past few years?

I think, partly as a result of the shift to digital platforms, we hear from executives that there is less command and control in their leadership styles because it no longer works. They have to lead more from the middle by being collaborative and gaining knowledge and depth from those around them at different levels.

So, for our work, as well as helping clients engage with their peers we are starting to look at setting up internal boards at different levels in the organization to help CEOs engage more with their teams.

What lessons would you leave for those wanting to improve their executive engagement strategies?

Number one is that you need to engage with senior executives on their own terms. You have to understand the pressure and environment they are in. Remember that your engagement programme can be a very small part of their existence. Try to help your teams figure out how to walk in their customers' shoes.

The second is that content matters. Yes, clients like to be well treated, but what sticks is the discussions they have, those 'aha!' moments, and the learnings they get from you as a vendor and their peers. And finally, remember that senior executives are both professionals and human beings: they will welcome anything that helps them do their job better and advances their career.

Reproduced with kind permission from Farland Group

Things have certainly changed over the past 10 years since the Farland Group started and I interviewed Orange Business Services, and perhaps one of the most striking changes is the fact that almost everyone has an advisory council today. So, how do you make yours stand out as the one an executive wants to spend their precious time serving on?

Microsoft's award-winning Services Executive Board can teach us all a thing or two. With a focus on immersive experiences in locations that the executives themselves would not normally visit, the board is well planned and executed, and delivering great results for the company.

CASE STUDY
Microsoft's Services Executive Board

In 2016, two years after CEO Satya Nadella took over, Microsoft was at a crossroads. Faced with the $4.5 trillion opportunity in the digital transformation (DT) space, it realized that despite having a solution-centric approach, relationships between Microsoft Services and its customers had been with the customer technology decision maker (TDM). The TDMs were not close to the forces that were disrupting their industries. To truly help customers evolve and be successful despite the digital disruptions they were facing, the company needed to connect with business decision makers (BDM), specifically at the C-Suite and board levels. To continue being relevant, the company needed an initiative that could help Microsoft connect and learn from the customer C-Suite, while driving a cultural shift to a learn-it-all culture so that it could better serve our customers.

Programme objective

Microsoft started the Services Executive Board (SEB) to build and inform its services strategy and execution, outside-in, with direct guidance from its top DT customers. The programme is designed to create a cohort of global business leaders who are willing to learn from each other and are vested in each other's success. The organizational design is heavily inspired by the experience undergone by elite start-ups, from influential incubators like Y-Combinator with their legion of founders, successful entrepreneurs, and advisory boards of venture capitalists.

The SEB was designed to have 20 C-Suite customers (increased to 30 in 2018), who partner with Microsoft Services on their DT journeys and are willing to invest their time to advise the company's executive leadership on current and future business challenges. SEB members represent Microsoft's 17 geographical areas and six priority industries.

Customers have found the way the SEB is run to be unique compared to peers in the industry. They cite the transparency with which Microsoft shares its business challenges with SEB members and ask for their guidance, which helps the company craft strategies or test hypotheses before it starts to execute globally, to be the key differentiating factor. Microsoft never pitches at the SEB – no marketing/sales decks or demos of technologies are allowed – it's about listening and learning from customers. As a technology company, the 'no demo' policy is a constant challenge to uphold, but it has helped Microsoft reach its goal.

Programme execution

There were seven key elements responsible for the continued success of the SEB Programme:

1 **A clear program definition** that differentiated the mission for the programme versus other customer advisory councils, clarifying the cadence and scope.

2 **Executive sponsorship**, with engagement from the corporate vice president to unlock the budgets and have direct reports on board across delivery, technology, operations and sales.

3 **Recruiting through a multi-attribute decision model** that evaluated customers across 18 proprietary attributes, scoring each nominated board member. Quantifying this helped Microsoft to be objective in its decision making and track its progress, while at the same time having an analytic language to use when potentially sticky political situations arise, such as when top customers, sales, executives and quota come together.

4 **Content strategy** created by a dedicated program team in tune with industry trends, Microsoft's vision and divisional strategies. The company has tried different formats, from normal presentation/feedback meetings, through design-led thinking workshops, to using improvisation to explore behavioural changes and having immersive world-class inspirational tours.

5 **Experience design** to help engage SEB members to give Microsoft feedback, following three pillars that define the soul for SEB that it wants our members to feel: 'unique and local', 'creative and inspiring', 'unforgettable and exclusive'.

6 **Engagement and real-time feedback mechanisms** to capture feedback and use the data to drive the shift to a 'learn it all' culture. Microsoft launched a dedicated app for iOS, Android and the web that connects SEB members to each other, providing the next meeting agenda and past documents. An important feature of the app is its integration with real-time presentations, where the presenter's questions display as a poll, and as the SEB member types their feedback, a dynamic graphic (or word-cloud) appears in real time on the main PowerPoint screen. This was a critical implementation innovation to hear the voice of every single customer while minimizing biases in answers.

7 **Follow up with senior leadership and the SEB** where, at the end of every meeting, the conversation is captured in a report that contains the dialogue and all the data from the polls. This report also enlists the insights and clearly identifies accountabilities for actions agreed. This has helped track accountability with the leadership team and report back to the SEB members, which they see as a huge indicator of their impact.

Business results

Over the past three years Microsoft Services has slowly improved its culture, while expanding its membership, covering more than 60 per cent of division strategies with customers before implementation (see Figure 8.4).

FIGURE 8.4 Services Executive Board scorecard

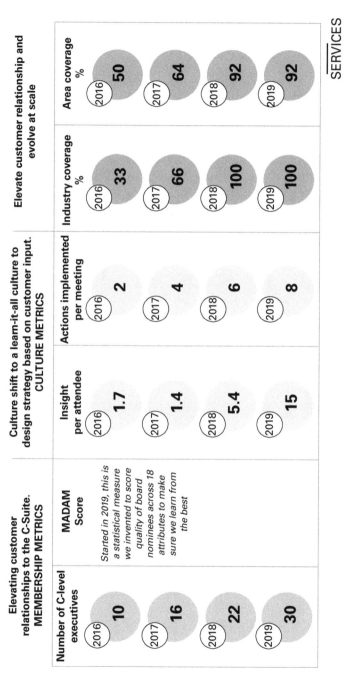

The growth of revenue for customers since joining the SEB has ranged from a rate of 98 per cent compound annual growth (CAGR) to 355 per cent CAGR, and the average deal size increased by a range of 2 to 10 times the size.

SOURCE ITSMA Marketing Excellence Award Winners summary booklet, 2019
Reprinted with kind permission from ITSMA

My own experience with advisory boards and councils leads me to add just three final recommendations if you are planning to include one or more in your engagement programme:

1   Make sure you have executive-level sponsorship and ownership in your own company by someone who is not head of sales or marketing (unless the executives you are targeting are from those functions).

2   Give someone the role to facilitate the discussion if your executive prefers to chair the meeting and take part in the discussion. It can be a challenging task and something that your executive doesn't need to focus exclusively on during a meeting.

3   Finally, don't let board members send deputies if they can't make a meeting – this will erode your executive attendance faster than anything else. Put the dates in the diary far enough ahead to secure the executives themselves, and invite enough people to your board to allow for a good meeting even if some can't attend each one.

Hospitality

Some roundtable discussions are held as a breakfast, lunch or dinner meeting, which borders on hospitality. Luckily, if the meeting is content led, and the refreshments within a reasonable per-head budget, they will still be seen as a serious meeting rather than a 'jolly'.

Pure hospitality is a useful way of building relationships with the executives that matter to you, and of introducing them so that they can expand their own networks. Particularly valuable are the events that they could not secure for themselves, or events that allow them to spend precious time with their families – or both!

Examples that I've been involved with in the past include advance film screenings (*Harry Potter and the Order of the Phoenix* at BAFTA on Piccadilly in London), advance viewings of exhibitions (the Chelsea Flower Show or the Tate's Rothko exhibition), private boxes at stadiums like Wembley or Twickenham for major games, stands at major sporting events (the Monaco Grand Prix or the Tour de France final leg in Paris), private meetings in symbolic venues (signing a partnership between a UK company and Swedish telecoms company, Ericsson, in the British Embassy in Stockholm), private tours of museums and historic buildings (the National History Museum or the Tower of London), private boxes at concerts (The Royal Albert Hall or the O2 Arena) and Christmas receptions and parties. Other popular options include golfing days, tickets to major sporting events such as tennis grand slams or the Olympics, or simply fine-dining experiences in a restaurant or hotel's private dining rooms.

As we saw in ITSMA's research, these are the things that executives are least likely to participate in, partly because their own company policy may make it difficult to do so. But when interviewing executives myself a few years ago, I discovered that they are more likely to attend if the event allows them to spend time with their families. In other words, for these exceptionally busy people whose lives are all too often dominated by work, if you can give them the chance to bring their loved ones to something they would value, it's a win for everyone (and the executives may get some brownie points back at home!).

To decide what would work best for your programme, go back to your research into the executives you're targeting. What are their hobbies and interests? What cultural organizations are they affiliated with, and what sports do they follow? This information will allow you to plan activities that they'll want to attend, if they can. And from there, the same rules apply as for other events – set your objectives, brief your team, plan the experience and follow up.

My final word on this is to recommend that before you do anything, you check with your own legal counsel about your own company's policy on providing hospitality, and act accordingly.

Summary

1   Executives themselves tend to prefer small group settings. They get to dig deeper into their issues, ask more questions and participate in hands-on activities to bring them to life and map out a route to solving them.

2   If an executive is going through a procurement process with you that is in the final stages of selection, they may not be able to attend any event that you invite them to outside of the formal procurement process.

3   In-person business seminars are not only the most preferred activity of the executives themselves, but are perhaps one of the most cost-effective, easy-to-run elements of a programme. Webinars are equally well used, but less preferred by executives.

4   Whether you are running a face-to-face or an online event, content and speakers are key for it to be successful, along with setting clear objectives, planning the executive's experience, briefing your team and adapting your approach based on event feedback.

5   Innovation workshops are popular with executives, and 89 per cent visit a supplier's innovation centre either during their purchase process or post-purchase, and 77 per cent describe the visits as valuable, claiming that their impression of the supplier improved as a result of the visit, they developed a stronger relationship and came away with a better understanding of the latest trends and developments relevant to their business and role.

6   Whether for peers from one company or from several, innovation workshops are about collaborative problem solving, and techniques such as design thinking are commonly used to define a context, explore alternative ideas, develop ideas and prototypes and agree action plans.

7   Advisory councils and boards are a trusted ecosystem of C-level executives who can feed into your organization's strategy and investments. These boards create reciprocal value as executives gain so much from the opportunity to learn from their peers and exchange perspectives on emerging trends in a facilitated, private discussion.

8   Some board meetings and small seminars are held as breakfast, lunch or dinner meetings, which borders on hospitality. If the meeting is content led, and the refreshments within a reasonable per-head budget, they will still be seen as a serious meeting rather than a 'jolly'.

9   Pure hospitality is a useful way of building relationships with the executives that matter to you, and of introducing them so that they can expand their own networks. Particularly valuable are the events that they could not secure for themselves, or events that allow them to spend precious time with their families – or both.

10 To decide what hospitality would work best for your programme, go back to your research into the executives' hobbies, interests and affiliations. And before you organize anything, check with your own legal counsel as to your own company's policy on providing hospitality, and act accordingly.

Notes

1   ITSMA (2019) 'How Executives Engage' survey
2   ITSMA (2018) 'How Executives Engage' survey

09

Engaging individuals

As we said earlier in this book, business buyers are people who buy from people, especially when they're spending a significant amount of money. So it makes sense that they need to trust those people before they'll buy from them. They need some form of relationship in place with them.

We know that executives prefer to have relationships with other executives, but will also accept SMEs, service delivery managers, account managers and, at a push, sales people. The type of relationship they want will vary, from a meeting of equals, through a professional consulting relationship, coaching or mentoring, to a friendship.

It takes time to build a relationship like this, which is why one of the key risk factors in any business-to-business supplier/client agreement is a change of staff – on either side. Even at work, people build relationships in the kind of stages their personal relationships go through. People are people.

This chapter looks at how to engage with executives one-on-one, both online and offline, to build relationships that will last. It also looks at how to engage the influencers that matter. Finally, it looks at the tools available to help you orchestrate and execute these engagements.

Relationships and how to survive them

There has been so much written on human relationships that it's difficult to add much more of value, but there are a couple of things to clarify, even if stating the obvious, in terms of executive-to-executive relationships. The first is about the type of relationship you want to develop, and the second is the way that personal relationships develop.

What type of relationship do you want?

Business-to-business relationships take different forms. I remember being really impressed by a presentation from strategic consultants McKinsey, where they defined the type of relationship that they aspire to compared to the types they saw other consultancies adopt. It held the line between purely professional and personal – a truly difficult balance to maintain, in my experience.

We've already heard about the research into what makes the most successful sales person – a challenger rather than a relationship manager. But given that executives prefer relationships with other executives, what does that look like?

The most straightforward is a peer-to-peer relationship of equals, where both parties are sharing their challenges and ideas. This can deliver great value to both parties even if it remains strictly professional and within these 'rules'. This is often the style of relationship most applicable where you have two companies in a reciprocal relationship, such as a bank providing financing and even personal wealth advice for partners in a professional service firm, who in turn are providing advisory services to the bank. When the CEOs of both companies meet to discuss how their relationship and contracts are progressing, it is likely to be a meeting of equals.

But some relationships go beyond the professional and blossom into friendship. There's nothing wrong with this. After all, it's a benefit to work with people you like (and working with people you don't get on with makes you miserable!). These people tend to meet at hospitality events, where appropriate, and seek each other out to have conversations that span both work and personal lives. They may even see each other at purely social events. Providing hospitality rules and other governance policies are adhered to, this shouldn't be a problem. (As always, check with your own legal counsel about what is appropriate.)

We should note here that it's not unheard of for the executives who form relationships between two companies to become romantically involved over time. I've seen this happen to a number of my own colleagues and clients. Typically this starts as a secretive liaison, but can be brought into the open once it becomes serious.

My own view is that this is a particularly dangerous boundary to cross, bringing with it conflicts of interest and creating discomfort for colleagues. A more extreme version of the friendship described above, these relationships should be declared and company regulations or policies followed, which may mean a change of role for at least one of the parties involved.

But there are other types of relationship that reflect a deeper engagement but remain strictly professional, such as the advisor or the coach. An advisory relationship is one where the supplier executive is providing a consultancy-style service to the client executive. I've seen this happen where the supplier is respected but not classed as a friend. There are no social meetings outside organized hospitality, and yet the client executive will contact the supplier for advice whenever they encounter a problem. This is the trusted advisor relationship in action – where the advisor is on speed dial! This is more akin to the relationship style that most professional service firms seek with their clients.

One step on from this is the coach, or mentor. This takes the relationship on from advising the firm and the individual executive on their role within it, to providing much more support for the client executive's personal development and career. This can be an enduring way to maintain relationships with executives as they move from company to company, but the balance between advising on what's right for the individual and what's right for the company can be a tricky one to maintain in this scenario. You need to follow your own and your organization's guidance on this.

In fact, you need to decide what guidance, if any, your organization will give those responsible for building relationships with your target executives in terms of the type of relationship to develop. Most firms leave it to personal discretion – I've seen very few guidance documents on this – with McKinsey possibly being the exception. But whichever type or relationship you are building, as I said before, it is likely to go through the natural stages of all human relationships. Note the difference with the purchasing process stages, since that represents the stages a group of buyers in one company go through when looking for a business solution. This is on a personal level. And we do it all the time.

The stages of relationship building

In one of my previous roles as a marketing director, we used to joke that what we were doing was effectively running an executive dating service, helping our executives to meet and build relationships with clients. We provided the conversation starters, the environment, things of value that could be left with the client and supported regular communication between them. We even ran events with speed dating-style interactions, where people moved between tables to meet as many others as possible at an event, looking for those who could help them with an issue. We weren't the only ones to make this observation, as you'll see in the Accenture case study in this chapter.

So, it seems appropriate to look at the phases of relationship development. There is lots of conflicting opinion on this, with various sources having multiple stages of development. Let's have some fun and use research from dating site eHarmony.[1]

THE SPARK

Within the first few seconds of meeting someone you have a response to them in terms of whether you are attracted to them and whether you think you might like them. In relationship terms, this is the spark. In business terms, this meeting is likely to happen at an event or in a scheduled appointment, and there are techniques you can learn to help you build instant rapport. These include mirroring their body language, matching your energy to the energy levels they are displaying and maintaining eye contact for an appropriate length of time. Talking to them about their issues and listening actively is a major factor here too. Actors in Industry, the London-based firm we met in Chapter 4, offers a great service to help executives get better at these techniques.

THE HONEYMOON

This phase is where you are happy and the relationship is still exciting. In business, a client executive is thrilled that a new supplier may be able to help them with their challenges and opportunities and bring a new perspective. And it's where your own executives are excited that they may be landing a new client relationship and working on new and exciting projects.

INTIMACY

The intimacy phase is exactly that! In our personal lives, it's when we might leave a toothbrush at our new partner's home and show more of our real selves. In business terms, this is where executives are comfortable with each other, and open up about the true nature of their operations. There may be a proof of concept or trial of working together. Suppliers are honest about their limitations as an organization, while clients are frank about the scale of their own challenges.

The politics of both organizations may come into focus and discussions held around how to navigate these. Personal and career challenges may also be on the table for discussion. At this stage, some business relationships may not continue – it may be too difficult or the challenges now visible, and to be met somehow, may simply not warrant the value each side will get.

COMMITMENT

This phase is where, in our personal lives, we may introduce each other to our respective families and even move in together. In business terms, this is where the executives introduce each other across their respective organizations and networks and begin working together in earnest. They may do things to help each other's careers, such as speaking on each other's behalf at events, or making personal recommendations and introductions. Ideally, this is where the best relationships stay, with both sides balancing the comfort of their relationship with the effort of keeping it fresh and interesting as time goes by.

HEARTBREAK

Sadly, according to eHarmony, the fact is that most relationships break up. There are many reasons for this. Relationship counsellors Relate discuss arguing, affairs, lack of communication, breakdown of trust, money worries and a general dissatisfaction with the relationship as potential issues.[2] In business, this plays out when there are different views that can't be reconciled around a contractual issue or common problem, where a new supplier is being considered or a new valuable client won that is taking the attention of one of the partners.

It could be that communications are not open and transparent, or break down altogether, especially around service incidents. Or where there are financial disagreements and disputes over payments. Finally, a common complaint in business is that the supplier does not bring any innovation to the client once the contract is signed, except just before the contract is due to be renewed. I'm sure I don't need to spell out the personal relationship parallels here with comments like 'You don't bring me flowers anymore'.

So, it seems that there are things we can learn from all that is known about the way personal relationships develop to help us build and maintain stronger relationships at work. Accenture, known for the strength of their ABM programme, has made that leap of thinking and explored what ABM and executive engagement within an account can learn from online dating.

CASE STUDY
Lessons from online dating applied at Accenture

At ITSMA's 2018 ABM Forum in London, Rhiannon Blackwell, Accenture UK Client Marketing Lead, took an unusual approach when she reflected, slightly tongue-in-cheek, on how running an ABM campaign for key clients could be compared to her previous life in the world of online dating. What's so interesting is how apt the parallels are.

ITSMA: *ABM and online dating?*

Blackwell: A few years ago, when I was single, I had a really clear vision of what I wanted my future to look like – my happily-ever-after. I moved from Germany to London with the sole goal of finding a boyfriend. I wanted a tall, dark, handsome man who lived in London and wanted to be my boyfriend – all before I turned 29. It was a SMART objective: Specific, Measurable, Achievable, Relevant and Time-boxed.

To bring this back to ABM, you have to be really clear on what the client wants, what the account team wants, and what you as marketers want to achieve. The first thing we do in any campaign is seek to understand the aspirations of our client. Let me bring this to life with an Accenture campaign. Our client, a major UK retail bank, wanted to drive through a fundamental transformation, from how they worked and the technology they used to their overall culture, so that the bank would be future-ready to deliver market-leading customer experiences.

In terms of business outcomes, the account team wanted to achieve a 10 per cent sales growth within the following 12 months. To enable this, the key sales objective was to get selected for a panel of transformation partners. This would put us first in line for new opportunities, help us build those C-level relationships and become a trusted, strategic partner.

From there, we were able to distil our marketing goal: increase preference among those key decision makers and buyers and keep us front of mind during the campaign. The objective was to engage over 70 per cent of those target stakeholders through our marketing activity.

How do you go about setting measures of success in a campaign like that?

Even dating has KPIs! What we do during the initial goal-setting phase is work with the sales team to decide and define what success looks like. For example, we look at audience growth, client perception and engagement, value of marketing to sales and revenue growth.

Let's look at the second ingredient, insight-led.

To carry on with my dating story, it wasn't long before arriving in London that I decided to download the infamous dating app, Tinder. After a lot of swiping I found someone, Tom, who caught my eye (and met my criteria!). Within two minutes I had looked him up on Facebook, Twitter, LinkedIn and the electoral roll, and I knew where he worked, who he lived with and, most critically, what his ex-girlfriend looked like!

In parallel, the first thing we did with our account team was to start mapping out who the key players were, to really get the lie of the land. This stakeholder mapping enabled us to identify the decision makers, the approvers, the influencers and the recommenders. We also worked out who from Accenture owned each relationship. We then took that list and started to apply our online detective skills.

What were your main sources?

We used a lot of different ones, including all those I used for my date-stalking! But we also looked at things like speaker engagements, media and our own CRM systems. How have they responded to events and hospitality? To e-mail? How do they use social media?

This started to inform our strategy for particular individuals as we got a better understanding of what they were passionate about, their interests and the best way to reach them. We then had an audience workshop with our account team. This was the exciting part because we began to get anecdotal insights from those people who knew our targets really well so we could build up enriched profiles.

We also talked about what a successful relationship would look like. Where we have a small target audience, we go on to create engagement plans at an individual level to deliver that success.

How did you keep on top of the process?

As the online dating site eHarmony says, the phone can be your greatest tool. We kept in constant touch with the sales team with weekly calls about the stakeholder engagement plan. We would go through each individual and discuss how sales or marketing had engaged them, what we had learned, and what was – or should be – our next step.

Your next ingredient is about being differentiated. How did that work?

Well, it's one thing finding someone on Tinder but writing your first message so that it stands out among the many others he might be getting is the hard part. As I flicked through Tom's photos, I saw one of him at Machu Picchu and I thought, great: I love South America, he loves South America, we have common ground and that was going to be my way in.

We had a collaborative workshop with the account team and really challenged them to put themselves in their clients' shoes to get that clear insight on *what* would help them and how Accenture – above anyone else – could make this happen.

This is where it can be very effective to get people from other areas into the room. We might have our vertical marketing leads, for instance, who can ensure that what we are coming up with is in line with the broader go-to-market messaging. Or we will get people who have previously worked for the client into the room because they have a really good understanding of the culture and the language used on the ground. From that we distil a set of core messages, possibly with a copywriter to come up with something punchy.

With this particular campaign we went one step further and created a messaging playbook. This articulated the value proposition and core messages, and provided stories our people could tell on the ground at the client's premises.

We had maybe 200 people working at that client who were not all involved in this opportunity but who, through their personal relationships with the client, could act as brand ambassadors. They had to be able to tell the story we had created. Finally, we engaged a designer who articulated and translated the messaging into a unique visual identity for all of our marketing and sales assets.

How did you approach personalization?

I know I said that writing the message is the hard part, but actually trying to be entertaining on dates is on a whole different level, especially if you are dating more than one person at a time. They can start blurring into one another if you aren't careful. How can you have a meaningful conversation if you don't know (or can't remember) what they like!

Personalization was key to our marketing strategy. We had a two-pronged approach. One was aimed at equipping the sales team to attract, connect with and engage those target clients while the other was launching the channel strategy that would engage clients through content and events relevant to each stage of the buyer journey.

When it came to the client, we didn't just want to bombard them with everything we had. We based it on where each was on their buyer journey, from awareness to interest to confidence, and then mapped out the relevant content for the relevant stages. We also customized some of our existing thought leadership to bring it in line with our story. Throughout this, we had a number of targeted channels in play the whole time, such as nurture e-mails, social media, personalized web pages and events.

Did it work?

With this campaign, we have actually engaged with 80 per cent of decision makers and influencers so far, while winning 100 per cent of the work packages related to this opportunity to date. We have also seen a 25 per cent uplift in sales with the account.

And yes, I finally got my outcome, my happily-ever-after, and married the man I met on Tinder!

SOURCE Extracted from 'How to Run a Successful ABM Campaign: Lessons from online dating', ITSMA, 2019
Reproduced with kind permission from ITSMA

Engaging one-on-one

In ITSMA's 2019 survey, 'How Executives Engage', the respondents cited one-on-one relationships with other executives as the third most valuable way to engage with their suppliers. They also said that to become a trusted advisor, you need to meet with them regularly without trying to sell them anything. So how do you do that?

Well, as we've said already, the simplest way to do this is through one-on-one meetings and briefings that talk about the existing business you're doing with them, and/or bring them new, valuable ideas and information. Ideally, this would be executive-to-executive all the time, but that's impractical given the other responsibilities your executives have.

The next best thing is to field your SMEs, particularly where you have new ideas and innovations to recommend to your client. Service delivery managers will be able to meet and discuss the status of current projects and hopefully suggest ways that operations could be improved based on the data collected by those delivering the service. This was always a very popular approach for us at Fujitsu, where our lean service methodologies, including a sense-and-respond approach, allowed us to spot where common problems were occurring and develop innovative ideas for improving our client's business operations and outcomes.

Coordinating the many meetings between your team of preferred players is one of the most important things you can do. Another thing is shaping the regular meetings that sales and account teams have with client executives so that they're not all about selling. Executives do value their account managers and sales specialists, but they want a range of things from them aside from their core sales role.

The things client executives expect from sales fall into three categories: seller, conduit and thought leader (see Figure 9.1). In the seller role, clients expect to receive information on the solution they're considering, help with navigating alternatives and support in building a business case. Outside of this role, they want their account manager or sales person to act as a conduit to SMEs, to point to where more information is available online, and to introduce them to other clients. As a thought leader, they want their account manager to bring them unique perspectives on the market and potential solutions, to educate them on new issues and provide ongoing advice so that they make the best decisions. They want access to benchmarks and best practices, and to be challenged in their thinking. This is by far the biggest set of expectations.

FIGURE 9.1 The three things expected from account managers

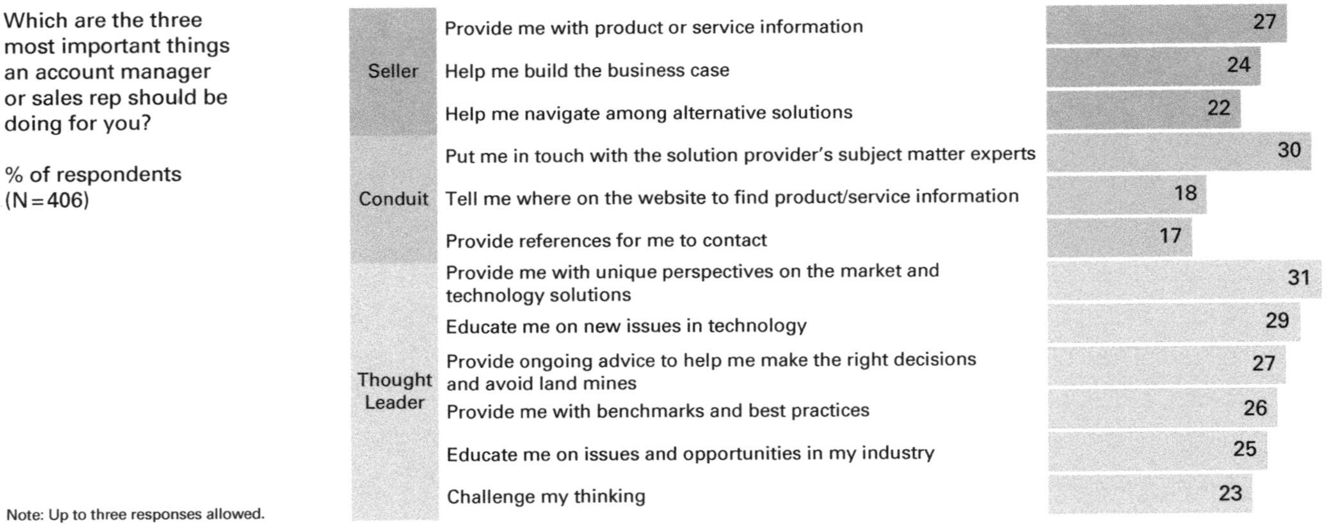

Which are the three
most important things
an account manager
or sales rep should be
doing for you?

% of respondents
(N = 406)

		%
Seller	Provide me with product or service information	27
	Help me build the business case	24
	Help me navigate among alternative solutions	22
	Put me in touch with the solution provider's subject matter experts	30
Conduit	Tell me where on the website to find product/service information	18
	Provide references for me to contact	17
	Provide me with unique perspectives on the market and technology solutions	31
	Educate me on new issues in technology	29
	Provide ongoing advice to help me make the right decisions and avoid land mines	27
Thought Leader	Provide me with benchmarks and best practices	26
	Educate me on issues and opportunities in my industry	25
	Challenge my thinking	23

Note: Up to three responses allowed.

SOURCE ITSMA 'How Executives Engage' survey, 2019

At least some of the meetings that sales people have with client executives need to be focused on this thought leadership and conduit role, and not on selling. You need to prepare them for that, using all of the types of content we've discussed so far in this book.

Of course, some of the one-on-one engagement will be online, not offline in face-to-face meetings (especially with millennial executives). We'll talk more about some of the technologies that can help you engage, coordinate and track your activities later on, but for now, a word about engaging on social media platforms.

These are by far the most common means of online engagement on a one-to-one basis, and yet for many executives they remain a bridge too far. I've met lots of executives who just aren't comfortable reaching out on social media. This is fine, so long as the executives they're trying to build relationships with don't like social media either. But that is increasingly not the case. The answer is not to palm the job off onto your executive's personal assistant or the marketing department, since that will not be your executive's authentic voice and could damage the relationship you're looking to develop.

Here are a few simple guidelines for engaging one-on-one via social media. The first step is to identify which platforms your target or client executive is using. That's where to meet them. Predominantly today, in the West at least, it will be LinkedIn, Twitter, Instagram and, to a lesser extent, Facebook.

The next step is to understand what interests them and what they post about. This will tell you where to focus your own engagement efforts. For example, one of my clients is passionate about how technology can solve the world's biggest issues, and regularly posts or comments on articles about that topic. Liking these posts and comments, sharing them, writing your own posts and sharing content they have missed are great ways to start and maintain a relationship with them online. It's what millennials do naturally.

But before you can start engaging on the topics that matter to your target executive, you have to get your own house in order and complete your executive's own profile on these media. The first thing they will do is check out who you are and what you care about, so you have to help your executives be ready for that. This is an important foundation, and one I've found your executives need a lot of help with, typically.

Most companies have someone identified to help get this done and provide guidance, whether internal or an external specialist. You might want to ask for their help in conducting an audit of your own team's social presence and activity today, and then for their help in educating your team on both.

There is some debate about how much personal information we should ask our executives to put on social media platforms, such as Facebook especially. This issue is akin to balancing the professional and personal in executive relationships overall. My recommendation is never to ask someone to do something they're uncomfortable with, and while it's OK to comment on interests such as societal issues, charities and even sports team success, it's rarely or never acceptable to comment or like content on a target executive's children. If in doubt, err on the side of caution, and check with your legal counsel.

A small company that created a fabulous platform for engaging with executives on a big industry and societal issue is Source Global Research. Set up to provide data-driven advice to help professional services firms develop their growth strategies, Source Global Research identified that a major issue within professional service firms was a lack of diversity at partner level, specifically a lack of women partners. They looked into this issue, and based on what they found, designed a campaign to help their clients address the issue, leveraging their relationship with female executives across the sector.

CASE STUDY
Creating emotional engagement at Source Global Research

Source Global Research is a leading provider of information about the management consulting market. Set up in 2007, the company serves both consulting firms and their clients with expert analysis, research and reporting. Its services include acquisition strategies, strategic intelligence and design, thought leadership and marketing effectiveness, and the market data and analysis critical to the performance of professional services firms around the world.

#foreveryninemen

For every nine men who make partner in a professional service firm, there is just one woman, despite these firms' stated ambition to change the status quo and a range of diversity policies to make it happen. In 2017 the company carried out a research project on what it called the 'pinched middle' in professional services firms. These were women at manager and senior manager grade – in their late 20s and early 30s – who, just as they expected to be at full throttle with their career, were also becoming busier at home as well, and giving up on their ambition to make partner.

As the report noted, this was the point in their lives where they reflected on the trade-offs they were willing to make to have the life they wanted. And despite the diversity initiatives in place in many firms, the research found that just over a third (34 per cent) of female senior managers said that the person they directly work for ignores the policies their firm has in place to help people in their position.

As a result, many women took the decision that to try to make partner was neither doable nor worth it, and so left the firm and the profession. This was damaging to an industry struggling to embrace a wide range of talents in the face of a changing business environment.

The need for role models

One of the key problems identified was the lack of viable female role models to show these women what was possible. So, when sharing the results of the research at an event on International Women's Day on 8 March 2018, the company announced that it was going to profile a few senior women with revenue-generating responsibilities to provide these much-needed role models.

The goal was to collect anecdotal stories that would go beyond the well-known statistics to create emotional engagement. The original aim was to interview just five senior women. But the sheer enthusiasm with which those interviewed embraced the idea, and recommended others to the researchers, meant that the project quickly snowballed well beyond that number. And every member of the team got involved in the interviews, reaching out and meeting some of the most impressive women working in professional services around the world today.

Getting personal

Because of these women's seniority, they felt less reluctance to share more personal information than their younger counterparts might have felt, which made for much more authentic, compelling and useful stories. According to Fiona Czerniawska, Joint Managing Director: 'These people were senior in their organization and had revenue-generating responsibility so they had little need to participate in this for recognition. I think they felt talking in this more personal way was contributing to something important. It was giving them a chance to recall the effort they had to go through to get to where they are today, and in some cases what it cost them to do so, and to help other women facing the same challenges.'

Celebrating the difference

The result is a series of compelling and, at times, moving stories about how these women around the world have overcome difficulties to rise to their senior position, their attitudes to the promotion of women at work and a range of anecdotes that powerfully illustrate the journey they have taken to get to the top. Many also have practical and encouraging guidance for young women forging careers in professional services.

There are a number of qualities the interviews revealed that these women share. They are universally competent and confident and, significantly, they are comfortable being women and not trying to act like men, notes Czerniawska: 'Many of them talked about the fact that women do business differently, and it can be immensely powerful when you throw that into the mix. And confidence feeds into that because you have to have to confidence to be different.'

Showcasing the results

Source Global Research created a bespoke website to showcase each interview as it was published. E-mails and social media alerted those on the rapidly growing mailing list, made up partly of the company's client base but also the increasing number of women opting in to receive their stories. 'As the project began to take on a life of its own and demand massive group effort, we decided some sort of endgame was required', recalls account executive in charge of the project, Hayley Urquhart.

In the pink

The result is an eye-catching coffee-table book in shocking pink. But it's not aimed exclusively at women: they are hoping it will help overcome what the research for the 'pinched middle' found was the rose-tinted view some men have of the difficulties women face in climbing the professional ladder.

For the firm, the culmination of all this work was the hugely successful event on International Women's Day in March 2019, attended by the interviewees and a host of other influential people.

Goodwill as the measure of success

What did Source Global Research get from it? This project began with the idea of building on the research findings of the 'pinched middle' report and identifying a few role models that could help women advance in professional services, rather than as a marketing campaign as such. And yet the goodwill it has generated will enable the firm to nurture a range of important new relationships, explains Czerniawska: 'We were quite clear about the fact that we would be creating goodwill. It was a way to engage with firms we might not speak to a lot but it had nothing to do with revenue as such. We had a bigger, more universal ambition in mind, to give more support to the future senior women in professional services.'

Reproduced with kind permission from Source Global Research

Source Global Research's approach of spotting an issue that matters to its clients, designing an innovative way to help and engaging executives one-on-one in a big vision and idea, is an excellent example of the way to build strong executive relationships and meet those executives without a sales agenda. In effect, the firm created a group of influencers in the sector, in this case as role models. But you may need to engage with existing influencers one-on-one as part of your executive engagement programme. Let's look at this briefly now.

Engaging influencers

We know from Chapter 4 that influencers can be an important part of an executive's network, and even of their decision-making unit. As such, they should be a part of your engagement programme, and while analyst or media events may be a useful way to get them together for briefings on your company's strategy and offerings, the best way to engage them is as individuals.

Who are they? The kinds of influencers that senior buyers of complex business solutions listen to include management consultants, industry analysts, sourcing advisors, trade and professional association staff and the media.

These influencers love nothing more than having a direct relationship with your own executives and SMEs, and with the people delivering your services. They are not fans of sales and marketing people, who will give them the latest sales pitch or brand story. So, you need to support your team in building relationships with influencers in the same way you would your target or client executives.

But given that these people are already short of time and need to get round to meet all the client executives in your programme, how do you decide which influencers they should also meet? The answer is to prioritize and to do as much online as possible.

Lee Odden of TopRank Marketing, an influencer marketing specialist, recommends looking for five things to judge the strength of a B2B influencer (his five Ps):[3]

- **Proficiency.** B2B influencers have to have domain expertise. They have to know their stuff. They can't just look good and take lots of selfies.

- **Popularity.** B2B influencers have to be popular in the sense that they have an active network paying attention to what they have to say. They need to be creating content in some form or another, and that content needs to have reach and distribution.

- **Personality.** While everybody is influential about something, some people do it with more finesse. Personality helps. Unfortunately, a lot of B2B influencers are lacking in this area.
- **Persuasion.** The best influencers have passion for their topic and are able to communicate that passion.
- **Power.** When this person talks, people act.

Odden adds:

> In reality, influencers don't need all of these things, but when all are present, the influencer is more effective. Ultimately, the power of influence is the ability to affect action. When that person communicates, do people change their way of thinking? When that person engages, do people change their behaviour? If they do, that's the person you want to work with. They might be what we call a 'brandividual', such as a famous keynote speaker or book author, or they might be a 'micro influencer' who has a tight group of 25 people who pay attention to every single word that person says.

He recommends four stages to engaging influencers in a campaign situation:

1 **Do your homework and compile your list of influencers.** In one of Odden's case studies, the company he was working with actually published the list as a way of formally recognizing the influencers.

2 **Invite influencers to contribute content.** Historically, we've reached out to influencers with content in the hope that they'll tell our story. Odden's recommendation is that we provide them with a platform to share their content instead, and ask them to contribute to whichever campaign or programme we're running, be it as a guest speaker, guest blogger or as part of a steering group designing thought leadership research.

3 **Be creative and interactive.** Odden cites techniques such as immortalizing the influencers in one programme with caricatures, and creating a Candy Crush-themed quiz, something that you don't usually find in the financial planning and accounting software category. In another example, he ran an 'Easy as pie' campaign for a software as a service (SaaS) company, invited the influencers to share details of their favourite pie and then sent them one of those pies. A bit of fun, as Odden insists that B2B doesn't have to be 'boring-to-boring'. It resulted in the influencers sharing photos and videos of themselves with their pies while they also shared content about the company and its proposition to their networks.

4   **Promote the anchor asset.** Odden suggests working with influencers to create blog posts, long-form interviews and general social amplification to drive executives to an interactive experience that, in turn, leads to the core content of any campaign you are running in your programme, such as an in-depth thought leadership report.

This is all great stuff. But, don't forget, one of the most powerful things you can do is map your own people to target influencers, and support them as they build long-term relationships and trust with those influencers, just as they would with client executives. This clearly takes more orchestration than a traditional marketing campaign, but luckily, there are tools on hand to help you.

Tools that support individual engagement

We've already discussed many of the central social media platforms that support the development of one-on-one relationships with target executives. To look further at how technology can help, both online and offline, I spoke once more to Kathy Macchi, a senior associate of ITSMA & Vice President, Consulting Services at Inverta.

CASE STUDY
Tools that start conversations and support relationships

Bev Burgess: *Kathy, you gave us a great overview in Chapter 3 of the tools that can help marketers understand their target executives and what they value. What types of tools are available to move beyond understanding and start engaging with those individuals?*

Kathy Macchi: There are a range of tools that support engagement online and offline, and help to orchestrate that relationship development across teams.

Tell us a bit about the tools people use to start conversations and build relationships online.

There are marketing automation platforms, interactive tools and AI-enabled sales coaching tools. Marketing automation platforms (MAPs) are used for rules-based outbound e-mails to executives, tracking responses, monitoring website visits and general marketing workflow management.

Interactive tools are technology- and data-enabled tools that help executives build a business case, offer industry benchmarks, calculate ROI or provide an assessment on demand, and so help start and support executive-level conversations.

AI-enabled sales coaching tools can monitor interactions for tone, objection handling and response length. These tools are used to refine the conversation in the context of the executive's priority scenario.

And what about the tools that support offline activities or face-to-face meetings?

The first is tactile marketing tools, which automate the delivery of gifts and other items as part of a coordinated set of marketing and sales activities. For meetings and workshops, you can use interactive tools that focus on delving deeper into your executive's priorities, such as by capturing brainstorms, drawings or design-thinking sessions.

Given that executive engagement is a team sport, with account teams, SMEs, business leaders and marketing working in close concert with one another, what tools are available to synchronize this behind the scenes?

Three main categories of tool come to mind here: account mapping, orchestration and CRM tools.

First, account mapping and relationship strength tools help to map the executives in an account and visualize the strength of your relationship with each one, ensuring that you have a 360-degree picture of all the personalities in the decision-making unit.

Second, demand orchestration tools are used to coordinate specific activities between marketing and sales in service of a shared goal, such as when pursuing a sale or getting an executive to attend a meeting. For example, marketing may want to know when a sales counterpart sends a personal e-mail to an executive. Orchestration tools allow shared visibility into the tactics used by different members of the team.

Third, CRM tools allow the account team to keep track of their interactions with the account's buying centre. Many relationship management tools have integrations to other marketing and sales tools in an effort to present a holistic view of both an individual executive's and an account's interaction with your brand.

It's worth checking what tools you have available already in your organization and then work with your technology team to plan an investment roadmap for the others that you need. They will help you create the business case for this investment, or may even make the tools you need part of their own investment plans. So much the better!

Summary

1   Business buyers are people who buy from people, especially when they're spending a significant amount of money. So, it makes sense that they need to trust those people before they'll buy from them. They need some form of relationship in place with the people from whom they are buying.

2   B2B relationships take different forms, from a meeting of equals, through a professional consulting relationship, to coaching or mentoring and even to friendship.

3   Often you find yourself running what is, in effect, an executive dating service. The phases through which that relationship develops can be described as the spark, the honeymoon period, intimacy and then commitment.

4   The final phase of a relationship is heartbreak when it breaks down. Typically, the contributing factors to this stage include different views that can't be reconciled; a new supplier being considered or a new valuable client won that is taking the attention of one of the partners; where communications are not open and transparent; a lack of ongoing innovation; or financial disagreements and disputes over payments.

5   The simplest way to engage is through one-on-one meetings and briefings that talk about the existing business you're doing and/or discuss new and valuable ideas.

6   Executives prefer relationships with executives. SMEs and service delivery managers are also strong candidates. Executives do value their account managers and sales specialists, but they want them to act as a thought leader and a conduit to others, as well as being a sales person.

7   One-on-one engagement will also take place online (especially with millennial executives) by engaging on social media platforms such as LinkedIn, Twitter, Instagram and Facebook. Find out where your target executives are and meet them there, engaging on the topics that interest them. But first, make sure your own team's profiles are up to date, and don't let them get too personal.

8   Prioritize the management consultants, industry analysts, sourcing advisors, trade and professional association staff and the media contacts that influence your target executives, and develop relationship plans for them too.

9   There are a range of tools that support engagement online and offline and help to orchestrate that relationship development across teams. Work with your technology team to leverage what you have and plan investments in those that you need.

Notes

1   Hosie, R (2017) 'The five phases of a relationship', *The Independent*, 9 December
2   https://www.relate.org.uk/relationship-help/help-relationships (archived at https://perma.cc/65WL-DGSE)
3   ITSMA (2019) Using content and influence to drive B2B marketing success, ITSMA Viewpoint

10

Measuring success

As we know by now, executive engagement is about building relationships with senior buyers in the organizations with which you want to do business, and with other senior executives whom those buyers trust. It is a long-term business development strategy aimed at creating mutual value for everyone involved. How do you know if it's working?

The first thing to be clear on is what you hope to achieve with your programme. What are your objectives? SMART objectives (see below) are measurable by definition, and this leads you to the metrics you can use to judge your success. Ideally, those objectives will go beyond starting and strengthening relationships with the executives in your programme, and include goals for how the programme will help to build your company's reputation and, of course, lead to growth in profitable revenues.

This chapter recaps the kinds of objectives you may set yourself before moving on to explore the importance of outcome-based metrics and the three measurement categories of relationships, reputation and revenues. Finally, it looks at the nature of performance dashboards and the challenge of building them and keeping them fed with the latest data.

Why engage?

As we said in Chapter 2, the first question to ask yourself when you're designing your executive engagement strategy is what you're trying to achieve:

- Is your goal to grow your business with your most important customers, or are you trying to win work with new customers?

- Is it all about creating advocates who will speak on behalf of your organization and recommend you to other executives?

- Or is it more about your reputation than about business development? Are you trying to reposition your brand in an existing market or introduce it into new markets?
- Are you trying to gain a larger share of voice in the media?

All objectives you set should be SMART: specific, measurable, achievable (not pie in the sky), realistic (not too easy) and time bound. The best way to think about the objectives for your programme is in three categories: building your organization's reputation, strengthening its relationships with customers and influencers and growing revenues. Once you've defined what you want to achieve, in specific and not general terms, and with a clear timescale in mind, it's time to set some measures of success so that you know you're on track to deliver against your objectives.

Measuring outcomes

There is a balance to be had between tracking performance metrics that help you continually refine what you're doing in your programme and tracking outcomes that your business leaders will care about. Traditionally, marketers running programmes such as executive engagement have done too much of the former and not enough of the latter.

The knock-on effect of this focus on activities is that the marketing function is seen as a support function, not delivering strategic value to the business.

Figure 10.1 shows a continuum of metrics you can measure, ranging from activity based (counting effort and tracking costs), through to more output based (counting results and measuring efficiency), to outcome based (reporting outcomes delivered and even anticipating and forecasting future outcomes).

The metrics on the right-hand side of Figure 10.1 are those to report to your business stakeholders. Those on the left are more for your marketing colleagues and leadership. As you decide how to measure the success of your programme, consider what your internal stakeholders for the programme will want to see as well as what those running the programme need to know.

But what about return on investment? Isn't that the ultimate outcome? Well, ROI is a finance calculation that measures the real or expected gains from a *capital investment*. But your executive engagement programme is likely to be classed as an *expense*. Additionally, ROI is calculated for a defined period. Any ROI calculation will vary depending on the period over

FIGURE 10.1 Moving from activity to outcome-based metrics

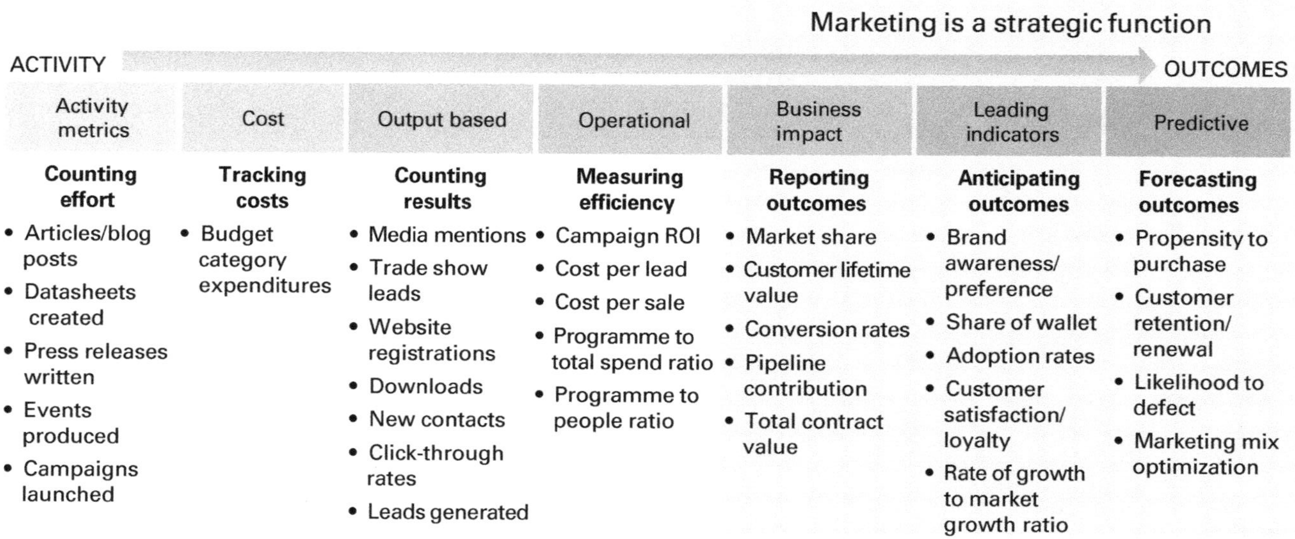

Marketing is a strategic function

ACTIVITY							OUTCOMES
Activity metrics	Cost	Output based	Operational	Business impact	Leading indicators	Predictive
Counting effort	**Tracking costs**	**Counting results**	**Measuring efficiency**	**Reporting outcomes**	**Anticipating outcomes**	**Forecasting outcomes**
• Articles/blog posts • Datasheets created • Press releases written • Events produced • Campaigns launched	• Budget category expenditures	• Media mentions • Trade show leads • Website registrations • Downloads • New contacts • Click-through rates • Leads generated	• Campaign ROI • Cost per lead • Cost per sale • Programme to total spend ratio • Programme to people ratio	• Market share • Customer lifetime value • Conversion rates • Pipeline contribution • Total contract value	• Brand awareness/preference • Share of wallet • Adoption rates • Customer satisfaction/loyalty • Rate of growth to market growth ratio	• Propensity to purchase • Customer retention/renewal • Likelihood to defect • Marketing mix optimization

SOURCE 'Measuring What Matters to Improve Marketing Performance', ITSMA, August 2019

which it is measured: ROI does not stand on its own, but must be tied to a specific interval. Finally, the point of calculating ROI is to evaluate multiple possible investments of the same size over a specific period to decide on the best one to pursue. This is an important way for organizations to make trade-off decisions.

It is sensible, then, that ROI measures are also used to evaluate the performance of an investment over a given period. If you are going to use ROI to measure the success of your executive engagement programme, focus on measures and time frames that make sense for the objectives you have defined.

In fact, you'll need to decide on the time frames for all of your measures of success in each of the three categories of relationships, reputation and revenue. While these time frames should reflect your unique business context and the objectives you've set, I tend to think in terms of short term being around three months, medium term being six months and long term being a year or more.

Let's look at the three categories and the metrics you could use for each one now.

Strengthening relationships

It seems obvious that you will want to set objectives and track the performance of the way you are starting new relationships and deepening existing ones among the executives in your programme. But what exactly will you measure? And how long will it take to see any results?

For many, developing relationships to the point of trusted advisor status will be the defining long-term goal here. Oracle has exactly that goal for its customer engagement strategy, aiming to achieve what it calls an 'architecture partnership', but its measures also include tracking a shift in internal mindset, efficiency in delivering the programme and the number and value of any opportunities generated.

CASE STUDY
Oracle: Earning the right to be a trusted advisor

Oracle Corporation is multinational computer technology corporation selling cloud infrastructure and cloud applications. In 2018, the company appointed Jacqueline Gummer as Head of Customer Engagement Strategy to strengthen the relationships that a team of senior executives had with their customers by earning the right to be seen as strategic and trusted partners. The team of 160 people consisted of a mix of business, industry and technical customer architects from across Oracle International.

Gummer, who had previously been in a senior ABM role, knew that this would be a big challenge, since it was more about fundamental behaviour change than process and technology. 'It was really a strategy and planning role to help the team be more consistent in the way we engage with customers, and have someone in place to orchestrate that engagement', she says.

The vision was clear: shift the relationship from Oracle being perceived as a company selling its services to one that could understand and build on customer needs and success. This would be accomplished by breaking down the many 'siloed' value propositions to a single, connected proposition and communication for customers facing unprecedented challenges in their goal to become more future-relevant or future-ready.

Changing behaviour

Gummer realized from the start that this was about instilling a new mindset. As she explains, 'My focus is customer engagement. Customer engagement is about behaviour. For me, engagement is all about earning the right to have the conversation and encouraging our customers to interact and share in the experiences we create for them. Our goal is to help our customers find evidence to support change and experience how to achieve it. Repeatedly doing this is the way we help our customers get to the future.'

When executed well, she believes a strong customer engagement strategy will enable Oracle to become a trusted business partner. To achieve this as a team there needs to be some discipline in terms of the process they all follow. There must also be a message that is relevant to the needs of the customer at the time and, of course, the right Oracle cloud capability to make it happen.

But, most importantly, the team needs to understand its purpose, she stresses: 'This is the consistent idea we all align behind. I don't think about what to say anymore, I think about how can I help – and I mean genuinely help – our customers get to the business outcome they desire. If you don't have purpose, the risk is you are just creating noise. Whether it is account-specific noise or persona-based noise, it is still noise.'

This makes a big difference, she says: 'If you tool the teams in the right way by aligning everyone behind the right approach – a purpose plus a focus on delivered outcomes – but with enough room for the team to be individuals, then I've seen the team's energy become truly infectious. They support, learn from and celebrate each other; they energize each other and bring everyone along on the journey.'

'In this instance it is their attitudes and behaviour that has changed', she says. 'Their attitude – their belief in what they are doing has driven that change in behaviour. And why is this important? Because we are all people. This is about bringing people together with a simple purpose.'

This unified approach to executive engagement was designed to deliver numerous benefits, including:

- consistency in creating added value for customers;
- efficiency and effectiveness, enabling the company to execute programmatically by repeating a known approach to engagement at scale;
- clarity for internal audiences about the approach, and improved alignment with other teams around the organization.

Developing a workable and measurable framework

Within a defining framework analysing 'where are we today and where do we want to be', Gummer began to break down this challenging brief into different streams of activity to make it more workable and measurable. The first stream, for example, examines how to help the chief customer architects (CCAs) shift from discussing what the company does to how the company could enable customers to achieve their goals.

According to Gummer, 'We wanted to equip them to talk more about how Oracle can help customer executives adapt to this fast-changing world rather than just discuss the right solutions design. These should be conversations about something that addresses today's need but leaves customers with a compelling vision of what we could do for them tomorrow to enable them to be more ready for future change.'

How do they measure this change in behaviour? 'We trained people region by region, and, importantly, we gave them time to challenge and input because they need to feel like they have contributed and shaped. After the training they had to present back a version relevant for their customers.' In addition, all customer-facing material is peer-reviewed, while the team is encouraged to contribute to a blog, which is reviewed by an SME and Gummer, who looks for purpose rather than noise. This is a gradual process of change.

The second stream focuses on approaches to ensure the team earn the right to be seen as strategic and trusted advisors, and come in at a much earlier stage in the buyer's journey than is currently the case. As Gummer explains, 'This is done by identifying the right account, the right audience, the right timing (Have we invested enough time into the account? Is the customer open to this approach?), and the right message in terms of how the company could create added value.'

In terms of measurement, this has been structured as an engagement plan, with progress measured against all the actions. After interviewing everyone in one region, Gummer created a template for the team to use, tested it in principle with the team's leadership, tested it with one account and then trained people on how to fill in their own version. The role of managers was largely to help remove obstacles. It gave the team an action or execution plan to discuss progress in one-to-one reviews.

A third stream looks at how to make the subtle shift from discussing process as such to how the company could help customers get where they want to go. The fourth stream emphasizes the importance of creating and sharing intellectual property across the business by establishing standards of quality and format, and rewarding staff who willingly do this as part of their role. The final stream is about how to demonstrate to other lines of business in a consistent way the progress being made with customers.

As Gummer says, 'If the customers sense you aren't sure what you are talking about, the relationship comes unstuck quickly. So, people have to be encouraged and rewarded for knowing when they need to pass a customer and an opportunity on to someone else, even when it's their account.'

Building on success

A year on, Gummer has already seen substantial changes. For example, they reviewed all management metrics and stopped those that were measuring activity or output from the team and refocused on measuring the right type of behaviour. In addition she has seen changes in the way the team members are talking to customers.

The ultimate measure, she says, is how many accounts the company has got that trusted relationship with:

> We measure this by the number of accounts where we have achieved what we call an Architecture Partnership. The activity out of this is a regular meeting which reviews work done and plans for the future. These reviews are a significant investment from both Oracle and the customer, both in terms of pre-work and people attending. It is essentially a commitment that without a doubt will pull through more revenue. And we measure this by where each new opportunity comes from.

Significantly, that fundamental shift in mindset has since been encouraged from the top of the company with the introduction of an extensive brand relaunch and change programme to support Gummer's mission.

Here are some other examples of relationship measures you may wish to track and report, from activity, through output, to outcome-based.

Percentage of executives with complete insight profiles

An activity metric, this is important in terms of understanding each executive you are targeting, being able to communicate with them and tracking your ongoing engagement with them. It can be a short-term metric with a 100 per cent target.

Number of events or opportunities to engage created

Another activity metric, this is a count of the number of things you are running as part of your programme that give your team the opportunity to engage with executives, such as events, social media outreach activities or thought leadership research interviews. This can also be a short-term metric with a target to suit your objectives, strategy and resources.

Number of C-level executives active in the programme

If your goal is to raise your relationship levels in your target account, then you may wish to track the number of C-level executives who are participating in your programme. You could also track this as a percentage of those you invite or of your top priority accounts against whichever target you set for yourself. This is an output metric that can also be tracked from the short term.

Number of advisory board participants

Similar to the number of C-level executives participating, this is a narrower group of possibly the most senior executives within your most important existing or target accounts, again tracked against the target you set yourself. It is also an output metric that can be tracked from the short term.

Percentage of customers rating their experience 'good' or 'excellent'

For each individual event or interaction, you may wish to ask for event-driven feedback, helping you to improve the way you design future interactions. You may wish to set a target based on your historic performance or on industry benchmarks. This is an output metric that can also be used from the short term.

Relationship strength

Many companies have some definition of the strength of their relationships, whether on a negative–neutral–positive scale, or from detractor to advocate. The important thing is to have a definition you can communicate and understand. This is an outcome-based metric that can be impacted in the medium to long term and tracked against a near 100 per cent target for advocates.

Increase in customer net promoter score (NPS)

NPS is typically a periodic score, perhaps checked annually or via a pulse survey – a sample of your programme participants on a more regular basis. This is an outcome-based metric that you will be able to track and report in the medium and long term against a target of 90 per cent plus, scoring you at least 9 out of 10.

Number or value of customer-solution decisions influenced

If, like Oracle, you can track the opportunities coming in from companies with participants in your programme, and identify those who were influenced by the executives' participation in your programme, this is a very powerful metric over the medium to long term as you see their advocacy in action. You could give this a target based on your target pipeline or revenue for the year and the percentage you would like to see influenced by executives in your programme.

There may be other measures of success that relate to your own specific objectives, and these are best co-created with your internal stakeholders and team. But for now, let's move on to reputation.

Building reputation

For many years now, I've been talking about B2B reputations, since this seems to be an easier concept for those running large B2B firms to get their heads around than to talk about brand, which they tend to associate with consumer goods. This is a pragmatic choice, which you may decide not to take, and instead you'll want to talk about your brand strength here.

Your executive engagement programme is a great vehicle for you to decide and promote what you want to be known for as a company. What do you want these executives to say about you when you're not in the room? The strength of your reputation will influence how your communications to the market – and to the executives – are received. Indeed, it will influence whether they are opened at all, and whether anyone wants to engage with your company and brand.

Here are a few things you may wish to track and report on as your executive engagement programme works to build your reputation, again working from activity to outcome based.

Number of content pieces created

You may wish to set yourself a target based on your share of voice in the market or your competitors' activity levels. An activity metric, this can be reported on in the short term against a target you set for yourself.

Number of website visits

An output metric, this will be useful for you to monitor what executives are responding to best and what doesn't interest them. It is linked to page traffic and click-through rates and the actions executives then take on your website. You can create a target based on your historic levels of interaction or on industry benchmarks, and performance can be tracked from the short term.

Campaign response rates

Similar to the above, this links with e-mail opt-ins and open rates, covering responses to invitations, podcasts listened to, or thought leadership reports downloaded, for example. Again, you can set targets based on your historic levels of interaction or on industry benchmarks, and performance can be tracked from the short term.

Customer references

An output metric, the number of customers acting as a reference on your behalf will influence your public reputation. You could set targets based on your historical performance in this area and objectives for executives in the programme becoming reference customers. This can be tracked from the short term.

Customer references are notoriously hard to secure, so I recommend that this be a specific objective of your executive engagement programme, since they are so valuable in terms of building long-term business. Indeed, you may already have an initiative within your organization to track and co-promote your customer's success, such as the one described in the Unisys case study, where customer feedback is taken seriously and acted upon in order to build mutual value and strong advocates for the company.

CASE STUDY
Client first at Unisys: Closing the loop to strengthen relationships and loyalty

Closing the loop with customer feedback is a critical element of building loyalty. Companies spend a lot of time listening to the 'voice of the customer' but those who reap the rewards go beyond simply listening. They take action on customer feedback. How a company responds to feedback says a lot about the value it places on customer relationships and loyalty.

Conducting customer surveys creates expectations that you will take some form of action based on the results, whether it be a follow-up call to address issues or simply a thank you note while sharing results. Asking for feedback and not following up can create more harm than not asking for feedback in the first place. One company that has perfected the art of closing the loop is Unisys.

Unisys' mantra of 'client first, then the account executive, then everyone who thinks they need the results' is the driving force behind the company's client satisfaction programme (CSAT). Since 2009, Unisys has designed, developed and evolved a customer-centric programme that has improved overall client satisfaction, deepened relationships and driven profitable business growth.

Unisys leaders highlight six key success factors with the CSAT programme.

Fostering a customer-centric culture

In 2008 the company lost one of its largest customers and no one saw it coming. Unisys' then-chairman and CEO declared this unacceptable and immediately directed his business unit presidents to do whatever it took to get closer to customers and develop a culture of service delivery excellence. Customer experience is now central to Unisys' business strategy.

Creating a process to ensure follow-up

Unisys has implemented a closed-loop process that ensures timely response and accountability. Client satisfaction information and enhancement plans are integrated into Salesforce.com and the system alerts account teams (and their managers) when action is needed. In some cases, Unisys also has clients sign off on remediation actions, keeping clients in the loop on what is being done to address their concerns.

Addressing systemic issues as well as account-level issues

Too often, companies that measure customer loyalty and satisfaction respond to feedback only at a tactical level. At Unisys, the feedback is addressed at both the account level and the strategic, company-wide level. For example, when client feedback pointed to a need for more proactive innovation, Unisys implemented a company-wide Innovation Program. An element of the programme is innovation workshops that engage clients in brainstorming sessions with SMEs on relevant topics. Unisys also provides clients with opportunities to provide input to solution roadmaps and has recognized clients with awards for their innovation with Unisys solutions.

Communicating with all stakeholders

The senior leadership team sends letters to clients to share the findings of the survey and to confirm their focus. Additionally, business unit presidents send personal recognition e-mails to hundreds of Unisys associates who are named by clients for contributing to their success.

Driving additional business with client satisfaction information

Unisys continually develops and evolves supporting systems to ensure that client satisfaction information is easily accessible and used regularly to help deepen relationships and grow accounts. For example, the programme includes individual dashboard reports for each account to show a rolling view of client satisfaction over time. Account executives use these reports with clients to discuss progress over time and in proposals to win additional business.

Creating client advocates

The company leverages client satisfaction feedback to create a pipeline of potential references by identifying clients who indicate willingness to refer Unisys to others. The programme has confirmed more than 300 client references.

For Unisys, the commitment to closing the loop has generated significant business benefits. Unisys' NPS is higher than average for B2B companies and is on its way towards best-in-class. This greatly strengthens the ability of sales executives to highlight Unisys' commitment to service delivery excellence with clear customer evidence.

Ultimately, of course, the goal is deeper customer engagement. Unisys' investment and commitment to listening and closing the loop have generated tangible results, including improved relationships and business growth.

SOURCE 'Client First at Unisys: Closing the Loop to Strengthen Relationships and Loyalty', ITSMA, 2016
Reproduced with permission from ITSMA

Media coverage and sentiment

Many companies talk about owned, earned and paid media, with the goal of achieving greater earned media coverage through their activities, since this is a cost-effective way of building your reputation. Hopefully, your thought leadership content and executive references, together with your influencer outreach, will secure you positive coverage in your target media. This will build a virtuous circle for your programme and the executives who want to participate in it. As an outcome-based metric, you can set a target based on your historic performance versus your competitors' share of voice in the market. Practically, it will take you a while to get your first coverage, so this can be tracked and reported from the medium term onwards.

Customer brand perceptions, awareness and knowledge

Your target customers' awareness, understanding, consideration and preference of what your company's brand stands for are a great measure of success. You can track these things among the executives in your programme to see shifts over time as they participate and get to know you better. Targets are likely to be based on historic performance and competitor scores, with visible shifts occurring over the long term.

Growing profitable revenue

Executive engagement strategies are put in place to build the future revenue streams of the company, delivering value to both your own organization and its clients or customers. To that end, it makes sense to include success metrics around revenue growth, and indeed, increases in profitable revenue.

Here are a few possible measures of success to consider in this category.

Number of proposals or proof of concepts delivered

An activity metric, this may be a leading indicator of future revenue growth, and you would hope to see this number increase among those organizations participating in your engagement programme as you build trusted relationships with their executives. Targets can be set based on historical performance levels, and performance tracked from the short term.

Expenditure against budget

An activity metric, tracking your expenditure on the programme against budget, both in terms of how much you spend and when you spend it versus when you forecast you would spend it, is important for the financial professionals to manage cash flow and profitability in your organization. This can be tracked from the short term.

Pipeline identification, progression and acceleration

In addition to new opportunities arising from among the companies represented in your programme, you may wish to track the progression and acceleration of existing opportunities in those accounts as their executives engage more with you. An output metric, you can set targets and compare this with pipeline levels and length of sales cycle before the programme was up and running, and with opportunities in accounts that are not in the programme. I would suggest this can be tracked over the medium term, depending on your typical sales cycle.

Pipeline growth

You may also wish to set a target around the growth of pipeline in accounts participating in the programme. An outcome metric, this can be tracked over the medium term. Again, you may wish to compare pipeline growth rates between accounts in the programme and those not participating.

Revenue growth

Growth in the absolute revenue secured from organizations participating in the programme is an outcome-based metric. You should be able to set targets when considering your objectives for the programme and track performance against those targets from the medium to long term (probably more the latter, despite the inevitable pressure you will face to deliver results as soon as possible).

Size and profitability of deals

The size of your deals is likely to increase as a result of your engagement programme, as is their profitability, since you may increasingly be selling more complex solutions or be invited to propose sole-sourced deals. Again, you may wish to set targets based on your historical performance, perhaps as an objective for your programme. These outcome-based metrics can be tracked over the long term.

Global professional services firm Avanade has a 'Most Valued Client' programme with many objectives and performance metrics, including an increase in the larger, transformational types of solution that it can deliver for clients, as outlined in the following case study.

CASE STUDY
Avanade: Best-in-class engagement

Avanade is the leading provider of innovative digital and cloud services, business solutions and design-led experiences on the Microsoft ecosystem. Founded in 2000 as a joint venture between Accenture and Microsoft, the company has grown to 38,000 professionals across the globe, and is one of the world's largest communities of Microsoft specialists.

In early 2019, Avanade embarked on an ambitious and carefully structured element of its Client Experience (CX) programme, the Most Valued Client (MVC) strategy – its goal to strengthen and deepen executive relationships with its key clients. The MVC strategy is overseen by Julia Martin, part of the Global CX Team, who was previously the North America ABM lead. She, in turn, reports to a top-level CX executive.

As Martin explains, the initiative was set up to: (1) segment the client base – a far more challenging task for B2B companies, like Avanade, owing to highly complex buying structures and practices, wide-ranging requirements, and trust and expectation factors; and (2) develop a programme that creates a differentiated experience for key accounts.

The premier league

Avanade started by creating a pilot programme called Orange Premier as a test ground for a new approach to deepening executive engagement. According to Martin, 'Avanade's vision is to create great experiences and our goal with Orange Premier is to provide a curated set of experiences over time that are closely aligned to what we know our clients value, as well as an execution framework for our account teams. The emphasis is on being distinctive, intentional and consistent.'

Avanade's determination to take a more proactive approach to executive relationships stems from client feedback, says Martin. Clients have reported that they want a deeper form of engagement, particularly in areas such as thought leadership and innovation, with leading-edge ideas being offered with more vigour and force. This underlines Avanade's reputation as a premium provider of high-value consulting services and deep Microsoft expertise.

Selecting the accounts to include in this high-value initiative is carefully done. The targeted clients are those with whom Avanade has had a significant depth of relationship, technology compatibility, and who are aligned to Avanade's expertise in growth and transformation skills. Key targets are also those industry disrupters with an embedded culture of innovation and where opportunities exist for co-creation.

Mapping the journey

The internal impact of this strategy is just as important as its external results, Martin explains: 'We look at our whole client experience programme as changing the hearts and minds of our people. In particular, what we want to impart to all our employees is that good client experience is not good enough. We have to be exceptional and to do that takes focus, intention and a very coordinated approach.'

The process begins with a discussion with the senior account owners so that they can gain a full understanding of just what it means for a client to be part of Orange Premier and explore whether the fit is right. The next step is to broaden that out to the account team as a whole to gather critical intelligence and understand each client's value drivers. That leads to the development of a detailed client experience roadmap for the next 6 to 12 months that Avanade commits to delivering.

Participating clients have been quick to appreciate the value of this, Martin says: 'What's been so interesting is that we have now started to share the experience roadmaps with clients, discuss our intent and get their feedback. This co-creation is leading to real engagement and synergy.'

Measuring success

The pilot phase has been valuable in highlighting how to make the programme attractive to account teams by showing the added value the Orange Premier framework can bring to their clients. The longer-term focus of the programme is not easily measured by short-term metrics, admits Martin, so increases in client advocacy, more than revenues as such, can be a useful way to judge progress.

For example, how willing are those clients to speak jointly about the work they do with Avanade? 'That's a real proof point for us because when clients talk about the work we do, it tends to show they feel good about the relationship and their attitude to our collaborative innovation', Martin explains. 'We also ask, are we expanding into those more transformational kinds of programmes with clients? If so, that means we have brought in the right thought leadership.' Longevity of the relationship will also be a key measure over time.

Another key metric is to what extent Avanade is fulfilling its vision for clients to be inspired, cared for and confident, based on client feedback. Scores can be compared for those 'most valued' clients against the rest of the client base. For example, is the inspiration score for someone who is part of the programme much higher than that of another client?

Looking ahead, the next stage will be to decide how to scale up such an intensive, time-consuming programme without the risk of diluting it. Martin explains, 'In a perfect world, you would have the ability to create unique and distinctive experience maps perfectly aligned to individual client needs for everyone.'

Win rate

Another outcome-based metric is the proportion of deals you win out of those you compete for. You will expect your win rate in competitive bids to improve in those accounts that participate in your engagement programme. Set targets to improve on your current performance, and compare your win rate among organizations in the programme with the rate among those not participating. You should see improvement over the long term.

Share of wallet

Finally, your share of the money that executives in the programme spend on the kinds of solutions you can deliver should increase over the long term. This should be one of your objectives, as the executives get to know more about what you have done for others and can do for them. Set a target based on your current share, and track it as it increases over the long term.

The specific combination of metrics you choose to judge the success of your programme will reflect your business context and the objectives you set. Tracking and reporting your success can be a manually intensive task, unless you can leverage technology to help you get the data, in as close to real time as you need it (which could be quarterly, if that's how frequently you are going to report the data and take decisions based on it). I recommend you use some kind of measurement dashboard to provide an overview of how you're performing against target, and to help you make decisions to course-correct if needed.

Building a measurement dashboard

Much has been said about measurement dashboards. Creating a useful dashboard that shows data that business stakeholders want to see without taking a day or more to compile them (which could be spent doing something more valuable) remains a challenge for many companies. When Tom Fishburne decides to create one of his wonderful cartoons on a subject, you know people are struggling with it. Figure 10.2 sums up some of the more problematic aspects of creating a valuable dashboard for your programme.

I recommend that you create something simple that has outcome metrics against your programme objectives at the top level, with the ability to drill down into the data beneath if necessary and depending on your audience.

FIGURE 10.2   The marketing dashboard

Reprinted with permission from the Marketoonist.com

TABLE 10.1a An illustrative performance dashboard

KPI dashboard	Short term	Medium term	Long term
Relationships	• Account coverage: 10 targeted contacts • Increase in touchpoints • # executive briefings • # client meetings • Attendance surveys	• Coverage: 50 targeted contacts • Account engagement: 25% lift in executive engagement • Client introduction to target contacts • Innovation centre visit • 10% lift in relationship strength with key stakeholders	• 50% lift in executive engagement • 25% lift in relationship strength with key stakeholders • Solution innovation
Reputation	• Sales and account team interaction and satisfaction • Social reach and engagement	• Sales and account team satisfaction • Brand perception with X stakeholders • More executive meetings • Event attendance • Customer satisfaction	• Sales and account team satisfaction • Brand survey • Brand perception with 2X stakeholders • Invitation to scope projects • X references and advocacy activity • Testimonials, referrals to others
Revenue	• Pipeline acceleration • Increase in RFP invitations	• $XM pipeline • Contract signing • New opportunity with custom solution • Revenue growth • Deal size and type	• $XM pipeline • $YM revenue • Account penetration • Portfolio penetration • Share of wallet/win rate

TABLE 10.1b An illustrative performance dashboard

Relationships	Reputation	Revenue
More/increased percentage of executives with whom we have a trusted advisor relationship	Increased positive media coverage achieved in priority media	Growth in pipeline
Improved net promoter score (NPS)	Improved brand awareness, knowledge and preference	Growth in revenue
More/higher value of solutions decisions influenced by executives in the programme		Growth in deal size and profitability
		Improved win rate
		Increased share of wallet

Looking back over the metrics described above, a few in each of the three categories were outcome based. Together, they could form the dashboard shown in Tables 10.1a and b.

But, even with this design in mind, the question still remains: how you populate the dashboard? Where will you get your data from? How will they be fed into the dashboard (as automatically as possible, ideally). Inevitably, this will rely on leveraging the systems and technologies that your organization already has, plus possibly a few third-party sources. We've talked about the tools that can support your programme a couple of times now, and it's true that some companies have made an art out of creating sophisticated digital infrastructures to support customer engagement strategies such as this. But not everyone can run to the type of investment a company like Cisco can make (see Figure 10.3).

Described by Scott Brinker of Chiefmartec.com[1] as 'a fantastic example of an elegantly organized, best-of-breed marketing stack', he says that this is 'a master class in real-world marketing technology management condensed into a single slide'. It's a slide that I find slightly alarming, and I'm sure many of you reading this will take one look at it and run.

The good news is that you don't need to go to these lengths. I recommend that as you design your own executive engagement strategy, you involve a technology specialist who can help you work out which tools you really need to provide insight on your target executives, to support and coordinate your efforts to engage them both online and offline, and to help you keep track of the fantastic results your programme will deliver for your business.

FIGURE 10.3 Digital enablement at Cisco

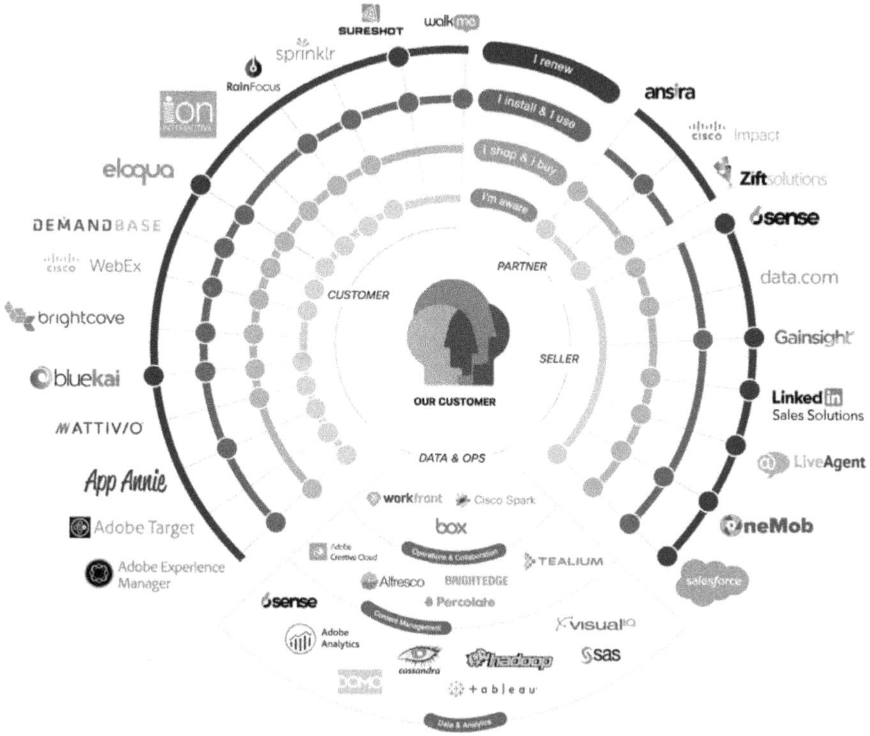

SOURCE ITSMA Webcast 'Next steps for marketing with customer experience and success', March 2018

Summary

1 The first question to ask yourself when you're designing your executive engagement strategy is what you're trying to achieve. All objectives you set should be SMART: specific, measurable, achievable (not pie in the sky), realistic (not too easy) and time bound.

2 The best way to think about the objectives for your programme is in three categories: building your organization's reputation, strengthening its relationships with customers and influencers and growing revenues.

3 There is a continuum of metrics you can measure, ranging from activity based (counting effort and tracking costs), through more output based (counting results and measuring efficiency), to outcome based (reporting outcomes delivered and even anticipating and forecasting future outcomes).

4   You'll need to balance tracking performance metrics that help you continually refine what you're doing in your programme, and tracking the outcomes that your business leaders will care about.

5   If you are going to use ROI to measure the success of your executive engagement programme, focus on measures and time frames that make sense for the objectives you have defined.

6   You'll need to decide on the time frames for all of your measures of success, in each of the three categories of relationships, reputation and revenue. While these time frames will need to reflect your unique business context and the objectives you've set, short term is typically around three months, medium term six months and long term a year or more.

7   For many, developing relationships to the point of trusted advisor status will be the defining long-term relationship goal and measure of success.

8   Your executive engagement programme is a great vehicle for you to decide and promote what you want to be known for as a company. What do you want these executives to say about you when you're not in the room? Customer references are a valuable measure of success and a great way to influence your reputation.

9   Executive engagement strategies are put in place to build the future revenue streams of the company, delivering value to both your own organization and its clients or customers. To that end, it makes sense to include success metrics around revenue growth, and indeed, increases in profitable revenue.

10 Create a simple performance dashboard to track and report your success, showing outcome metrics against your programme objectives, and with the ability to drill down into the data beneath if necessary.

Note

1   'Next steps for marketing with customer experience and success', ITSMA, March 2018

INDEX

CPSIA information can be obtained
at www.ICGtesting.com
Printed in the USA
BVHW022346081122
651520BV00010B/55

9 781789 661927